The Economics of Edwin Chadwick

For Bob Hébert and Bob Tollison, friends beyond compare and collaborators for four decades, with unending admiration and respect.

R.B.E.

To my wife Janet, and our children Edward, Colin, Holden, and Caroline. Thanks for keeping me smiling, and busy.

E.O.P.

The Economics of Edwin Chadwick

Incentives Matter

Robert B. Ekelund Jr

Auburn University, USA

and

Edward O. Price III

Oklahoma State University, USA

Edward Elgar

Cheltenham, UK • Northampton, MA, USA

Published by
Edward Elgar Publishing Limited
The Lypiatts
15 Lansdown Road
Cheltenham
Glos GL50 2JA
UK

Edward Elgar Publishing, Inc.
William Pratt House
9 Dewey Court
Northampton
Massachusetts 01060
USA

A catalogue record for this book
is available from the British Library

Library of Congress Control Number: 2012935328

ISBN 978 1 78100 503 3

Typeset by Servis Filmsetting Ltd, Stockport, Cheshire
Printed and bound by MPG Books Group, UK

Contents

Figures and tables

FIGURES

TABLES

Preface

The name of Sir Edwin Chadwick (1800–1890) adorns any list of pioneers in the engineering of sanitation, public health, and water resources. Knighted by Queen Victoria in 1889 for these accomplishments, only a year before his death, Chadwick retains a place of honor in the engineering and social aspects of public health, Poor Law reform, and administration. Far less known are his incredible economic excursions into utilitarianism. These inventions, promulgated over his long life and career, include nothing less than an invention of some of the essential tools of modern microeconomics applied to economic policies. Consider some singularly important and contemporary questions:

- Do air bags and seat belts create moral hazard; that is, by lowering the cost of reckless driving do the regulations create a danger to self and public?;
- Are government regulations of mining conditions or elimination of greenhouse gases best handled by regulations (a regulatory body) or by establishing liability provisions?;
- Is the state licensing of physicians or florists (a restrictive regulation in the state of Louisiana in the United States) necessary to protect consumers of such products and services?;
- Should Amtrak be regulated or owned by the federal government in the United States or, alternatively, should it be owned by the government but leased out to private enterprise for particular periods?;
- How should 'overuse' of the communally provided police and criminal justice system be curtailed and/or streamlined?;
- What is the effect of immigration, legal and illegal, on national productivity?

It would be absurd to say that Edwin Chadwick answered these particular questions, but he did provide a clear economic framework with which to answer them, within the often-turbulent domestic economic environment of nineteenth-century England. Problems of moral hazard, asymmetric information, liability placement, 'natural monopoly,' and labor productivity were, it turns out from reading Chadwick, as much

recognized problems in his day as in ours. But we do not wish to 'reincar-
nate' Chadwick as a 'modern' but rather plan to let him speak for himself
and to leave it up to the reader to decide 'how modern' he was. However,
we note that parallel to the contemporary questions and issues mentioned
above, Chadwick analyzed:

- How insurance 'clubs' in which children of the poor could be
  covered created a moral hazard for the lives of the children
  themselves (see Chapter 5);
- How accidents on the railways and in the production of other services could be prevented or mitigated by appropriate assignment of
  liability-creating incentives for prevention (Chapter 2);
- The manner in which asymmetric information impeded the appropriate functioning of urban markets for funerals of all classes
  (Chapter 5);
- A new means for regulating national transport industries (in
  Chadwick's case, railways) that left operation to private enterprise
  but ultimate control to the government (see Chapter 4);
- A trenchant analysis of the inefficiencies and ineffectiveness of the
  police and criminal justice systems, one with particular relevance to
  today's problems (see Chapter 7);
- An argument supporting open Irish immigration as increasing
  England's productivity, one which has relevance for contemporary
  issues regarding Hispanic (Mexican) immigration to the United
  States (see Chapter 6).

These and other brilliant insights and a coda on how they might relate to
problems in the twenty-first century are the subject of this book.

Chadwick is most certainly not an elusive and unknown thinker in
some areas. Prior research however has focused almost exclusively on his
role in social, administrative, and sanitation reforms. Excellent works on
these topics include Marston (1925), Lewis (1950), Finer (1952) and, more
recently, Brundage's *England's 'Prussian Minister': Edwin Chadwick and
the Politics of Government Growth, 1832–1854* (1988). It is no exaggeration
to note that Chadwick is an almost singular progenitor of public health in
the UK and elsewhere. The one hundredth anniversary of his death (1990)
and the one hundred and fiftieth anniversary of the first Public Health
Act (1848) was an occasion for serious and deserved plaudits for him in
the United States (Krieger and Birn 1998) and abroad (Hamlin 1998). His
prowess in sanitation engineering has also been duly noted (Hamlin 1992).
These excellent works appropriately feature Chadwick's role as one of the
two or three most important policymakers of nineteenth-century England.

There is a serious gap in our knowledge of his substantial achievements, however, for no work focuses on Chadwick's startling advances in economic theory and their application to then-critical and similar contemporary problems. Our interest in Chadwick contrasts with all previous approaches and it stretches back almost forty years. In the early 1970s, Ekelund read Chadwick's long essay of 1859 with the unwieldy title 'Results of Different Principles of Legislation and Administration in Europe; of Competition for the Field, as Compared with Competition within the Field of Service,' published in the *Journal of the Royal Statistical Society* (1859c), in connection with modern papers on franchising and in connection with Crain and Ekelund (1976). The inventions of that essay led to a decades-long quest, one supported by Professor Ronald Coase (then at the University of Chicago) and the late Alfred Chalk of Texas A&M University, which continued and continues to reveal an amazing understanding of economic approaches to policies related to cases of, or cases purported to be, failures of the market to perform efficiently. Portions of this research were conducted by the authors at Texas A&M University during the 1970s. Additionally, in that and the following decades, research was conducted by Ekelund with Price and others on aspects of Chadwick's thought and on the utilitarian approach to economic policy. These include papers written by Ekelund at Texas A&M and Auburn University on ideas relating to Chadwick, John Stuart Mill, regulation, and utilitarian thought generally. (See W.M. Crain and R.B. Ekelund Jr, 'Chadwick and Demsetz on Competition and Regulation,' *Journal of Law and Economics*, 19 (1976): 149–62; R.B. Ekelund Jr and R.D. Tollison, 'The New Political Economy of J.S. Mill: The Means of Social Justice,' *Canadian Journal of Economics*, 9 (1976): 213–33; R.B. Ekelund Jr and Edward O. Price III, 'Sir Edwin Chadwick on Competition and the Social Control of Industry: Railroads,' *History of Political Economy*, 2 (1979): 213–39; Melvin Cross and R.B. Ekelund Jr, 'A.T. Hadley on Monopoly Theory and Railway Regulation: An American Contribution to Economic Analysis and Policy,' *History of Political Economy*, 12 (1980): 214–33; R.B. Ekelund Jr and R.F. Hébert, 'The Proto-History of Franchise Bidding,' *Southern Economic Journal*, 48 (1981): 464–74; R.B. Ekelund Jr and Douglas M. Walker, 'J.S. Mill on the Income Tax Exemption and Inheritance Taxes: The Evidence Reconsidered,' *History of Political Economy*, 28 (1996): 559–81; E.O. Price III, 'The Political Economy of Sir Edwin Chadwick: An Appraisal,' *Social Science Quarterly*, 65 (1984): 975–87; R.B. Ekelund Jr and G.S. Ford, 'Nineteenth Century Urban Market Failure?: Chadwick on Funeral Industry Regulation,' *Journal of Regulatory Economics*, 12 (1997): 27–51; R.B. Ekelund Jr and Cheryl Dorton, 'Criminal Justice Institutions as a

Common Pool: The Nineteenth Century Analysis of Edwin Chadwick,'
Journal of Economic Behavior and Organization, 50 (2003): 271–94.) We
are grateful to these co-authors and the journals for use of some of the
materials included here and express deep appreciation to Bob Hébert
and Bob Tollison for that as well as for reading and commenting on
earlier drafts of this book. Matthew McCaffrey was a great aid in editing
our work as were Tara Gorvine and Christine Gowen of Edward Elgar.
We are also indebted to Professor Nick Tyler, Chadwick Professor of
Engineering at University College London and to Special Collections
Librarian Dan Mitchell for information regarding Chadwick's voluminous papers (more than 250 file boxes) housed at University College
London. Investigations into Chadwick's incredible productivity and the
mass of his writings reveal and, in all likelihood *will continue* to reveal,
new and startling concepts and approaches to economic and social issues.
Indeed, his contract bidding scheme for the provision of public goods in
public-private collaborations for such goods as water provision (Hanke
and Walters 2011) remain in use in many countries today, including
France. Hence, the reason for putting Chadwick's ideas on economics
between two covers for the first time.

Finally, our research on Chadwick casts light on a long-standing debate
among intellectual historians; at least, those interested in the history of
economic theories and ideas. Does tool development have 'a life of its
own' in that there is a steady progression in the value of economic analysis
when applied to economic problems? Or does environment play a crucial
role in the development of economic theory, as argued by famous historians of economics from the past such as Wesley Clair Mitchell? Put
more directly, did Chadwick empirically observe economic and social
problems engendered by the Industrial Revolution and urbanization in
England, only *then* developing tools to analyze and deal with them? Or did
he simply apply tools already extant to deal with pressing economic and
social matters? We comment on this issue as our discussion progresses.
Fundamentally we argue that Chadwick's message to the world is that economic policies relating to actual or presumed failures in markets – in the
nineteenth or twenty-first centuries – are all seeded with the *same* problems
and that best evidence must be mounted to support or reject regulation
or market interferences. Chadwick's famous contemporaries – political
economists David Ricardo, John Ramsey McCulloch, Robert Malthus,
and James Mill – almost completely eschewed the empiricism that was
Chadwick's trademark. They certainly did not devise the solutions to the
kinds of actual or potential market failure that so intrigued him. That is
because Chadwick, while certainly acquainted with Adam Smith and his
direct intellectual progeny, was possibly, along with his good friend John

Stuart Mill, the chief acolyte of Jeremy Bentham. Chadwick (and to a lesser extent John Stuart Mill) pushed utilitarianism to its logical limits, although Chadwick's desired abrogation of property rights in order to achieve utilitarian ends far exceeded that of John Stuart Mill. Chadwick actually wanted to *realize* the goals of utilitarianism. These issues, ever fresh, concerning the role of government in a market-oriented society deserve a new reading. The problems faced by highly developed first-world countries are, given technological advances, remarkably similar. Chadwick, armed as he was with proto-modern economic tools, was able to offer unique and inventive solutions that still deserve close attention.

Robert B. Ekelund Jr
Auburn, Alabama

Edward O. Price III
Tulsa, Oklahoma

PART I

Introduction

1. Who was Edwin Chadwick?

INTRODUCTION

Today a quick Internet Google search of the name Sir Edwin Chadwick (1800–1890) will reveal more than 600 000 entries, a degree of attention that would certainly compete with that paid to many modern Nobel laureates in economics. But the vast majority of economists – many directly connected with the history of the discipline – draw a blank when they hear the name. Who could this man be, living and writing over the high period of classical economics? More to the point, why would economists of the twenty-first century be interested in his massive body of nineteenth-century policy work? In his masterful and still unmatched biography of Chadwick, S.E. Finer makes the following observation:

> He was a bore, a really outstanding specimen of bore in an age when the species flourished. He was too keenly aware of his own merits; while on the other hand he had no patience with fools, and his definition of a fool was a very wide one, taking in as it did, nearly everyone who disagreed with him. With a wholesome suspicion of power wielded by others, he managed to combine a boundless confidence in the benefits of power in his own strong hands, and every scheme drawn up by Chadwick seemed to contain a provision at some point for giving more power to Edwin Chadwick . . . He stirred up a great deal of mud, and it is a tribute not a reproach that so much of it was thrown back at him by his critics. (Finer 1952: 3–4)

Such a description could hardly explain the importance of the man. Indeed, it would seem a reason for neglect.

A survey of Internet sites or a look at the Social Science Citation Index gives a great deal of information on one important aspect of Chadwick's fame – his early statistical investigation into the sanitary state of Great Britain entitled *On an Inquiry into the Sanitary Condition of the Labouring Population of Great Britain* (1842b [1965]). This classic study, one of the two or three most important social documents of the nineteenth century, forcefully brought out the causal relationship between the aseptic state of the country and the progress of disease. In response to this condition, Chadwick devised what he called the 'arterial' drainage system, the forerunner of the modern sewage system.[1] He was also the driving force behind the practical implementation of sanitary science. The long debate over sanitation was finally won with the passage of the Public Health Act of 1875, which mandated local Boards of Health, medical examiners, and inspectors of 'nuisance' throughout England. For this work Queen Victoria knighted Chadwick in 1889, just over one year before his death in 1890.

But there is much more about Chadwick even in the potted history of the period. Specifically, he made pioneering contributions in almost every area of British public policy: tropical hygiene, criminal justice institutions, policy towards funerals and interments in urban areas, school architecture, Poor Law reform, water supply, drainage, utilization of sewage, military sanitation, and pauper education, to mention only a few. In almost every area Chadwick's statistical methods of investigation produced 'policy results' – one reason for the opinion of Finer noted above. Chadwick, as reflected in these policy concerns, was most certainly interested in what became known as the 'public good.' For example, John Stuart Mill, Chadwick's close friend and associate, offered the following assessment of him in Chadwick's unsuccessful bid for a parliamentary seat:

> I have touched only on the main points; for, to go through all the minor, but still important matters of public interest which he has helped forward, would take up far too much time and space. I may say in brief, that he is one of the organizing and contriving minds of the age; a class of minds of which there are very few, and still fewer who apply those qualities to the practical business of government. He is, moreover, one of the few persons who have a passion for the public good; and nearly the whole of his time is devoted to it, in one form or another. (Mill 1972: 1432)

This interest in the social and economic policy designed for the public good led Chadwick to use statistical investigations as support for his policy views. Elsewhere Mill clearly stated that he always deferred to Chadwick on matters of fact. One of the greatest 'bean counters' of the nineteenth century, Chadwick was said to have been the only man who had actually counted the rats in London prisons. Chadwick was clearly one of the first writers to use extensive anecdotal 'evidence' to support policy conclusions. In this sense he was an early 'statistician.'[2]

These achievements in social and economic policy, numerous and important as they are in an administrative and sociological sense, have been the principal but not the only source of Chadwick's fame. Economic historians have centered on other aspects of Chadwick's career. For example, he provided evidence and collaborated on the writing of the Poor Law Act of 1832, later serving as secretary to the Central Board appointed to administer the Act.[3] He was the chairman of the committee which investigated the employment of children in factories, as well as the author of a report on the optimal organization of the police force. He testified before committees investigating drunkenness, the treatment of railway laborers, the construction and maintenance of highways, the organization of the civil service, and numerous educational inquiries.

Historians and economic historians have also focused on Chadwick's 'academic' involvements. He contributed to such diverse organizations as the Institute of Civil Engineers, the National Association for the Promotion of Social Science, the Royal Statistical Society, the British Association for the Advancement of Science, and the Royal Society of Arts, serving on the executive committees of the latter two organizations. The publications of these organizations are replete with Chadwick's thoughts on an ever-wider range of topics. The use of sewage as manure, machinery and the laborer, the reorganization of the railways, pollution, legislative procedures, electoral corruption, and public measures to promote head-to-foot washing are but a few of the topics upon which Chadwick expounded. He was an incessant discussant or session chairman at the meetings of these organizations and an early and faithful participant in the London Debating Society and the Political Economy Club – organizations that were forums for the Philosophical Radicals.

While historians have not missed the exploits and achievements of Chadwick in several realms, the economic historian's attention has been confined to particular issues surrounding his work. One of the earliest of these papers dealt with Chadwick's intervention on behalf of the railway laborers and is an attempt to set the record straight concerning Chadwick's reputation as an oppressor of the workers (Lewis 1950). Pedro Schwartz recounts his interchange with J.S. Mill on the issue of the London Water Companies (Schwartz 1966). His name appears throughout discussions of public policy stands of the classical economists (for example, Coats 1971), including his role as the author of an early British Factory Act (Marvel 1977). In 1964 Mark Blaug re-examined the 1832 Poor Law Report with an emphasis on the accuracy of Chadwick's testimony, concluding that Chadwick's statistics were biased and over-estimated the operating costs of the Old Poor Law. Indeed, more than any other topic, Chadwick's involvement with 'welfare reform' has received the most attention from economic historians.[4]

WHY WAS CHADWICK 'MODERN'?

The magnitude of this attention would suggest that Chadwick's role in the development of economic analysis applied to social and economic policy would be clear and well settled. We argue in this book that nothing could be further from the truth. It is our purpose to show that, alone among all classical writers of the nineteenth century, Chadwick understood the nature and role of market failures in a functioning industrialized economy. Only one part of Chadwick's brilliant and original contributions to the *theory* of economic policy have received any attention – his theory of 'competition for the field.'

The Contract Management Principle

The best-known economic principle attributable to Chadwick – the so-called theory of contract management – was actually an extension of Benthamite utilitarianism. It gives new meaning to 'competition' and riddles Chadwick's treatment of markets. Competition, as actual behavior rather than a formal theory, finds meaning in the notion of rivalry. There are, however, two distinct notions of rivalry, each associated with a different structure of property rights. The first notion – ascribed to Richard Cantillon and Adam Smith – is that of a contest open to all rivals in the sense that each has equal access to relevant economic markets. This requires a structure of property rights that permits ownership to be atomistic, decentralized, and participatory. In this system, legal institutions generally uphold property rights in commodities traded so long as they are acquired in good faith without force or fraud.

A second form of rivalry, also with an ancient pedigree in the economics literature, is described by the contest to obtain an exclusive right to serve. In this notion competition is temporary and discontinuous. It often takes the form of competitive bidding to secure a franchise, the monopoly status of which is subsequently sustained by legal force. Property rights, far from being dispersed, are held by the franchise-granting agency. As a principal means of rent-seeking by authoritarian (monarchical) governments throughout history, this kind of 'competition' is well known.[5] In codified form, so-called 'franchise bidding' has a short but distinguished history. French military engineers, including one Bernard de Belidor writing in the early eighteenth century (1729) envisioned the entrepreneur as a government contractor who bids competitively on contracts for the execution of public works. (Franchise bidding continues to exist in the provision of goods and services at all levels of government.)

Jeremy Bentham's major interest was law, not economics, as is well known. As the premier utilitarian policy wonk of all ages, Bentham viewed the contract as the most formal type of obligation – it was a means of acquiring property rights over services. In briefest terms, it was a means whereby the State could define obligations and punishments in such a manner that private interest would be brought by artificial means to coincide with public interests. It goes without saying that the world Bentham envisioned was not that of Adam Smith, wherein an invisible hand always (or almost always) produced the greatest good for the greatest number. This legalistic, contractual device was inculcated into the works of Bentham's greatest 'student-practitioner' of utilitarianism – Edwin Chadwick.

Chadwick, in numerous contributions and in an important statement published in 1859 (see 1859c), extended this contractual principle into many areas under the rubric of 'competition for the field.' Chadwick believed that open competition resulted in economic inefficiency in the form of market imperfections or excess capacity and the remedy for such 'economic waste' involved substitution of competition *for* the field in place of competition *within* the field. Practically speaking, this meant collectivization of property rights under Bentham's principle of contract management. Chadwick argued (1859c: 385) that:

> [T]he whole field of service should be put up on behalf of the public for competition – on the only condition on which efficiency, as well as the utmost cheapness, was practicable, namely, the possession by one capital or by one establishment, of the entire field, which could be most efficiently and economically administered by one, with full securities towards the public for the performance of the requisite service during a given period.

With allowances for the perpetual inelegance of Chadwick's prose, it is clear that he was advocating an entirely different system of 'competition' for the provision of goods and services. Importantly, however, Chadwick's conception of competition required property rights alterations via contract in a system where both property rights and contracts were variables within the economic system. More than any writer, before or since, Chadwick believed that such alterations would bring about economic efficiency in markets. But this system, so different from the classical and neoclassical economists who were his contemporaries, contained enormous difficulties in implementation. Undeterred, Chadwick wished to apply franchise bidding to a whole plethora of industries, services, and economic activities. His solutions in this area, which have received some contemporary attention (Crain and Ekelund 1976; Dnes 1994), raise issues that are highly contemporary and critical for modern day provisions of all kinds of goods and services in transportation, telecommunications, and power utilities.[6] But the concept of shifting property rights in order to create economic efficiency was only one aspect of Chadwick's remarkable originality.

Information, Market Failure, and Common Pools

The modernity and importance of Chadwick's applications of economic theory to economic and social policy has been generally conceded in the area of 'franchise bidding.' But as in so many areas of Chadwick's thought, there is far more to be found in a careful reading of his work.

Adam Smith's famous theory of exchange suggested that, in large numbers bargaining situations, exchange that was beneficial to both parties unambiguously increased the welfare of society. In short, there were no 'third-party effects' in Smith's invisible hand. However, Bentham's utilitarianism suggested the possibility that two-party exchanges could affect third or x-party individuals. In a world where these problems have been made familiar to economists by Ronald Coase (1960), problems of market failure are commonplace in the economic literature, but many aspects of the concept are not without criticism (Demsetz 2011; DiLorenzo 2011). But problems relating to the costs of information, externalities, and public goods were analyzed in detail by Chadwick, often with statistical accouterments, long before Benthamism took a 'practical turn' in the twentieth century.[7]

Theoretical utilitarianism proceeded apace in the nineteenth century to be sure. John Stuart Mill was a leading theoretical proponent of Bentham's ideas, defending utilitarian principles against all comers.[8] British intellectuals, including Henry Sidgwick (1838–1900), and later, A.C. Pigou (1877–1959), continued that tradition which ultimately led to the 'Coase Theorem' and its many developments in the second half of the twentieth century.[9] But traditional economists did not attempt to label and *apply* the concepts of Bentham. Chadwick's uniqueness lies not in the theoretical extensions of Bentham per se but in the direct application of utilitarianism to economic policy. Mill was much more of a 'utilitarian theorist' while Chadwick applied theory. We attempt to show that encased within these interesting applications is a fully developed theory of market failure. But while Chadwick has sometimes received the simple appellation of 'utilitarian practitioner,' his achievements go far beyond that. They include:

1. A clear analysis of how sunk costs and other market imperfections may underlie extra-market restrictions on property (the so-called 'contract management problem');
2. An understanding of how the legal shifting of liabilities might achieve market results consistent with the 'public interest' in particular policies;
3. An analysis of information cost and what is now called 'asymmetric

information' supporting market failure and the necessity of some form of market intervention;
4. A development of the externalities problem – with third party effects – and the means through which public goods are created;
5. A thorough understanding of how common pools dissipate resources through adverse incentives on the part of market participants, and;
6. A well-formed understanding of how time is calculated within and affects economic markets.

If all this sounds modern, as in the twentieth-century contributions of James Buchanan, George Akerlof, Gordon Tullock, Paul Samuelson, Gary Becker, George Stigler, and a host of other contemporary economists, it is because Chadwick – certainly at the level of policy application – plainly scooped modern thought in many of these areas. He showed that 'institutions' such as property and contract were *variables* that affected economic outcomes and that they could be manipulated to produce results in the public interest. While it is the purpose of this book to demonstrate and dissect some of Chadwick's important achievements in these areas, we do not argue that he was always (or ever) 'right' or accurate in his assessments or calculations concerning economic markets. We do argue that the *means* through which he arrived at his market assessments were and are of critical-and-as-yet-unrecognized importance in policy assessment. Before turning to an introduction of a wide range of Chadwick's economics in Chapter 2, after which several of his proposals and analyses are considered in detail, a short biography of this remarkable man provides some insight into the forces that shaped his thought.

IN BRIEF, WHO WAS EDWIN CHADWICK?

To a great extent, Chadwick's career and life were shaped by his early experiences as a son of the English middle class that developed as a result of the industrial revolution. Andrew Chadwick, his paternal grandfather, was a distinguished religious leader and a close friend of John Wesley, the founder of Methodism. Andrew had the opportunity to amass a large estate through real estate acquisition but eschewed material wealth on religious grounds. Andrew's forfeiture of material wealth was a blow to Edwin's father, James, whose inclination was toward the philosophical and the esthetic, rather than the practical. James excelled in academics, was an accomplished cellist, but had no aptitude for business; a number of businesses he started ended in bankruptcy. Witnessing the French revolution, James became a confirmed radical and vigorously supported the human rights movement. One trip to Paris to celebrate the revolution and James returned Francophile – just as his son was later to be – and the editor of a radical newspaper. The Chadwick family moved to London.

Edwin, James' eldest son, was born on 24 January, 1800 and had a normal education until the family moved to London. There Edwin was tutored by his father's radical friends with a focus on modern languages, particularly French. Early on, the young Chadwick was taught that French administrative knowledge was the example to be adopted for England's social and economic problems, a position he held throughout his life. When his father became editor of a Devon newspaper in 1816, Edwin stayed in London with distant relations and, in 1818, at the age of 18, he entered an apprenticeship as an attorney.

The legal profession was at that time one of the few socially acceptable means for an individual to improve his station. Chadwick entered the profession as an apprentice attorney – the field with the least amount of esteem since apprentices served only to prepare and not to argue cases. In 1832, with two years remaining in his apprenticeship, Chadwick decided to become a barrister (a lawyer who actually took cases to court) and was forced to start another seven-year apprenticeship. When Chadwick was finally certified to practice law, his first case was the defense of a bigamist. At first blush, the case seemed straightforward; but, upon investigation, Chadwick became convinced of his client's guilt – a fact his client eventually admitted. Chadwick could not accept the doctrine that his first obligation was to his client, irrespective of the person's guilt or innocence, and forsook law as a career.[10]

While a legal apprentice Chadwick supplemented his income as a freelance writer for the London newspapers. London slums provided copy for his stories and he would often be found touring prisons and the side streets of lower-class London. Chadwick, viewing suffering first-hand, developed a hatred of waste and a desire to cure the social ills of London. On these excursions, moreover, he fell into the company of Neill Arnott and Southwood Smith, medical students and devout utilitarians. They became lifelong friends and associates but they were not, however, responsible for introducing Chadwick to the group known as the Philosophical Radicals. Chadwick volunteered his services to numerous governmental investigative committees and shared a committee assignment with John Bowring who, according to Finer (1952: 10–11), introduced Chadwick to the Philosophical Radicals. Chadwick became an active member of the group, participating in the London Debating Society and the Political Economy Club and, in due course, created the one of the closest and most important friendships of his life with John Stuart Mill.[11]

Chadwick's introduction to the Philosophical Radicals was not the start of a conversion to utilitarianism; rather, it was the fulfillment. As a law student Chadwick had assiduously studied the works of Bentham, holding that Bentham was the theoretical master of correct social doctrine. The intellectual kinship was profound: both were inclined to sweeping changes and had a deep-seated mistrust of tradition; both stressed prevention as the means of promoting the public good, and both had an incessant desire for haste in reform. Consider Bentham on the latter issue (1776–82 [1962]: 423):

> Ought it not – this and every reform – ought it not to be temperate? Well then – to be temperate, it must be gradual – to be well-done, it must be gradually done. Fellow citizens! As often as you meet with a man holding to you this language, say to him, 'Sir, we have our dictionary; what you are saying we perfectly understand; done gradually means left undone, left undone forever if possible.'

The statement could have been Chadwick's and similarities between Bentham and Chadwick in almost all matters meant that Chadwick was a doctrinaire utilitarian and a Philosophical Radical prior to his formal induction in the group, and to his first meeting with Bentham.

The year 1829 was auspicious for Chadwick. As we have mentioned, Chadwick gave up a law career on principle! While another budding career, as a journalist, was closed to him. In a journal edited by John Bowring, Chadwick published a scathing article accusing the daily newspapers of intentionally distorting articles on parliamentary meetings. The editor of *The Times* was particularly incensed and persuaded other editors to blacklist Chadwick while at the same time letting it be known that he would stop his actions if Chadwick would publish an article exempting *The Times* from his accusation. *The Times* claimed innocence, vowing to fire any reporter proven to have distorted the facts. In a tone that was to become his hallmark, as Finer reports (1952: 33), Chadwick replied that *The Times* 'would not be the first paper to sacrifice an individual for what was the systematic practice of all newspapers and not merely all papers, but of *The Times* in particular.' Needless to say, it was years before Chadwick received any good press in that newspaper.

Coincidentally, Chadwick was asked to contribute to a new journal under the co-editorship of Nassau Senior. By chance, Chadwick had an article ready for press, one that he had prepared on crime and police protection for a government committee but which (according to some accounts) had been misplaced by a clerk.[12] Entitling this article 'Preventive Police' (1829) Chadwick turned it over to Senior. The article created a great commotion amongst the Philosophical Radicals, 'combining as it did, Bentham's *Principles of Penal Law*, his *Rationale of Evidence* with the practical working of the "French Code . . . the hand was Chadwick's but the spirit Bentham'" (Finer 1952: 30). Bentham, who was enthralled with the article and then in the process of writing his *Constitutional Code* (1830, in Hume 1981), hired Chadwick as his personal secretary and assistant in organizing the manuscript.

The utilitarian crowd, recognizing the temporary nature of Chadwick's work for Bentham, set about to find a permanent occupation for their most promising young disciple. Bentham himself continually tried to find a career for Chadwick, proposing several schemes that were designed to give Chadwick a secure position. At one point, Bentham offered Chadwick a life's annuity to become the official expositor of Bentham's teachings. Chadwick declined the offer, having reservations concerning some of Bentham's works and thinking himself unfit to be the final authority on Bentham's philosophy. Shortly thereafter, Bentham became quite ill and died with Chadwick caring for him through his last illness. Then, when Senior was appointed to a Commission to inquire into the operation of the Poor Laws, Chadwick was hired as an Assistant Commissioner. Chadwick's true career as utilitarian policymaker had begun.

Chadwick was assigned the task of investigating the operation of the Poor Laws in London and Berkshire. His report, a massive document with copious statistics was not confined to simply enumerating the problems – it also proposed a solution. Chadwick was asked to elaborate his ideas and the resulting document generated an enormous amount of favorable public opinion. The Commissioners urged Chadwick to write the draft of the report to present to Parliament and Senior argued that if Chadwick was to have this responsibility, he should be a full Commissioner. The other Commissioners agreed and Chadwick was promoted.

At this time (April, 1833) there was a wave of worker unrest and agitation for some form of factory legislation. Chadwick was called away from the Poor Law Commission to head the Royal Commission on the State of the Children Employed in Factories. Due to the pressures of political unrest, the Commission was given just six weeks to report. Chadwick himself designed the questionnaires for the collection of information and caused a brief controversy over the private nature of the questions (number of births, miscarriages, and so on). Chadwick, with incomplete information, proposed that no limit be placed on the hours of adults, but that the labor of children be limited to a half-day (the other half to be spent in school) along with an organization of independent inspectors to enforce the new law. Chadwick's original plan was adulterated to make it politically acceptable and he returned to his Poor Law work disillusioned and embittered with 'politics.'

Chadwick set about drafting administrative arrangements for the new Poor Laws. His plan was to centralize administration through a board of three Commissioners – with contempt powers as well as powers to appoint Assistant Commissioners – working through mandatory workhouses operated by Local Boards of Guardians. In addition to centralization, Chadwick wanted to prohibit outdoor relief, that is, payment for services and duties outside the workhouse. Parliament incorporated much of Chadwick's plan into the new law but did not grant the enforcement powers that would be required for the Central Board to maintain the ban on outdoor relief.

Naturally Chadwick expected to be appointed to the Central Board but the three positions, given to J. Shaw-Lefebvre, Franklin Lewis, and George Nicholls, were apportioned on the basis of politics rather than merit and only one of the three (Nicholls) had experience with the operation of poor relief. While recalcitrant at first, Chadwick heeded the call for his expertise and accepted the offer of the position of Secretary to the Central Board. Bitter feuds between Chadwick and the Board followed, particularly over the 'less-eligibility principle' which held that subsidized work in the workhouses had to be at least as onerous in real terms as that in the market (else the demand for poor relief would be intolerable).[13] The conflicts within the administration, particularly between Lewis and Chadwick, became personal, more so since the Board could not fire Chadwick who appointed all of the Assistant Commissioners (the Central Board's local extension) and administered the day-to-day operation of the Law. Lewis set about trying to reduce Chadwick's influence through changes in the Board's procedural rules. The tactic worked. Though Chadwick complained to higher authorities – complaints that were taken as insubordination by the government and the press – his influence waned. Chadwick's popularity was already in decline due to his defense of the use of workhouses which, he believed, were a necessary evil for the proper administration of relief. The Commission, under Lewis, delayed the introduction of workhouses that fanned public hatred and permitted Chadwick to be depicted as the oppressor and Lewis the savior of the poor.

The conflict between the Board, the government, and Chadwick continued, with Chadwick being passed over for promotion to full Commissioner on a number of occasions. Lewis' son replaced him on the Board, inheriting his hatred of Chadwick from his father, and an Irish Commissioner was added to the Board, but Chadwick remained Secretary though increasingly eliminated from the Board's activities. This did not mean that he was inactive however, and as so often happens, seeming defeat brings new opportunities. In this case it had two important effects on Chadwick.

A major problem and high cost of the operation of the Poor Laws were medical expenses and Chadwick, seeking to determine a means to minimize costs, began researching what was to become his most famous report

– the *Sanitary Report*, eventually published in 1842. But this scholarly quest was interrupted by a call for information for a centralized police force. By 1838 public sentiment towards the Poor Laws had turned to hatred. Violent disturbances were beginning to occur. In light of these developments Chadwick revised his 'Preventive Police' article of 1829, deleting references to Bentham and the French Penal code – which the British always believed was inhibitory of liberty – and publishing the revision as the *Constabulary Report* (1839a). Chadwick started a campaign to sway public opinion to pressure Parliament into adopting his proposals.[14] The campaign backfired, however, because the public viewed the proposed central police force as being designed to enforce the Poor Law Acts.

The Poor Law Act was up for renewal in 1839, but because of the controversy generated, Parliament wanted to amend it. No agreements could be reached however and the Act was renewed year-by-year for a number of years. In the midst of these developments Chadwick was ready, in 1842, to publish his *Sanitary Report* – without doubt his (and one of England's) most important pieces of research. A brief historical perspective to this report is instructive.

London, a city approaching two million inhabitants, was disastrously weak on sanitation infrastructure and, importantly, medical science was 'in progress' as regards a multitude of diseases and their causes. Cholera epidemics punctuated the early nineteenth century and terrorized the city in the 1830s and 1840s killing thousands of Londoners. A great debate embroiled medical circles and scientist-physicians over the causes of the epidemic. Chadwick was completely aware of the discussions amongst politicians, scientists, and within the medical profession. One school of thought placed the causes at 'foul air' or person-to-person transmissions of various sorts. Chadwick thought differently and set out to survey physicians and local authorities on sanitation conditions of all kinds.[15] Vested interest against such an exposé and publication of the report was strong from both the Prime Minister and from the younger Lewis on the Board, the election of a new government and the intervention of the Irish Commissioner paved the way for publication. Lewis consented to having the report published provided that it carry *only* Chadwick's name.[16] When the report was favorably accepted by the public, Chadwick received full credit as the author. Fully titled a *Report to Her Majesty's Principal Secretary of State for the Home Department, from the Poor Law Commissioners, on An Inquiry into the Sanitary Condition of the Labouring Population of Great Britain*, and presented to both Houses of Parliament in July 1842, Chadwick's report became an instant classic amongst critical social documents of the nineteenth century (Chadwick 1842a). Most certainly the *Sanitary Report* is the capstone of Chadwick's fame as a 'social' reformer. We will show (in Chapter 5) that his 'supplementary report' published the following year (in 1843) titled, *Report on the Sanitary Conditions of the Labouring Population of Great Britain: A Supplementary Report on the Results of a Special Inquiry into the Practice of Interment in Towns*, carries far more importance as an 'economic' document. Chadwick's *Sanitary Report* focused the nation's attention on the importance of sanitary measures. In 1844, the Health of Towns Commission was formed to examine his recommendations and, although he was not named to the Commission, he had great control over it. He selected issues that were to be investigated and nominated about half of the Commission, which focused on engineering and legislative problems involved in sanitation, ignoring medical issues. The force of Chadwick's report was such that public pressure built for the formation of private associations, foremost of which was the Health of Towns Association. Chadwick was one of the organizers of this association and anonymously authored several pamphlets in support.

Chadwick remained secretary to the Poor Law Central Board but had only minimal duties vis-à-vis operations. In 1845, charges of unusual cruelty were made against a workhouse master, and an Assistant Commissioner was sent to investigate. The Commissioner was conscientious in preparing a thorough report although the newspapers accused him of showing partiality to the master. This led to brouhaha with G.C. Lewis, who failed to support his actions and subsequently fired the assistant for insubordination. A Parliamentary Commission was formed to investigate the original scandal and the assistant's dismissal. Chadwick was called to testify and revealed what had been occurring within the Poor Law administration since it was formed. The public, this time, firmly supported Chadwick against Lewis; however, Lewis was politically influential and Chadwick was blamed for Lewis' downfall. Political pressure mounted to dismiss Chadwick on grounds that he had betrayed his superior and preparations for a massive parliamentary battle were made. However, the issue never reached Parliament and was settled beforehand; Chadwick agreed to resign his post as Secretary and was promised another position in a different department.

In 1847 Chadwick was appointed to the Royal Commission for London Sanitation and for the next seven years served in numerous government positions, all of them dealing with sanitation reform. In 1848 he was appointed to the General Board of Health and the Metropolitan Commission of Sewers. The latter appointment created yet more difficulties – the local authorities who were to be replaced fought tenaciously to maintain their identity. The battle was nominally over the type of sewer system to be installed; Chadwick's tubular drains or the old-style bricked drains. Local authorities (backed by the rent-seeking manufacturers of the old-style drains) successfully fended off Chadwick's attack. For the next seven years, Chadwick was constantly forced to defend the integrity of his original plans against individuals seeking to subvert them for private gain.

As usual, Chadwick could not stay out of the fray. By the mid-1850s, Chadwick was complaining about the effectiveness with which the Public Health Bill had been enforced. Chadwick blamed Parliament for allowing the non-enforcement of the Bill and alienated many members of Parliament. Ill fortune had arranged that the General Board of Health was up for renewal and it was obvious that the Board would be allowed to expire if Chadwick remained a member. It was for this reason that Chadwick agreed to be pensioned off with the knowledge that he would be recalled when his services were needed. Finally, after many years of controversy, Edwin Chadwick retired from public service. For twenty-two years he had made his presence felt – loudly in most cases – through public administration. Although 'retired' Chadwick turned his prodigious energies elsewhere and was to live another 36 years.

Chadwick essentially spent the remainder of his life disseminating ideas and theories through academic societies. One of his most important essays – one distinguishing between competition 'for the field' and competition 'within the field' – was published under the auspices of the Royal Statistical Society in 1859 (see Chadwick 1859c). This essay, mentioned above, contemplates an entirely different mode of 'competition' than that in the traditional competitive theory developed among the classical writers. This 'new' principle was not invented by Chadwick, but he was its most forceful exponent until the second half of the twentieth century. By 1866 Chadwick was interested in the railway 'problem' as it related to ownership, subsidies, and 'coordination,' contributing an important essay on the subject in that year in the *Journal of the Royal Society of Arts*.[17] In 1868 Chadwick was elected to the council of that Society and served as one of its Vice-Presidents from 1872 to 1886. In 1860 Chadwick became Vice-President of the section of Economy and Trade of the National Association for the Promotion of Social Science and in 1877 took over as President of the Public Health Section. His interest in policy, particularly as regards to sanitation and crime, never waned (for example, see Chadwick 1863 [1887]; 1876–77 [1887]; 1887b). Honors continued to flow to him, and in 1862 he was elected to the prestigious Institut Français.

Retirement was spent in relative calm, marred only by an occasional controversy. He maintained his mental faculties until his death in the face of deteriorating general health. Chadwick died on 6 July, 1890 (being knighted the previous year by Queen Victoria) and his last will and testament reflected the issues that concerned him most. His estate was to be used to sponsor annual prizes for the 'sanitary authority which shall have obtained the greatest reduction of the death-rate' and another for 'the managers of a Poor Law district school who could show the largest proportion of scholars got into productive industry' (Finer 1952: 512–13). Tributes to Chadwick abounded at the time of his death. One mentioned by Finer (1952: 512) is particularly apt:

> The faults which were imputed to him may be generalized as faults of over-eagerness . . . Mr. Chadwick, beyond any man of his time, knew what large fresh additions of human misery were accruing day by day . . . and the indignation which he was entitled to feel at the spectacle of so much needless human suffering is not an ignoble excuse for such signs of overconfidence as he may have shown.

And Finer added his own assessment: 'Where others were unmoved, Chadwick cared. Whatever his errors of judgment – and they were many – this is his supreme justification' (1952: 6). Who could ask for anything more?

PLAN OF THE BOOK

It would seem that a man of these vast accomplishments in the realm of sociology and economic history would have been investigated to exhaustion and, indeed, his contributions (and failures) in these areas have been widely discussed. We argue, however, that there are critical aspects of Chadwick's thought – contributions to modern economic theory and their applications to economic policy – that are virtually unknown. This book is an attempt to begin to remedy that gap. In general we will show that the utilitarianism of Chadwick (schooled by Bentham before him) enabled him to conceive of *individual* behaviorist principles and how their action, in the presence of specific institutions, *could* lead to market failure. His understanding of these principles led him to theories about how to deal with what were essentially *economic* problems – problems that had social consequences. A mere history of Chadwick's participation in the social problems of his day overstitches a unique theoretical understanding of markets and market failure. His advanced knowledge of these principles, beyond any of the theoretical and applied policy analyses of the classical or early neoclassical writers, made him 'modern' in that market problems are handled in the same way by economists today. It is Chadwick's 'modernity' and economic sophistication that will be described in this book.

Our account opens in Chapter 2 with a discussion of the overall dimensions of Chadwick's thought. Here we analyze aspects of Chadwick's uniqueness. In particular, we look at his ideas in relation to well-known classical principles, at his mastery of basic modern economic principles, and at the nature of his Benthamite inheritance. (The latter sets the stage for specific examples of his applications of utilitarianism to follow.) The volume of Chadwick's writings is vast and the central portions of our book can only investigate selected topics in Chadwick's huge oeuvre of more than 500 books and manuscripts.

The central focus of Part II entitled 'The Regulation of Markets' is on Chadwick's most famous – but not the most original – economic principle. The so-called theory of contract management, while not invented by Chadwick, was perhaps best explicated by him. In Chapter 3 we develop Chadwick's particular version of 'franchising,' discussing in detail not only his view but bringing his analysis up-to-date as it appears in contemporary economic theory. The relation between Chadwick's conception of competition and the theory of natural monopoly and imperfect competition is a central part of our discussion. The discussion of Chapter 3 creates the background for understanding two of Chadwick's most interesting specific applications of the idea of 'competition for the field.' We have selected two: one (Chapter 4) deals with nation-wide regulation of an industry – the railways of England; and another (Chapter 5) concerns service provisions in urban populations – the supply of funerals and burial grounds. In these examples we begin to understand Chadwick's uniqueness as a sagacious thinker who was able to make keen *theoretical* generalizations from masses of data and facts. Further, we develop the important point that the franchise bidding scheme was only *one* possible institutional response to problems of market failure. To the best of our knowledge, for example, Chadwick was the first writer to ever claim that high information cost and/or 'negative' externalities create market failure, justifying forms of intervention and, possibly, property rights alterations.

Part III of our book is devoted to Chadwick's extensive work on issues relating to law, crime, sociology, and economics. Chapter 6 dissects Chadwick's views on the social condition of the laboring classes of England as a 'utilitarian' problem. In particular we analyze Chadwick's uniqueness on labor issues when contrasted to classical writers, his views on labor productivity, and his analysis of the role of education. In Chapter 7 Chadwick's contributions to the conception of a 'common pool' are developed at length. A penetrating analysis of the English crime problem, both historically and in his own time, led Chadwick to propose solutions that reduced dissipations of utility within the common pool created by the government take-over of crime and criminal justice. Few writers, of his or later times, have ever offered a more complete and able analysis of the whole criminal justice system as Chadwick. While Chadwick's 'solutions' may not be acceptable to some modern populations, his discussion offers possibilities of contemporary relevance. Chapter 8 considers the broad outlines of the utilitarian agenda and its relation to Chadwick's views on sanitation reform, information as a public good and his understanding of the *economic* nature of politics. Our concluding chapter, Chapter 9, discusses how and in what manner Chadwick was unique in the entire realm of nineteenth-century economic thought. Throughout our excursion into Chadwick's economics we will contrast his approach with those of British and non-British contemporaries, particularly that of his good friend and fellow utilitarian John Stuart Mill. That Chadwick was influential in his own time is beyond doubt. More importantly, perhaps, we believe it demonstrable that his brilliant policy excursions provide guidance – positive *and* negative – to policymakers of the twenty-first century.

NOTES

1. He is also credited with ordering the first experiments to determine the engineering parameters of the tubular drainage system (that is, necessary diameters, gradients, and water flow to provide a self-cleansing system). Chadwick's involvement in the engineering aspects was so intense that 'the first glazed earthenware drainpipe in England was baked at Chadwick's insistence' (Finer 1952: 293).
2. The use of probability and statistical inference came somewhat later, in the contributions of F.Y. Edgeworth, Francis Galton, and Karl Pearson (see Stigler 1986).
3. His early espousal of separate housing for male and females in order to prevent unwanted pregnancies led wags to label marriage as being 'Chadwicked.'
4. Blaug's (1963) analysis of the dynamics of the labor market concludes that the Poor Laws were a means of tempering the effects of agricultural structural unemployment, and his conclusion is confirmed in a statistical analysis of Poor Law data.
5. See Ekelund and Hébert (1981).
6. Without recognizing the 'myopia' of Chadwick's concept of 'economic inefficiency,' for example, Harold Demsetz (1969) proposed that there was no clear link between the theory of natural monopoly and monopoly price (creating economic efficiency). Franchise bidding for the exclusive right to serve, in this scenario, could obviate the link between natural monopoly and monopoly price. Whether or not such a system would eliminate, or in what ways it would attenuate, the need for administrative regulation is unclear in practical cases however. See Chapters 3, 4, and 5 of this book for details on this and related matters.
7. We argue that 'sunk costs,' wherein scale economies lead to a single supplier, are a kind of 'market failure' in that, under freedom of property rights, a monopoly is produced.
8. Mill debated and defended utilitarianism throughout his life. It would appear, as we suggest throughout this book, that Mill's utilitarianism made him extremely wary of centralization or socialism. The influence of Ricardo and other classical free market economists is also present in Mill's recommendations for economic and social change.
9. The linkages between Sidgwick and Pigou in the development of modern externality theory are discussed in O'Donnell (1979).
10. This experience, wherein Chadwick bitterly attacked British practice of 'client over truth' and the willful intimidation of innocent witnesses, became a cornerstone of his attack on the criminal justice system of England, as we show in Chapter 7.
11. Mill, a man of incredibly generous spirit, never veered in his support of Chadwick (and

a number of other young scholars and reformers), if not all of Chadwick's inventions and ideas. In the early years, Chadwick and Mill apparently walked together daily and discussed utilitarian doctrine. As some of Mill's early letters suggest (for example, Mill 1963: 516), Mill served as a sounding board for many of Chadwick's articles, acting as editor and advisor. Mill also introduced Chadwick to Nassau Senior and requested that Senior consider one of Chadwick's articles (the 1829 article on crime prevention) for publication (Mill 1972: 1955). This was the article that eventually led to Chadwick's introduction to Bentham.

12.   There seems to be some disagreement as to whether Chadwick actually presented evidence before this early committee on crime. Emsley (1983) states that Chadwick presented evidence before the select committee, but Finer (1952) disagrees, believing Chadwick was asked by Peel to present the evidence, but that the manuscript was lost by an assistant and not found in time, as we report in the text. Brundage (1988) felt that despite Chadwick's ambition, he was unable to influence the committee or present the evidence he had prepared. A look thorough the committee's report reveals no recorded evidence credited to Chadwick or mention of him as a witness (*British Parliamentary Papers* 1968a; 1968b). His manuscripts are collected at the University College London (UCL) library. The Edwin Chadwick Papers held at UCL is an immense archive of more than 250 boxes. The interested reader may do a search on 'Chadwick' in the Calm catalogue http://archives.ucl.ac.uk/. Descriptions of the holdings appear at the file but not the item level. We are grateful to the Chadwick Professor at UCL, Nick Tyler CBE, Chadwick Professor of Civil Engineering, for information on Chadwick's papers.

13.   Chadwick's position on the 'less-eligibility principle' is identical to Mill's (see Mill 1834). Chadwick held this as a sine qua non if the new law was to be effective whereas T.F. Lewis (one of the three Commissioners) thought it was only superficially necessary and thus reasoned that the workhouses were an unnecessary evil. In fact, under Lewis' guidance, the institution of workhouses proceeded at a snail's pace and was eventually disbanded.

14.   We argue that one brilliant result was his paper on criminal procedure in the 1841 issue of the *Westminster Review*, which we analyze in detail in Chapter 7 of this book.

15.   Parliament was goaded to act when, in 1847, more than 10 000 persons were felled by cholera. Again, while Chadwick's assemblage of sanitation conditions convinced him that cholera was spread by unclean water, this was not confirmed until the research of John Snow, a private physician, who identified contaminated drinking water as the culprit. What Chadwick knew by intuition was later proved scientifically. Yet another epidemic took place in 1854 providing even more urgency for a restructuring of urban sanitation infrastructure. A fascinating look into these horrendously frightening epidemics may be found in a book by Steven Johnson (2007), *The Ghost Map: The Story of London's Most Terrifying Epidemic – and How It Changed Science, Cities, and the Modern World*.

16.   There is a preamble to the report, which carries the three Commissioner's names (George Nicholls, George Cornewall Lewis, and Edmund Walker Head).

17.   That essay is entitled 'On the Proposal that the Railways Should be Purchased by the Government,' see Chadwick (1866b).

2. Chadwick's modernity

INTRODUCTION

The long ninety-year life span of Edwin Chadwick (1800–1890) covers the most seminal and fruitful period in the development of modern economics. It encompasses what has become known as the 'classical period,' the marginal revolution, and the beginning of neoclassical economics in both English and Continental incarnations. To place things in time, consider the following: Chadwick entered an attorney's office to study law the year David Ricardo's *Principles of Political Economy and Taxation* was published (1817 [1969]), was still an attorney's clerk when Malthus' *Principles of Political Economy* (1820 [1951]) went into print, and engaged in close personal contact with such economic luminaries as Nassau Senior, John Stuart Mill and J.E. Cairnes. Furthermore, the Francophile Chadwick was as aware of the French 'neoclassical' writers on political economy as he was of the English 'pioneers' in marginalism such as Jenkin and Jevons.[1] Chadwick was also fully cognizant of the romantic and historical criticisms of English political economy and the nascent mathematization of economics. He lived long enough to see the publication (and promulgation) of Walrasian economics, dying only in the year when Alfred Marshall published his monumental *Principles of Economics* (1890). Yet, while not totally unaffected, the thrust of Chadwick's economic analysis and the source of his modernity were different from all of these developments. The purpose of this chapter is to explain, at least in brief, *why* and, to a degree, *how* this was so.

The ultimate source of Chadwick's uniqueness (and modernity) were his roots in utilitarianism and his study of its outcomes when forms of self-interest did not create the Benthamite mantra often phrased as 'the greatest good for the greatest number.' But it was more than that. As we will see in later chapters, Chadwick added a unique empirical component to utilitarianism. No other writer of the classical or neoclassical periods made greater inroads into the economics of social policy because no other writer had a greater command of, and respect for, data. As we will see, Chadwick was a statistical fanatic, offering extensive statistical proof for every proposition that he developed – not formal analytical statistics but through number gathering. In this, Chadwick was interested in 'applied utilitarianism' – devising social policies which equated public and private interests. In taking this approach to social problems Chadwick was inexorably drawn beyond the traditional realm of economics in the treatment of social ills. Social problems *were*, as modern economists such as Becker and Posner have shown, economic problems. This extension of economic analysis into new areas of public policy constitutes the uniqueness of Chadwick as a political economist.

But it is not enough to simply assess Chadwick as an expression of inventive utilitarianism. A focused picture requires a more comprehensive view of his thought which, as a gifted intellectual, would constitute the mélange of influences and interests in his life. Thus, in the present chapter we canvas Chadwick's insights into and criticisms of classical economics, his use and understanding of standard microeconomics and anecdotal statistics, and his approach to some particular solutions to economic and social problems. This somewhat prolonged introduction readies the reader for much more detailed discussion of his applications to specific problems and reveals some of the uniqueness of Chadwick as a thinker. Throughout the discussion, we believe it will become apparent that Chadwick, while undoubtedly absorbing some intellectual influences of nineteenth-century savants, was *not* a man of his age but was far closer to one of our own.

SELF-INTEREST AND ARTIFICIAL INTERESTS: BENTHAM'S CRITICAL LEGACY TO CHADWICK

Human egoism and the self-interest axiom have prevailing explanatory variables in the organized study of economic phenomena. In order to understand Chadwick's philosophical preconceptions it is necessary to describe self-interest. Its origins are in the intellectual environment which characterized the beginnings of social science. The two decades surrounding the turn of the eighteenth century marked a major revolution in the physical sciences and are especially important. Newton had reduced physics to a finite number of theoretical propositions upon which a new understanding of man's physical environment was to be built. Newton's success sparked a desire in social thinkers to achieve a similar reformulation of social environment, that is, to found a social science based on a minimum of universally true, verifiable principles. The works of Locke, Gay, Hartley, and Hume exemplify the application of Newton's method of scientific reasoning in order to reduce social science to a set of common denominators (Hartley 1966; Hume 1978). One of these principles was that individuals are essentially hedonistic, seeking pleasure and avoiding pain.[2] Hume (1936; Appendix I) pointed out that pain and pleasure may be quantitatively different between individuals and, therefore, individuals must react to their own needs or in their own self-interest. This characterization of individuals acting in their own self-interest has survived to become the primary basis of modern economic theory, thanks predominantly to Adam Smith.

Smithian Self-Interest

Adam Smith introduced self-interest as the mainspring of economic activity. Although Smith considered sympathy as the single most important factor in guiding behavior in *The Theory of Moral Sentiments* (1759 [1976]), he underwent a marked transition by the publication of the *Wealth of Nations*.[3] In the *Wealth of Nations*, Smith abandoned sympathy as the universal emotion in favor of self-interest as a common denominator. As one famous quotation indicates:

> It is not from the benevolence of the butcher, the brewer or the baker, that we expect our dinner, but from their regard to their own interest. We address ourselves, not to their humanity but to their self-love, and never talk to them of our own necessities, but of their advantages. (Smith 1776 [1937]: 14)

Thus, Smith ruled that individual behavior could be predicted on the basis of which activity served to maximize the utility of that individual.

The doctrine of man as a self-interested creature was indelibly inscribed in the fabric of economic thought within Chadwick's era. Chadwick's own characterization of the role of self-interest reflects the methodological influence of the Newtonian scientific revolution; that is, the search for 'natural' laws. According to Chadwick, 'Self-interest is the most constant – the most uniform – more lasting, and most general feeling; and it appears, when traced in its ultimate actions to be really one of the most powerfully beneficent' (Chadwick 1846: 26). The constancy of self-interest makes it useful as a predictive variable in the development of public policy and Chadwick went so far as to maintain that there were national differences in the general efficacy of this emotion. Dealing with problems of mine safety, for example, he notes that:

> We Anglo-Saxons were, perhaps, somewhat more susceptible to a pecuniary interest as a motive power, and would display greater vigour in the prosecution of the principle. Instead of leaving the application of mechanical science to the promotion of casual and feeble benevolence, the managers and owners would themselves take them up, issue large rewards for them, and prosecute them with vigour. (1859b: 44)

The relative predilection of the British for the promotion of individual interest implies that predictions based on an analysis of incentives would produce greater accuracy and consequently, provide a comparative advantage to those who might wish to control behavior.

The ability to predict and control behavior through self-interest is two-sided. One application is to control individual behavior, which may be intellectually distasteful on Lockean grounds of 'interpersonal utility evaluations.' But this tactic may be abandoned in that it deals with an individual and not the community as a whole – a *raison d'être* for social science as a discipline. The second application of the self-interest doctrine lies where individual behavior affects society generally or where an anomaly appears between the interests of individuals and that of society. This has become the orthodox use of the principle and thus the problem becomes a matter of relationships between private and public interests.

The Insights of Halévy

Given that utility may be subjectively different between individuals, Élie Halévy in his *The Growth of Philosophical Radicalism* outlines the problem as follows: 'If my pleasure is the natural object of my desire, and my pain the natural object of my aversion, how is it conceivable that the moral sense which inspires me to pursue the greater utility and not my private interest should be a constituent part of my nature' (1928: 13). What, in other words, brings about an identity of private and public interests? Assuming the identity of interests is the preferred situation, there are three philosophical frameworks under which the identity of interests is produced. Halévy identifies these three doctrines as the fusion of interest theory, the natural harmony or natural identity of interest theory, and the artificial identity of interest theory (1928: 13–34).

The 'fusion of interest' argument presupposes the possibility of conflict between private and public interest, simultaneously assuming away a fruition of the conflict. Halévy argues that '. . . it may be admitted that the identification of personal and general interest is spontaneously performed within each individual conscience by means of the feeling of sympathy which interests us in the happiness of our neighbor' (1928: 13). In modern terminology, individual utility functions are interdependent with sympathy a reconciling force wherever individual and public interests are opposed. Individuals voluntarily sublimate their strict self-interest to the public good.

Use of the fusion doctrine as a philosophical foundation for social science eliminates the necessity of public policy. Under this doctrine, private and public interests are automatically equated and individual actors will automatically maximize social welfare. Within this framework, social science becomes simply a descriptive profession and no longer satisfies the Newtonian philosophical basis of science.[4] However there is a fundamental contradiction in the assumptions underpinning the fusion of interest doctrine. The first assumption is that utility is quantitatively and qualitatively different among individuals and that this interpersonal difference cannot be subjectively determined. The doctrine then assumes that, through the emotion of sympathy, individuals take the necessary actions to maximize social welfare, which implicitly assumes that individuals can evaluate interpersonal utility levels. There lies the contradiction: knowledge requirements logically prohibit such evaluations. Additionally, this doctrine bears the added imperfection of being inconsistent with the facts. Criminal behavior would be unlikely if sympathy were a controlling factor in human behavior.

The 'natural harmony or natural identity of interest' doctrine played a decisive role in the development of economics as a discipline distinct from the other social sciences. It was a basis for the rise of economic liberalism and was cast in a leading role in the *Wealth of Nations*. The fusion theory and the natural harmony theory have much in common, but the latter fared better intellectually. Both doctrines posit an egocentric, hedonistic behavioral pattern as individuals are viewed as being concerned with promoting their own utility. Both reach similar conclusions with respect to the identification of private and public interests and the automaticity of that result is the same. In both, social science is 'descriptive,' but the paths through which individual action creates the public interest differ. In the natural identity doctrine individuals *unintentionally* (passively?) and *by assumption* advance the public interest whereas the fusion of interest doctrine utilizes the emotion of sympathy to (actively?) elicit the identity of interest. Halévy summarizes the natural identity doctrine by noting that '. . . since it is recognized that the predominating motives in human nature are egoistic, and further that the human species lives and survives, it must be admitted that the various egoisms harmonize of their own accord and automatically bring about the good of the species' (1928: 15). Action is based solely on the individual's utility considerations but such actions necessarily promote the public interest.

The natural identity of interest doctrine rests on two implicit assumptions:

- That the public good is the sum of individual situations (this so-called 'additive' assumption is basic to utilitarian philosophy in general) and;
- That there are no externalities or 'third-party effects' in the social system.

So long as all costs and benefits are internalized, the voluntary actions of individuals will necessarily be to the advantage of society – utilitarianism dictates that voluntary activities are always calculated to increase net welfare. However, if externalities or third-party effects are admitted to exist, the possibility that individual actions may be detrimental to social welfare becomes significant. In other words, private interests may diverge from the public interest by virtue of unexploited positive externalities or non-compensated negative externalities. Under the fusion of interest doctrine, these externalities were reconciled through the mechanism of sympathy and benevolence. No such mechanism exists within the natural harmony of interest doctrine because the problem is *assumed not to exist*.

Smith's Identity of Interest

Although the natural harmony of interest doctrine ignored an empirically verifiable fact recognized in the fusion doctrine, the new paradigm was swiftly incorporated into the emerging discipline of economics. The idea that society would be best off when individuals were allowed complete freedom in their economic activities was the philosophical justification behind the rise of economic liberalism during the eighteenth century. The doctrine, with important antecedents in the work of such writers as Bernard de Mandeville, reached its zenith in the writings of Adam Smith.[5]

The *Wealth of Nations* (Smith 1776 [1937]) represents an almost complete acceptance of the natural harmony of interest doctrine as applied to political economy. Whatever the empirical content of this doctrine (and there are many interpretations), Smith set out to delineate those factors which increase overall happiness.[6] He discovered that the things serving to increase production of goods and services (exchange and the division of labor) were motivated by the desire of individuals to further their own interest. However, Smith did not rely on unbounded self-interest to direct society to its most preferred position, employing as he did the institution of competition to provide the limiting constraints. Within a competitive framework individuals could be allowed to follow their self-interest, with the result that this would promote the public interest. The process is summarized within the 'invisible hand passage,' so well known that we need not repeat it here (see Smith 1776 [1937]: 423).

Competition is the process which harmonizes private and public interests. This reliance on competition to bring about harmony hinges upon whether or not the competitive process is viewed as natural. If the competitive framework is a natural phenomenon, then the harmony will be 'natural.' But individuals will attempt, in their own self-interest, to monopolize markets when they are not constrained from doing so. Thus, competition itself must be protected against the actions of self-interested officials – a fact Smith noted. It would seem therefore that competition must be maintained through artificial means. The naturalness of this harmony inevitably depends on the definition of 'naturalness' – a non-quantifiable variable.

However 'natural' the natural harmony of interests actually is, Smith's doctrine suffered the same fate as the 'fusion' theory and, at least partly, as a result of other ideas and opinions that Smith himself issued in the *Wealth of Nations*. The natural harmony of interest doctrine, in strictest terms, assumes no externalities, and therefore, the competitive market need not be transcended or redirected by other forces. Smith himself pointed out that this was not true, in that there were legitimate roles for collective action. Thus, Smith recognized the existence of externalities and market failure. Confrontation of the 'theory' with the 'facts' of the real world yielded yet a third variant in the quest to describe the relation between private and public interests.

'Artificial' Identities of Interest: Enter Bentham and Chadwick

Yet another revision of interest theory has been called (by Élie Halévy) the 'artificial identity of interest' doctrine. This thesis was employed primarily in a theoretical framework by Jeremy Bentham, and later, in an empirical setting, by Edwin Chadwick. Halévy (1928: 17) describes the doctrine as follows:

> [W]hile still admitting that individuals are chiefly or even exclusively egoistic, it is yet possible to deny that their egoisms will ever harmonize either immediately or even ultimately. It is therefore, argued that in the interest of individuals, the interest of the individual must be identified with the general interest, and that it is the business of the legislator to bring about this identification.

This alternative conceptualization was a prominent theme, though not the only one, of the work of Jeremy Bentham (see Bentham 1776–82 [1962], Vol. 1: 1–2). It enlists the utilitarian view of behavioral patterns and the utilititarian view of social welfare. The artificial identity doctrine is also flavored by the fact that Bentham was more adamant about the egocentric view of man's nature than most writers. It was not simply one facet of human psychology to Bentham, but a necessary element in social organization. As he put the matter (1776–82 [1962], Vol. 1: 339):

> Every individual has for his constant occupation the care of his own welfare – an occupation no less legitimate than necessary; for suppose that it were possible to reverse the principle, and to give to the love of others superiority

over self-love, the results of this arrangement would be most ridiculous and disastrous.

Bentham's artificial identity thesis diverges from the natural harmony argument and aligns itself with the fusion argument in its position on external effects. The doctrine accepts as an undeniable fact that the existence of spillover costs and benefits may involve disinterested third parties. The doctrine also emulates the natural harmony thesis in discounting the efficacy of sympathy as a motivating force. The existence of externalities and the ineffectiveness of benevolence produce a conclusion that differs from the parent doctrines – which means a conflict of interests may exist.

Acceptance of the possibility of setting up an artificial identity of interest through various methods paves the way for a more active role for the social scientist. The social scientist becomes a promoter of the public interest and there are two distinct philosophical solutions to a divergence of interests. One may:

1. Reorganize the social structure and assign the responsibility for the public interest to a public body – that is, a benevolent government; or,
2. Redirect private interests in such a manner that the identity of interests is brought about artificially.

Clearly Bentham espoused and defended the second alternative. Alterations of personal interests working through the auspices of government to coincide with the public interest become, for Bentham, the prime function of the social scientist. This was the thrust and central theme of Jeremy Bentham's life work.

Examples of the pervasiveness of the artificial identity of interest doctrine are contained in two of Bentham's many works: *The Panopticon Writings* (1791 [1995]) and his *An Introduction to the Principles of Morals and Legislation* (1789, originally written 1780). The theme of each of these works is to provide solutions to social problems by altering incentives to bring about an artificial identity of interests. The *Introduction* is Bentham's appeal, as Halévy put it (1928: 17–18), for the 'legislator to solve, by means of well-regulated applications of punishments, the great problem of morals, to identify the interest of the individual with the interest of the community.' *Introduction* deals with crime, and the book's conclusions investigate the proper design of a legal structure (in terms of laws and punishments) wherein it will become of individual interest to act in the public interest. The *Panopticon*, which also deals with criminal behavior, is a blueprint for a prison (called a Panopticon) based on utilitarian principles. Encompassing architectural and administrative details, the

Panopticon was to produce maximum rehabilitation at minimum social cost. Bentham's method was to resolve all conflicts of interest involved in custodial care of offenders by identifying the public interest (minimum cost and maximum crime prevention while maintaining humanitarian treatment of prisoners) with the pecuniary interests of the warden. It was on the self-interest of the prison administration rather than its benevolence that Bentham relied.[7] And it was Chadwick's 1829 article on 'Preventive Police' and his application of Bentham's principles that led Bentham to make him his trusted associate and last 'secretary.'

CLASSICAL AND CONTEMPORARY ELEMENTS IN CHADWICK'S THOUGHT

We are convinced that Edwin Chadwick had read and was fully abreast of the social and economic literature of his time, including the works of his contemporaries, the classical economists. However, Chadwick did not parrot classical theoretical ideas. Rather, his empirical and practical nature led him to challenge or modify a number of them. We glean this observation from Chadwick's approach to some of the cornerstones or founding elements and essential ingredients of classical economics – the division of labor, the Malthusian population doctrine, and Say's Law of markets.

Chadwick and Classical Cornerstones of Economic Analysis

It is well known that Adam Smith featured the division of labor as, to use the words of Schumpeter, 'practically the only factor in economic progress' (1954: 187). Chadwick, who had obviously read Smith, agreed with him on the division of labor and resulting productivity gains concerning the introduction of machinery. But, in this as in almost all cases, Chadwick extended or modified the basic classical idea to be more in tune with his policy-empirical predilections. Chadwick warned against 'unnecessary' divisions of labor. First there are the increased dangers of unemployment due to specialized production – that is, increased interdependence. Here he offers the example of the cessation of cotton imports during the American Civil War which resulted in great unemployment in the textile districts (1856b). More in keeping with Chadwick's policy interests, however, was the empirical observation that the division of labor did not translate into managerial efficiency:

> Division of labour in the arts derives its efficiency from combination, adaptation, and subordination to direction to one end; but that which appears to

be a division of labours in local administration is, in fact, an insubordinate separation, weakening the means of procuring adequate skill and power, occasioning obstructions and defective execution, and enhancing expense. Were pins and machines made as sewers and roads are constructed; shafts of pins would be made without reference to heads, – in machines, screws would be made without sockets, and it may be confidently stated, there would not be a safe or perfect and well-working machine in the whole country. (1842b [1965]: 380)

Here Chadwick is pushing for the centralization of authority by countering the argument that local authorities are more efficient due to the division of labor attendant in the separation of powers. He argues against dividing managerial processes into independent activities, as in Smith's pin example, maintaining that the division of labor (in this particular case, road and sewer construction) would only result in an inferior product at a greater cost.[8]

Population theory is yet another example of Chadwick putting his own policy stamp on one of the classical analytical cornerstones. Since the solutions to social ills of nineteenth-century England were dependent on the sheer numbers involved, Chadwick was acutely interested in population. Although there were many interpretations of the nature of population growth, the Malthusian doctrine – with food supply limitations, and positive and preventive checks – was the received theory during Chadwick's early forays into economics and sociology. It was used extensively by the classical economists as a predictive or explanatory mechanism and as an element of other theories. Chadwick, true to his interests, was concerned with its use as an explanation of real world phenomena, and in this mode he completely rejected the idea of the 'trap.' First, Chadwick rejected the notion on empirical grounds, citing comparative statistics on longevity. In particular Chadwick, again in his 1842 *Sanitary Report* (1842b [1965]), compared life spans in Geneva, Switzerland with those in parts of England, finding that 'The progression of the population and the increased duration of life had been attended by a progression in happiness . . . the probability of life is 45 years, and Geneva, which exceeds 27,000 in population, has arrived at a high degree of civilization and of *prospérité matérielle*' (1842b [1965]: 241). By contrast, some corresponding British life expectancies ranged from a high of 39 in the county of Rutland to a low of 17 in Liverpool. Most interesting is that Chadwick attributed the failure of the Malthusian trap in Geneva to a 'Beckerian' kind of restraint: '. . . as prosperity advanced marriages became fewer and later; the proportion of births were reduced, but great numbers of the infants born were preserved; and the proportion of the population in manhood became greater' (1842b [1965]: 241). As incomes rise, as in Geneva, the opportunity cost to childbirth becomes greater, and higher costs mean fewer children, other things equal.

Chadwick, again arguing from observation, refused to use the population theory as a description of reality. He refused to adhere to the notion, common in the popular opinion of the time, that unemployment, poverty, crime, and other social ills were the *result* of the natural tendency of the population to increase beyond its means. As he noted in regard to his and others' inquiries into the Poor Law reforms, '[in] the inquiry instituted by the Poor Law Commissioners into the circumstances of the rural population, and by parallel enquiry into the condition of a large proportion of the manufacturing population, instituted by the Central Board of Factory Commissioners, opposite conclusions were established' (1836: 241). Rather, Chadwick argued that the explanation for these evils could be attributed to the incentives provided by deficient institutions such as those relating to sanitary and medical science, information, and the lack of redress of externalities and market failures by government. While there were many disagreements over the population doctrine in the classical literature, Chadwick's view of it coincided with his careful empirical analysis and the policy orientation of his social research.[9]

One of the cornerstones of classical thought was the macroeconomic theory of Say's Law, popularly characterized as 'supply creates its own demand,' suggesting the impossibility of a general excess of production and a general excess of labor. There are essentially two versions: Say's 'identity' and Say's 'equality.' Say's 'identity' is a truism, as Mark Blaug has explained: 'Unless they were talking nonsense, they [the classical writers] could not have meant that aggregate demand is always equal to aggregate supply, regardless of variations in prices, and that no departures from full employment can possibly take place. Rather, they were driving at the idea that a perfectly competitive economy tends to full employment' (1978: 159). In Blaug's assessment, Say's identity is a logical impossibility of an oversupply of goods from the assumptions both of demand functions being homogeneous of degree zero in prices and of continuous equilibrium in the money market. Say's equality, on the other hand, does not dichotomize the pricing process and allows for short-run overproduction and labor market disequilibrium – indicating only a 'tendency' towards full employment for the economy.

Chadwick, as a clear empiricist, acknowledged the falsification of Say's identity and the possibility of macroeconomic disequilibrium.[10] In what is basically a Malthusian interpretation Chadwick clearly recognizes the possibility of unemployment in the short run and the possibility of government intervention to lessen the severity of the distress. But rather than call for government policies to guarantee full employment Chadwick

promoted policies such as education to increase worker mobility in order
to shorten the adjustment process. It is clear, moreover, that he was thinking in terms of 'real' disturbances rather than in the possibility that only
money market disequilibrium could create disequilibrium in the goods
market, a position taken by a number of classical writers, including J.S.
Mill (see Mill 1851 [1967]: 69–74).

Chadwick then, at least from a practical and workable standpoint,
was fully versed in the basic classical propositions. These propositions were primarily of a macroeconomic character. That he took an
empirical perspective on many of them – often offering contradictory
'evidence' – is hardly surprising given that a large part of his method was
to combine Benthamite principles of individualism with keen observation
of markets.[11] This was to be his hallmark, but it is also important to note
that Chadwick's empiricism led him to a clever understanding of some
now-standard microeconomic concepts.

Chadwick and Some (Now-)Standard Principles of Microeconomics

Chadwick's status as a bona fide economist is revealed not only in his
understanding of classical principles but through keen insights into some
fundamental microeconomic problems. As with the confrontation with
classical economics, Chadwick's prescience is revealed mostly within empirical discussions. Here we show that Chadwick's toolkit included an early
and formidable arsenal of standard microeconomic ideas: the concept of
opportunity cost, cost-benefit analysis, a clear specification of the demand
curve, and a workable concept of 'value.'

Opportunity cost played a major role in Chadwick's policy prescriptions, perhaps most especially in his analysis of sanitary reform.
Chadwick's vision of the benefits to reform went far beyond the direct
costs of the unsanitary state of the country, that is, doctor's fees, hospital
costs, medication costs, and so on. He included the benefits *foregone* due
to sickness and death as indirect (opportunity) costs, estimating that their
inclusion would involve a money saving in 'excessive sickness, excessive
funerals, and lost labour, amounting to no less than twenty-five millions
of money for the United Kingdom' (1885: 6). Chadwick was never more
thorough in wanting to use full opportunity costs than in his *Sanitary
Report* in order to promote the most convincing case possible for reform.[12]
As we shall see in the ensuing chapters, all of Chadwick's reforms are characterized by a similar thoroughness in the determination of opportunity
costs.[13]

For Chadwick, as for Adam Smith, individual self-interest was the key
to understanding behavior. Chadwick's application of it was, however,

in the tradition of Bentham. Individual behavior was always the result of a calculation of the utility gained by an action in contrast to the additional cost incurred. This matrix, so modern in spirit, was evident in much of Chadwick's contributions from the earliest to the latest of his written work. One example stands out. Chadwick's direct involvement with Peel's Select Committee of 1828 is the subject of some controversy, but the fact that he devised 'principles of action' to close up the gaps in private incentives to crime prevention and societal protection by 1829 is beyond doubt. Chadwick focused on *economic* crime – robberies – calling other kinds 'indoor crimes.'[14] His foundation and aim was to underline the institutional changes that would alter *marginal incentives* of perpetrators. Marginal costs of criminal behavior was equated to the marginal benefits obtained thereof (see Chapter 7). This kind of marginal calculation is the modern one underlying the 'economics of crime' as outlined by Gary Becker (1968), George Stigler (1970), and Issac Ehrlich (1973); and as excellently reported by Hébert (1977) it is the foundation for contemporary economic research in criminal enforcement. Chadwick, understanding the reciprocal nature of 'economic' crime, adjured individuals to protect themselves and others from crime, reducing the marginal benefit from robbery (1829: 272) and urged increased information in the form of 'property registries.' Potential victims could reduce the benefits accruing to miscreants from criminal activity. Marginal cost increases to criminals could be had by numerous means, including 'random' enforcement, better police technology (use of tricycles for speed, and so on) and, most particularly, by increasing the probability of conviction (Chadwick 1841). While we reserve a full discussion of this aspect of Chadwick's contribution to Chapter 7, we note here that Chadwick's policy prescriptions all involved changing the *marginal* incentives of criminals. This view of the calculating individual suffuses virtually all of Chadwick's policy work.

Most amazing, perhaps, is Chadwick's specification of the demand curve. In his 'Address on Railway Reform' of 1865, for example, Chadwick wrote:

> The prevalent railway administration is, however, at variance with a practical economical principle, which I enumerated thirty years ago, and proposed to develop as a law – of the increasing capacity of purchase in ratios proportional to the relative numbers of the different classes or strata of society, and to the reduction of the rates of charge. Thus, if in any community of the average proportions of different classes of society, there are found one hundred who can purchase a work or afford to pay for a service at a shilling, there will also be found more than double the number of purchases at sixpence; more than double the number of purchasers at threepence, than there are at sixpence; and so on in an increasing ratio with a descending price. (1865a: 83)

In this particular case Chadwick is arguing that the demand curve is elastic with respect to the prevailing railway fares. Chadwick's 'law' of 'increasing ratios of consumption' associated with price decreases applied, he thought, to a number of industries. Chadwick maintains that demand was elastic with respect to railway rates, water prices, newspaper taxes, cabriolet rates, and telegraph and gas rates. In each of these cases, Chadwick alleged that a decrease in price would result in an increase in total revenue and, as further evidence of the law, he habitually cited the experience of the penny post, which became profitable with the institution of greatly decreased rates. In general Chadwick was extremely optimistic about the overall effect of price reductions and he often assumed (as we will see in later chapters) that scalar economies were so great in some industries that costs would fall faster than price so that profitability would increase.[15] Chadwick's was one of the earliest formulations of a demand relation in England, relying probably on his familiarity with Continental literature.[16]

From the foregoing, it does not take much to conclude that Chadwick possessed a workable theory and understanding of exchange value. He espoused a relatively crude theory of supply and demand with supply being governed by costs of production and demand being a measure of utility. Within this nexus, Chadwick constantly emphasized the impact of 'better methods' and new technology on reductions in costs of production: mechanization in agriculture such as steam tractors and reapers; and fixed-factor consolidation in railway, postal, and telegraph rates would do the trick and, as noted above, in such cases Chadwick thought that increased output would offset cost increases resulting in average cost reductions. In all, then, Chadwick could not be called a 'theorist' but rather someone who had a quite workable theoretical orientation in the standard tools of classical economics and, especially, in some of the early fundamentals of microeconomics. His clear understanding of opportunity cost and, in particular, demand theory served as a fine backdrop to the theoretical interpretations and policy studies that made him unique among nineteenth-century thinkers.

CHADWICK'S MODERNITY: APPLYING BENTHAMITE PRINCIPLES TO SOCIAL PHENOMENA

Chadwick likely had utilitarian leanings even prior to his active participation with the Philosophical Radicals as our brief biography of Chadwick in Chapter 1 suggests. His association with the radicals and with Bentham, however, created the 'total utilitarian' and his entire career may be characterized as the application of Bentham's principles to economic and social phenomena. Chadwick used a wide variety of Bentham's ideas at one time or another, but it was the artificial identity of interest doctrine that Chadwick applied with the most success.

In understanding Chadwick's achievement, it is important to understand that Chadwick, while accepting Bentham's philosophical pleasure-pain hypotheses, concentrated on the importance of real and pecuniary self-interest – specifically, on self-interest as achieved through the individual's *equation of marginal benefits and marginal costs.* His great originality lies in proposals to adjust this principle through the establishment of regulations or institutions that redirected self-interest to creation of the public interest. In this Chadwick considered new problems and reassessed 'older' lingering social problems, most of which had been considered 'non-economic' in nature.

There are many examples of Chadwick's originality and his anticipation of concepts that became part of modern economics only in the latter half of the twentieth century. These include, as we will see, such notions as the voter paradox, the one-vote veto, the acceptance of crime as rational economic behavior, the value of time in economic decisions, the Coase Theorem, and a better understanding of bureaucratic behavior, to name but a few. Such concepts were developed within a wide range of social problems such as the protection of private property, personal safety, hygiene and sanitation, productive efficiency in markets, and public sector efficiency. The theme these problems and issues have in common is that they all deal with activities where private incentives are to be *redirected* for the public good due to a conflict of private and public interests. A number of these analyses are considered in detail later in this book. Here we consider only a sample of cases demonstrating and documenting Chadwick's remarkable ingenuity.

Time as an Essential Element in Economic Analysis

One of the most profound and useful additions to modern microeconomics has been a direct integration of the economic concept of time into the theory of consumer behavior, input and output markets, and economic sociology (Becker 1965; Becker 1981; Lancaster 1966). Time is, in essence, an opportunity cost that must be included as part of human motivation. These observations were an integral part of Chadwick's economic analysis. He was entirely cognizant of the importance of time as a parameter in the optimizing behavior of individuals and sought to apply time as a factor in analyzing diverse social problems. These problems include the use of time costs to explain transportation speeds, personal hygiene habits, legislative inertia, and the historical development of police systems.

Chadwick found himself embroiled in the controversy over rail nationalization in the mid-nineteenth century, the complete analysis of which
appears in Chapter 4. One interesting aspect of his analysis relates to train
speeds. One criticism made by the proponents of a nationalized rail system
was that English trains operated at speeds which were excessive when
contrasted to those of continental counterparts. Chadwick responded by
saying that 'It is true that on the Continent speeds are lower than with us;
but there the people do not like high speeds, it is only with us that there
is a due appreciated of the economic maxim, that time is money' (1856a:
803). Chadwick argued that higher speeds on English trains were simply
reflecting the desires of demanders, explicitly recognizing that individual
time valuations will affect economic activities.

Private activities were not the only sphere in which Chadwick argued
the importance of the value of time. He also sought to augment legislative productivity by more efficient use of parliamentary time. Specifically,
Chadwick attempted to streamline parliamentary procedures by requiring
that all evidence concerning legislative issues be submitted in print prior to
the start of the legislative session. This parliamentary reform was designed
to eliminate lengthy debates due to members' ignorance of the issues being
debated. Chadwick illustrates the problem:

> Mr. Chamberlain is reported to have occupied three hours and forty minutes in
> his exposition of the Merchant Shipping Bill. If it had been circulated in print
> in the morning, every member might have read it attentively, and in about a
> third of that time mastered it better than he could usually have done in hearing
> it. (Chadwick 1885: 59)

By eliminating unnecessary debate, Chadwick calculated that the dissemination of information before parliamentary action would save 'time of the
public value of some thousand pounds' (1885: 59). Chadwick arrived at
the monetary estimate using a twenty-five year old study estimating the
value of each member's time at five guineas per hour. As with the modern
analysis of the opportunity cost of time, Chadwick assumed wage rates as
a proxy for value.

Perhaps Chadwick's most explicit use of the value of time concept
was in his famous *Sanitary Report* (Chadwick 1842b [1965]). As noted in
Chapter 1, this document was the result of a thorough examination of the
sanitary conditions and habits of the English population, concluding that
sanitation was in a deplorable state. The cause: adverse incentives on the
part of individuals to practice sound personal hygiene.

A central feature of Chadwick's policies on the sanitary conditions
of England was to overhaul the existing water distribution system.
Extant facilities consisted of centrally located cisterns where consumers

purchased their water supplies – a system that required the internalization of transportation costs by the consumer. Chadwick's statistical analysis revealed that the pecuniary cost of water was well within the budget of the lowest classes but that the extensive use of water for home sanitation was restricted by the full cost of water usage, that is, when the time cost of hauling water was considered. According to Chadwick, 'under any circumstance, if the labourer or his wife or child would otherwise be employed, even in the lowest paid labour or in knitting stockings, the cost of fetching water by hand is extravagantly high' (1842b [1965]: 142). Thus, it is the high full cost of water that, in large measure, explained the low sanitary quality of the nation rather than some vague preference for unsanitary living conditions.

The solution, in Chadwick's analysis, was to reduce the full cost of water consumption by having water delivered directly to every home in the empire. This would obviously raise the money price, but by eliminating the necessity of hand cartage, full price (money price plus value of time spent) would in fact decrease. Again noting that the opportunity cost of time is approximated by the wage rate, Chadwick concludes that:

> In most towns, and certainly in the larger manufacturing towns, those members of a family who are of strength to fetch water are usually of strength to be employed in profitable industry, and the mere value of their time expended in the labour of fetching water, is almost much higher than the cost of regular supplies of water even at the charge made by the water companies. (1842b [1965]: 142)

Water demand is thus a function of its money price and the individual's wage rate and the change in quantity demanded by a move to a more expensive (in money terms) mode of delivery would be offset by the decreased time costs of consumption.

There are many contemporary applications of the value of time, including market applications to goods 'types,' advertising, fast-food restaurants, and concert attendance, to name only a few. Chadwick's applications of this principle – while certainly not a match for the technical virtuosity of modern work – was in the vanguard of 'value of time analysis' in numerous applications as early as the first half of the nineteenth century.[17]

Liability Placement and Law and Economics

The artificial identity of interest theory is nowhere more obvious in Chadwick's works than in his analyses of liability placement in the production of personal safety, a clearly modern concern. Here we briefly analyze two aspects of Chadwick's analysis: the protection of convict transportees and the protection of industrial operatives. These are fundamentally examples from what is now called 'law and economics' and both demonstrate the frequent impotency of benevolence when contrasted with pecuniary incentives.

Prisoner transport

Convict transportation was one of Chadwick's favorite examples of self-interest at work. The British government decided to relieve prison overcrowding through exile to the penal colony at Botany Bay, Australia. Shipowners were paid a flat fee for every convict embarked, with the expected results (at least in hindsight) since incentives could only be termed perverse. The shippers sought to maximize profits by maximizing the number of prisoners embarked and minimizing the costs en route. Under this payment system, the survival rate of prisoner-passengers fell as low as forty percent. Chadwick describes the problem and the solution:

> [I]n the first instance, a capitation payment was made on embarkation, and this resulted in the loss of half of the convicts put on board; by degrees that loss was reduced to one-third, but when, under the auspices of a new colonial administration, the system was altered to a capitation payment for all the convicts that were landed at their destination, the contrast was very striking indeed, and the owners of the vessel carried surgeons, and the best means were devised for landing the largest possible number at the port for which they were bound. (1866a: 252)

The transportee system was to remove criminals from English society – an aim achieved with great success. But a perverse result was that the mortality rate was unexpectedly high. Chadwick noted that these deaths were not part of the shipowners intent and that 'the shippers were, no doubt, honourable merchants, chargeable with no *conscious* designs against the lives of those being committed to their charge' (1846: 27, original emphasis). It was in the shippers' interest to minimize safety precautions because they had no interest in the safety of the convicts.

The private interests of the shippers were exactly opposite those of society.[18] Happily, a very minor change in the nature of the contract brought about an artificial identity of interests. The stipulation that payments were for the numbers of transportees debarked *created* a greater interest in the survival rate of convicts, and produced dramatic results. Chadwick illustrates that the production of personal safety responds to relative price changes, a conclusion he extended to include many aspects of industrial safety.

Accident prevention

Chadwick published an extensive work on the problem of railway construction accidents in 1846. Although we treat this tract more extensively elsewhere (in Chapter 6), the article contains an excellent example of the divergence of private and public interests, establishing a liability principle that has become a central feature of the economics of externalities. Chadwick, in this piece, presents copious statistics concerning the costs shifted to society by railway contractors. These costs include additional police costs (necessitated by the congregation of large numbers of workmen), the cost of supporting widows and dependents of men killed on the job, and the costs of supporting disabled workers and their families.

Such costs were shifted to society because liability for them was attenuated through a series of subcontracts and re-contracting. Chadwick recognized that at a lower price, a greater quantity of anything, even construction accidents, will be brought forth in the market. He concluded that the great frequency of accidents at railway construction sites occurred because those capable of preventing the accidents had no incentive to do so and indeed indirectly promote the accidents. This lack of incentive for prevention arose because of a lack of responsibility for damages. Contractors were also indirectly responsible for accidents due to the employment of workers ill-suited for safe construction of the railway lines. By the nature of the contract, wherein the subcontractor undertook the project for a fixed sum, the subcontractor's incentives were to complete the work at minimum cost. One way in which the subcontractors sought to minimize costs was to employ the lowest class of workmen at the lowest wages. Although the social costs of such employment were deemed to be higher than the amount paid, the subcontractor shifted a portion of these costs to society as a whole.

Strict definition of liability was necessary in order to properly assign costs resulting from industrial accidents. Chadwick was direct in this matter:

> I have elsewhere had occasion, in respect to fatal casualties occurring to labourers employed in other descriptions of works, to advance as a general principle of justice and as a measure of prevention, that those who erect machines or conduct large and dangerous works, or undertake public conveyance, should be pecuniarily responsible for all their unavoidable consequences. (1846: 18)

Assigning liability for damages to the firm elicits an incentive for the prevention of accidents to an economic agent with the ability to prevent losses from occurring. While such principles were well known as foundations of law and property rights, Chadwick extended the principle of liability to include damages resulting from forces beyond the direct control of the firm, for example, damages resulting from employee negligence. He argued that 'The way to obtain this end with the most certainty is to make it the pecuniary interest of the shareholders, or employers of the machinery, to obtain educated men, and that is to make them responsible for the pecuniary consequence of employing the uneducated' (1846: 26).

Chadwick would arbitrarily assign liability in order to bring about an artificial identity of interest with respect to accident prevention. By making accident prevention the sole responsibility of one individual, that individual will find that it is in his interest to produce an efficient level of prevention. Creation of allocative efficiency by an arbitrary assignment of liability for all costs is the essence of the Coase Theorem (Coase 1960) which, at least to some extent, Chadwick anticipated by more than a century.

Coase's proposed 'factory-smoke problem' and Chadwick's accident liability problem are analogous. Both represent situations in which the actions of a firm impose costs on society as a whole. As long as compensation is not required, the offending firm will produce at a socially inefficient output level. Coase reframed the question of liability by noting the inherent reciprocity of social cost, or 'the real question that has to be decided is: Should A by allowed to harm B or should B be allowed to harm A? The problem is to avoid the more serious harm' (1960: 2).[19] Coase demonstrates that the assignment of liability to the damaging firm (in Chadwick's case, the railway company) results in a socially optimal allocation of resources, confirming the appropriateness of Chadwick's solution. Naturally, Coase went further in arguing that resource allocation is efficient so long as the damaged party can effectively use side payments to induce the producer of the externality to cease or decrease the offending activity. According to Coase, 'the ultimate result [which maximizes the value of production] is independent of the legal position if the pricing system is assumed to work without cost' (1960: 8). Chadwick's formulation did not allow for the indeterminacy of the property rights assignment – a result that was correct for the specific problem Chadwick considered. His example entailed the imposition of costs on a collective entity, society as a whole. Given non-zero transactions costs, it would be inefficient to force the collective entity to organize a system of side payments – not to mention the free-rider problem that would evolve. Chadwick, then, may be said to have at least partially anticipated Coase's theorems relating to externalities.

Public Sector Economics

Chadwick did not restrict his analysis to the private sector. Some of his most trenchant insights related to the public sphere, and most especially to interactions between the public and private sector.[20] His goal, one which continues to haunt politicians, is to increase the efficiency of government in the presence of a *lack* of a harmony of interests within the public sector. Central to increasing the effectiveness of government was a determination of the existing cause of ineffectiveness.[21] Chadwick found one common element: it was not in the interest of the individual(s) empowered to act on behalf of the public to always act in the public interest. The extreme case where the interests of authorities were not merely neutral, but actually opposed to the public interest arose in many situations.

Nuisance Laws were in effect and directly applicable to all forms of pollution, including air and water pollution, in England's cities throughout the nineteenth century. In spite of these laws, the environmental quality of nineteenth-century London was infamously poor. How could this happen? Chadwick (1842b [1965]: 357) cites the opinion of an anonymous policeman on the enforcement of these laws with respect to air pollution:

> On inquiry of a peace-officer acting where redress is provided under a local Act, how it was that the dereliction of duty occurred that was visible in the dense black clouds that darkened the town, he replied that the chief members of the [local] Board were the persons whose furnace-chimneys were most in fault, and he appealed whether a man in his condition was to be expected to prosecute his patrons.

In this instance, it was counter to the individual's interest (job security) to promote the public interest (clean air) and the public interest was superseded. Chadwick went much further and advocated as a general principle the fact that one could not expect public agents to act in any other manner than to promote their own interests: 'On this topic, a large mass of evidence might be adduced, showing the unreasonableness of expecting private practitioners to compromise their own interests by conflicts for the public protection with persons on whom they are dependent' (1842b [1965]: 404). Recognition of this conflict of participants in non-profit activities opened the door to the development of policy to increase government effectiveness and efficiency through institutional changes creating artificial identities of interest.

This, of course, is a modern idea. Chadwick's rule for judging bureaucratic behavior was revived in modern economics. McKean (1972) argued that the property rights structure is such that the public agent cannot appropriate the rewards of being an effective civil servant. Without a claim to the results of his activity, the civil servant has no incentive to promote the public good. (One might add that this is an example of a 'government failure' in a modern view: see DiLorenzo 2011.) Additionally, the individual cannot be blamed for acting on the basis of his self-interest

(Chadwick's assertion). Recognizing that individuals are self-interested, McKean concludes that public sector effectiveness can be improved by altering the incentives of civil servants so that it becomes the individual's interest to promote the public interest. McKean analyzes the incentive structure of suggestions for the improvement of governmental efficiency, arguing that there are means to bring about an artificial identity of interest for civil servants. Chadwick's solutions, as we will see throughout this book, were to employ institutional devices, such as the reliance on contracts and centralization, to create greater economic efficiency in the supply of goods and services. Whether and to what extent 'contracting' was a means of avoiding the costs of bureaucratic behavior we leave to Chapter 3. However, the nature of Chadwick's argument that centralization was a means of avoiding self-interested bureaucratic behavior demands attention.

CHADWICK'S USE OF STATISTICS

Finally we come to one field in which Chadwick held a clear absolute advantage – his superior command over nineteenth-century English (and Continental) demographical data. Participation in numerous parliamentary commissions gave him access to all government data, and if the data did not exist, he collected it himself or had others collect it for him. At the outset a distinction must be made between probability-based statistics and simple inferences from data, sans probability. Stephen Stigler's excellent study of the history of statistics (1986) presents convincing evidence that the former investigation – at least statistics applied to social phenomena rather than astronomy and physics – was primarily a French development. The long and complex story of that critical evolution is told by Stigler, but the primary stirrings were in the writings of Adolph Quetelet (1796–1874) in the 1820s and 1830s. Quetelet wrestled with the application of 'scientific' statistical methods into social categories of population and crime (Quetelet 1827; 1835), developing propositions relating to the 'average man' and the 'normal distribution' exhibited by most social data. Further, he developed error measurements, expressed implied correlations, and understood the necessities of the use of concepts such as *ceteris paribus* (Stigler 1986: 175).[22] While it is probable and even quite likely that Chadwick was acquainted with such French literature (see Chapter 4) he preferred a more direct rather than a 'methodological' approach to statistics, as least as it then existed.

Suffice it to say that Chadwick detested 'theorists' – those who relied on deductive reasoning alone – always seeking to base his principles and conclusions on observed facts. Further, he was aware that the collection of data, per se, was of little use to the social scientist. The vital factor in determining proper public policy was the distillation of general principles from the available data. As Chadwick pointed out:

> I might fill a whole number of the [Royal Statistical] society's publications with the tables or figures which I have given only the totals. But laboriously prepared statistical tables are too often presented without any totals, much less any reduction, to determinate elementary standards, often indeed without reference to any economic principles whatsoever. (1859c: 383)

Generalizations based upon facts represent the goal of statistical science, a goal that Chadwick perpetually strove to meet. It would be incorrect, however, to argue that Chadwick was on the same road as the French writers of his time (such as Quetelet) in the use of probability theory in data collection and analysis. But while this scientific element was absent from Chadwick's work, no one was more vigorous in using data and data inference in support of public policy in the nineteenth century.

Chadwick's aim was to paint a less romantic-mythical and more accurate portrait of England's past and present through his statistical (*anecdotal*) investigations. Chadwick believed that these myths were a major hindrance to the design of effective social policy – policy being Chadwick's primary goal. No one was his match in this endeavor. A glimpse into Chadwick's intense passion to assemble numbers in support of arguments may be found in an unpublished autographed letter to J. Grant, Esq., a member of the Royal Society of Arts. Writing from Richmond, Surrey on 21 January, 1857, the leading sanitation reformer of his day requests statistics on sickness and mortality for parts of Lancaster in order that a Mr Owen can present them to a meeting of the Royal Society of Arts. Chadwick writes:

> I heard it stated that at those parts of Lancaster where cesspools have been removed a marked improvement in health and reduction of the cases at the dispensary have been observed. It is to be anticipated if the cesspools have been removed for any length of time a reduction of the proportion of deaths from zymatic diseases [those caused by fermentation or purification] will be found.

Chadwick then requests any and all information on 'the rates [of mortality], before and after the removal [of the cesspools].'[23] Chadwick's web of medical and other contacts throughout England were constantly pressed for data on disease, mortality statistics, and information on practically every subject imaginable. This is not, of course, the statistical method of the present day, but it reflects the most serious attempt to marshal evidence to support (or deny) programs and social and economic policies at all levels of government, particularly the British Parliament.

Although the accuracy of Chadwick's actual observations has not been challenged, the appropriateness of its application has come under scrutiny by at least one modern observer. Chadwick was (possibly) not above massaging data to fit preconceptions. Blaug (1964) concluded, in a detailed look at Chadwick's Poor Law evidence, that his analysis was biased. The bias originates from the fact that Chadwick made an incorrect classification of the data in order to prove the excessive costs of the administration of the Poor Laws. Blaug argues that the 'Allowance System' (whereby laborer's income was augmented from public funds) was not as prevalent as maintained in the Report compiled by Chadwick and, therefore, this system was not the cause of unemployment (the conclusions of the Report). Blaug concludes that:

> The evidence collected in the town and rural queries should have taught the commissioners that they had misinterpreted the consequences of the Old Poor Law. But their minds were made up, and where they did not ignore the findings, they twisted them to suit their preconceived opinions. *The Report of 1834* is not only a 'wildly unhistorical document,' as Tawney once said, but also a wildly unstatistical one. (1964: 243, original emphasis)

This one instance where Chadwick consciously or unconsciously misinterpreted the available evidence might cause one to doubt the appropriateness of all his uses of statistics. In Chadwick's defense there is an alternative explanation for the fact twisting in the Poor Law investigation. His initial involvement in the inquiry was as an Assistant Commissioner assigned to the collection of data. As it turns out, Chadwick was assigned the Berkshire district, the county where the Allowance System originated. Thus, Chadwick's own experience was with the district where the system had operated longest and where its effects were most pervasive. Chadwick's fault, therefore, might lie in over-generalization from an unusual local situation to the national level, and not necessarily from pre-conceived biases. But Blaug's important analysis and the foregoing suggest that an in-depth examination remains a task for cliometricians (which is beyond the purposes of this book). It is perhaps important to keep the intellectual status of data-gathering and 'statistical' analysis in the first half of the nineteenth century in mind when assessing Chadwick's achievement. Under these far looser standards, Chadwick stands out as a pioneer in the science that requires evidence for reasoning and conclusions regarding economic and social policy. A priori reasoning, by itself, was not for him.

CONCLUSIONS

This chapter has sought to establish some of the major elements in Chadwick's 'modernity,' acknowledging that to call Chadwick a 'modern' in full would be absurd. Born into Benthamite principles of creating an artificial identity of interest, Chadwick carried economics and policy analysis far beyond anything found in the literature of the nineteenth century. How did he do that? Chadwick was able to apply utilitarian principles to outcomes when individual and collective self-interest did not create the 'greatest good for the greatest number.' Thus, Chadwick's chief interest was in what created divergence between private and public interest and what could be done about (alleged) market failures of various kinds.

These cases and abstractions from the writings of Edwin Chadwick show that, as early as the late 1820s, he brought modern economics to the table in evaluating markets, public policy, and (what he believed to be) the appropriate division of roles between government and the private sector. Under the general rubric of applying the 'artificial identity of interest' doctrine learned from Bentham and early utilitarian sources, Chadwick understood and applied such contemporary concepts as knowledge as a common pool, information costs and how they affect behavior, the impact of time and time costs to market participants, elements of the Coase theorem relating to market failure, and some of the fundamentals of public choice. In the remainder of this book we will show, detailing specific cases, how he used these and other concepts to derive elaborate policy conclusions. Despite some exaggeration and posturing on his part, he was a pioneer in evaluating the welfare effects of alternative institutional structures. His great inventiveness in identifying modern principles of economics was only one aspect of Chadwick's originality however. He was also a pioneer in the use of statistics to analyze and amplify economic and social problems. In the rest of this book, we consider these aspects of his unique vision of public policy in the nineteenth century.

Inventive genius and what can only be called 'modernity' led Chadwick to establish, always using statistical analysis, studies of particular markets where he believed market failure existed. His conclusions concerning these markets, as we will see, were perhaps less important than the path which led him to policy prescriptions and the framework he established for analyzing them. His prescient use of concepts such as the 'common pool,' time and opportunity costs, the demand curve, marginal analysis, strategic behavior, public choice, implicit markets (as for 'accidents'), property rights and liability assignment, and more created the richest sort of toolkit with which to analyze nineteenth-century English economic and social problems. These tools, most of which have not been heretofore recognized or discussed in detail, were accompanied by a unique ability to collect and use statistics to illustrate societal problems and to offer solutions to them. Classical writers *suggested* theoretical solutions to observed societal problems; Chadwick actually *used* theory and evidence to analyze them. We have here only hinted at the depth and breadth of Chadwick's analysis. The remainder of this book examines specific applications of tools and evidence in particular markets – markets where, Chadwick hoped, he could press economics into the service of society.

NOTES

1. There is evidence that Chadwick, for example, was the first English writer to have read and appreciated the economics of French engineer Jules Dupuit; see Chadwick's *Address on Railway Reform* (1865a).
2. These writers are the philosophical precursors of Bentham's utilitarianism. Halévy (1928: 6) discusses pre-Benthamite statements of utilitarianism.
3. Smith's apparent change in emphasis from benevolence to self-interest as the dominating emotion has become known as 'the Adam Smith Problem.' Two basic explanations for the (apparent) differences between the two works exist. Jacob Viner (1928) maintains that comparing the two volumes is inappropriate and, therefore, no paradox exists. Others argue that there is no paradox and that the *Wealth of Nations* and *The Theory of Moral Sentiments* are logically consistent.
4. Halévy summarizes the philosophy of the Newtonian scientific method as follows:

   It is the universality of law which alone makes it intelligible. To say of any relation that it is necessary is to say not that it is intelligible but that it is constant. For me to be able to exert an influence on external nature it is not necessary for me to understand the relations of phenomena to each other as intelligible relations; but merely that these relations should be constant and that by producing a first phenomenon I can be sure to cause the appearance of a second phenomenon, which I desire to produce. (1928: 6)

5. Mandeville's *The Fable of the Bees*, published in 1723, carried the subtitle 'Private Vices, Public Benefits' (1723 [1924]). However, Mandeville's penchant for paradox may have delayed the explicit development of the natural harmony of interest thesis. Mandeville obviously viewed selfishness as a virtue, rejecting the contrary majority opinion. Thus, the paradox was only in the minds of those who judged self-interested behavior as a vice, not in those who considered economic freedom a prerequisite for the promotion of the general welfare.
6. An interpretation serves as an example. In an interesting essay on the 'meaning' of 'natural harmony of interests,' William Grampp argues that:

   The invisible hand is not a power that makes the good of one the good of all, and it is not any of a number of other things it is said to be. It is simply the inducement a merchant has to keep his capital at home, thereby increasing the domestic capital stock and enhancing military power, both of which are in the public interest and neither of which he intended. Smith's exposition discloses how his rhetorical sallies could disfigure his economics, confuse his argument for free trade, and make him play fast and loose with facts and the ideas of others. (2000: 441)

Grampp takes to task those, such as neo-Austrians, who argue that the 'invisible hand' is a metaphor for how a beneficial social order arises unintended as the result of human action. However this may be, it is clear that the policy-guidance of nineteenth-century laissez-faire liberalism sprung from Smith's philosophical observation.

7. See Stephen (1950: 193–205) for an exposition of the details of Bentham's argument.

8. This view is elaborated upon at great length in his famous *Sanitary Report*. According to Chadwick, for example, 'In the districts where the greatest defects prevail, we find such an array of officers for the superintendent of public structures as would lead to the *a priori* conclusion of a high degree of perfection in the work from the apparent subdivision of labour in which it is distributed' (1842b [1965]: 383).

9. Many classical writers would not have disagreed with Chadwick's assessment. Malthus himself came to the position that 'institutions matter' (private property, and so on) after the second and later editions of 'On Population' (Malthus 1798–1826). Senior, in his *Outline*, argues that it is economic institutions which determine the growth of population and that instances where data are best described by the population theory are instances of governmental failure: '. . . a population increasing more rapidly than the means of subsistence is, generally speaking, a symptom of misgovernment indicating deep seated evils, of which it is only one of the results' (Senior 1836 [1965]: 49).

10. In this realm the importance of policy rather than classical theory is foremost for Chadwick. As he notes:

    [W]hat may be done to avert or mitigate the periodical recurrence of distress and outcries for external sympathy and aid; for although it is to be hoped that nothing so extraordinary may again occur [the 'cotton recession'], as that which has arisen from the large loss of supply of the raw material, yet experience warrants the anticipation of recurring disturbances from overproduction, from underconsumption, from bad harvests, from changes of fashion and from improvements in machinery. Change must, therefore, be regarded as a normal condition of our manufactures to be provided for in the interests of ratepayers, as well as of the employed. (1865b: 10)

11. Another good example is Chadwick's treatment (or lack thereof) of the law of diminishing returns which was a cornerstone of classical rent theory believed to be a 'limiting factor' in economic development. Chadwick's reaction was basically to ignore that theory because he saw a rapid improvement in agricultural technology with the introduction of mechanical thrashers, steam powered tractors, and improved irrigation techniques. Observationally, therefore, Chadwick did not witness declining marginal productivity in agriculture. In a 'technology constant' world, however, Chadwick did see how marginal productivity worked, for example, in the use of town sewage as a fertilizer which was part of the system he presented for the improvement of British sanitation.

12. Chadwick compared the cost of drainage around the tenements of the laboring classes with the benefits they would derive showing a huge net benefit including 'the wear and tear of shoes and clothing, from having a well-drained and well-cleaned instead of a wet and miry district to traverse' (1842b [1965]: 291).

13. Chadwick's analysis of the benefits of railway reform, that is, the costs of continuing the old system, included the expanded trade due to lower transport costs, the effects of lowered population density through the opening of commuter rail lines, and the increased efficiency of government operations in terms of police and military efficiency from a unified system (see Chadwick 1867d; 1867a; 1875; and Chapter 4).

14. Later in his career, Chadwick analyzed incentives surrounding murder: see Chadwick (1863 [1887]). In this essay Chadwick linked property crimes to murder and argued that hoarding or the business practice of keeping large sums on the premises was an incentive to murder. He advocates (1863 [1887]: 402–3) methods of self-protection through the use of banks.

48   *The economics of Edwin Chadwick*

15. In addition to the defense of a universal reduction in prices, Chadwick called for a kind of peak-load pricing, proposing this pricing system with respect to the merging of the postal and telegraph systems. Acknowledging a proposal calling for a second class telegram, where the message would be delivered with the next available postage delivery (similar to the US Mail Gram), Chadwick argued that 'Secondary postal telegraphs of this sort would have the advantage of freeing the service from the excessive pressure now experienced at particular hours for the dispatcher of special messages' (1867a: 223). While this is not precisely peak-load pricing in the modern sense, the purpose of the system is the same: to reduce purchase at peak periods and to even out demand through time. This was a kind of marginal cost pricing or 'time of day' pricing described by A.C. Pigou in the early days of neoclassical economics.

16. Astonishing indeed is the *date* of Chadwick's (correct) specification of the law of demand in terms of the functionality of price and quantity. While this law was implied in much of his earlier writings, this clear description, coming as it did in 1865, was years before Fleeming Jenkin's (1870 [1931]) and William Stanley Jevons' (1871; 1879 [1965]). If his word is taken seriously, Chadwick knew of the law of demand by the mid-1830s, prior to Augustin Cournot (1838 [1971]) and Jules Dupuit (1844 [1952]). Dupuit, as Chadwick readily acknowledged, was his primary influence on demand theory. The latter probably read Dupuit's essays (1844 [1952]; 1853a [1933]) since he reproduced demand and revenue functions which appeared in both of these essays – reproductions which also included the *form* of the demand curve specified by Dupuit but not the full analysis. At some points in his discussion Dupuit defended an extreme convexity in demand, suggesting high elasticity, and he based this argument on the pyramidal form of income distribution in society, and upon two laws of demand (see Ekelund and Thornton 1991 for details).

17. We will have opportunity in the following chapters to further illustrate Chadwick's modern analysis of full price, as in Chapter 7 on crime prevention and criminal justice.

18. This does not mean that ship's captains did not treat prisoners responsibly due to religious, philosophical, or other motives.

19. An even more compelling case for property rights principles may be found in Coase (1959).

20. As we will see in the following three chapters, Chadwick designed a principle to resolve conflicts between private and public interests. The conflict was between profit-seeking behavior of individuals and the public's interest in an 'efficient' use of scarce resources in a wide variety of industries. His solution of franchising or 'contract management' was applied to both monopolistic and competitive industries. It depended upon prohibiting the self-interested behavior of firms and limiting the entry of firms, while at the same time taking advantage of the competitive process. As we discuss in Chapter 3, Chadwick believed that these goals could be reached through the careful application of competition for the field of service and the creation of an artificial identity of interests.

21. But see the critique of Coase's argument in Demsetz (2011) and DiLorenzo (2011).

22. While Augustin Cournot wrote the most important book of his day (and many others) on mathematical and *abstract* empirical methods in economics (1838 [1971]) and an early and important guide to probability (1843), he believed that the use of statistical probability applied to social data was quite problematical due to a 'selection effect' in the *post hoc* arrangement of data to analyze. Thus, at an abstract level Cournot was highly sympathetic to quantification but felt that applications would contain fatal errors. See Stigler (1986: 197 *et passim* and Chapter 5 generally).

23. Chadwick, autographed letter to J. Grant, Esq. dated 21 January, 1857 (collection of Robert B. Ekelund Jr).

PART II

The regulation of markets

3. Managing contracts: a means to social welfare

INTRODUCTION

Contemporary economics entertains a number of notions of 'competition.' Those dealing with small numbers competition have developed a theoretical underpinning to models containing underlying assumptions about conjectural behavior. Many of these models – generally called 'game theory' – have also led to empirical testing and new areas of 'experimental economics' and neuroeconomics. Alongside these developments there has been a continuance of the traditional textbook notion of competition. For example, the basic approach emphasizes competition as a model wherein there are many sellers, many buyers, homogeneous products, low or no transactions costs, free entry and exit, and a litany of characteristics producing an 'efficient' equilibrium. This familiar model and its static extensions into 'imperfect' competition, extant from around the time of Richard Cantillon in the early eighteenth century, was developed through several centuries of orthodoxy from Adam Smith to John Stuart Mill to Alfred Marshall to E.H. Chamberlin, J.R. Hicks, and Paul Samuelson. As noted, it survives today in the basic textbooks on the science of economics. It was also the prevailing notion of competition when Chadwick was seeking social reform in the nineteenth century.

Chadwick was undoubtedly aware of the Smithian theory of competition. Based on natural law and decentralized property rights, Adam Smith had argued that price-cost margins would be narrowed by entry and exit processes with social welfare being maximized by the 'invisible hand.' This notion, so familiar since the nineteenth century, was *not* accepted by Chadwick as *necessarily* efficient. Chadwick, as we will see in the present chapter, did not fully accept the fundamental institutional underpinning of Smith's famous idea of a natural law leading to a social welfare maximum in society. Chadwick, in his quest to maximize social utility, concluded that there were instances – a large number of instances – where productive efficiency could be increased by a re-allocation of property rights from the private to the public sector. In short, while extolling the benefits of 'competition,' Chadwick developed a model wherein the welfare benefits of competition could be achieved but with *limitations* placed on property rights. As we shall see, Chadwick's elaborate development (if not invention) of an alternative form of competition is yet another rationale for classifying him within the nexus of modern political economy.

In this chapter we examine the important antecedents of the 'Chadwick plan' which were probably European (French) in origin. We will show that its origin existed in alternative forms of property rights far more ancient than the eighteenth-century sources of situational or 'process' notions of competition. Next we will discuss Chadwick's applications of this form of competition in two situations: (a) where certain conditions, now called 'natural monopoly' exist; and (b) under imperfectly competitive conditions in the market. (While some of his applications of the principle will be discussed at this point, we postpone several of his most important models to Chapters 4 and 5.) Finally, we highlight the contemporary importance of the theory Chadwick developed for contemporary analysis of economic problems.

PROPERTY RIGHTS AND COMPETITION

The actual behavior called 'competition,' rather than its theoretical formulation, finds meaning in the notion of rivalry. But intellectual history holds two distinct notions of economic rivalry, each aligned with a different structure of property rights. Most commonly, use of the term competition is descriptive of a contest between two or more parties to achieve the same prize, for example, economic profits. In the contest, two or more parties are open to all rivals in the sense that each has equal access to relevant economic markets. This situation or process requires a structure or legal assignment of property rights permitting ownership to be atomistic, decentralized, and participatory, which in turn allows every seller an equal right to serve customers and every buyer the freedom to choose those goods he wants. Such wide freedom of action characterized the competitive 'model' of Adam Smith (and previously that of Richard Cantillon), who gave this familiar paradigm its most forceful early expression. In this market system moreover, legal institutions generally uphold property rights in commodities traded so long as they are acquired in good faith without fraud or force.

Another, and more ancient, kind of rivalry is described by the contest to obtain an exclusive right to serve. The rivalry described by this form of competition is temporary and discontinuous, as compared to the continuous and quasi-perpetual rivalry of open competition. It usually takes the form of 'competitive' bidding to secure a franchise, the monopoly status of which is subsequently sustained by force of law. In this case the State is the lawful repository of the property right it franchises. (Rights to television franchises, or to supply local water, electricity, or cable services readily come to mind as modern examples.) Under properly designed contractual safeguards, franchise bidding *may* result in the manufacture and sale of goods at minimum average total costs of production where scale economies (for example, natural monopoly) conditions exist in markets.[1] Of course, it may be applied in other *non-scalar* cases as well.

History of the Two Principles

A critical issue, certainly *the* critical issue with regard to Chadwick's use of the principle, is how far to apply it. When Chadwick forcefully introduced his ideas in an 1859 essay (Chadwick 1859c), his good friend and mentor John Stuart Mill opinioned in a letter that 'I have gone through your proof [of the efficacy of competition for the exclusive right to supply goods and services] . . . But I do not well see where your principle is to stop or at what place you would draw the line of demarcation between it and conflicting principles' (Letter, Mill to Chadwick, 26 January 1859, in Mill 1972). A satisfactory resolution of questions such as these depends in part on a brief but more complete understanding of the historical nature of the two types of 'competition.' Clearly, past institutions, in the form of law, custom, and the degree of authoritarianism, affected the form of competition commonly practiced, which in turn affected the nature of the theoretical abstractions that have formed modern economic analysis.

The eighteenth century – *prior* to Smith's *Wealth of Nations* in 1776 – was a pivotal time in the contrast between two systems of competition and the concept of entrepreneurship. One of the earliest writers to recognize that economic activity involves decisionmaking under uncertainty in an openly competitive process was Richard Cantillon (1729 [1931]). The mysterious Cantillon – about whose birth, death, and lifework little is known – created a theory of competition centered on the activities of a specific class of functionaries: entrepreneurs. Thus, the first explicit notion that competition consists of entrepreneurial activity is to be found in the economic literature of the eighteenth century. But Cantillon's theory is historically relevant to a society in which property rights are widely disseminated and entry is open to certain key markets. He had a modern vision of an economy as an organized set of mechanisms that operate to achieve a kind of equilibrium, with the entrepreneur as a pivotal figure who assumes the risk and uncertainty inherent in the system. Guided by price movements and the behavior of buyers and sellers, Cantillon's entrepreneur continuously brings particular supplies and demands into balance. Specifically, Cantillon's entrepreneur buys goods or resources at a certain (known) price and sells them in the future at an uncertain price, because he cannot foresee perfectly the extent of demand or the actions of his rivals (Cantillon 1729 [1931]: 39).[2]

While Cantillon's vision incorporates a conception of decentralized property rights with which open competition could take place, a very different system had been dominant throughout the history of nations and regimes – that based on concentrated, authoritarian rights and privileges.[3] For example, a different description of entrepreneurial behavior was offered in a work contemporaneous to Cantillon's by Bernard de Belidor (1729), a French engineer and author considered an expert in his field. Belidor's 'theory' of entrepreneurship grew out of his experience as a practicing civil engineer in the King's service. He treats the entrepreneur as a government contractor who bids competitively on contracts for the execution of public works. Each contract awarded an exclusive franchise to the entrepreneur and obliged him to pay the costs of construction and to complete the work within a given time according to specifications set down by the engineers. The government agreed to pay the contract price in installments according to progress made by the contractor and subject to inspection and certification of work performed (Belidor 1729: 46ff).

Thus, two very different concepts of competition existed side by side in early economic literature. Belidor stressed the administered contracts approach to competition. His participation in the public sector meant that he was operating in a sector of the economy where government exercised control over certain property rights. Cantillon, in contrast, emphasized a discrete transactions approach later championed by Adam Smith and classical economics because he was describing instead a sector of the economy in which all individuals had an equal right to serve.[4] In both 'competitive' systems, the entrepreneur confronts and reacts to uncertainty. Cantillon's system emphasized the notion of equilibrium and Belidor's system did not, but the interesting thing about their respective processes is how institutional practice constrained the form of entrepreneurial uncertainty. In Belidor's theory the entrepreneur knows his gross revenue, which is contractually set, but he does not know the costs of economic resources which must subsequently be purchased in order to complete the project. Cantillon's (and later Smith's) entrepreneur buys goods or resources at known prices, but faces uncertain demand in that other sellers are competing for the same customers.

A critical point is that, for many centuries and even millennia, franchise bidding of the type described by Belidor took place between rival entrepreneurs and monarchs or designated officials. Medieval monarchs, both those who held absolute power to tax (in the French case, for example) and those who did not (for example, the English), often augmented the royal treasury by the sale at auction of certain property rights that were reserved to them by virtue of their office. Franchise bidding schemes were devised either to maximize royal revenues as a form of rent-seeking or to minimize 'public' expenditures in, say, the provision of public goods such as defense (where this system is often used in contemporary settings). Further, monarchs might therefore auction to the highest bidder an exclusive trading right, or they might award to the lowest bidder a contract for the construction of military fortifications or other 'public' goods. So long as their control of property rights was absolute and centralized, European monarchs were under no compulsion to use franchise bidding (or *any* scheme for eliciting or encouraging the production of goods or services) in the public interest. But it should come as no surprise that, in France, there was an evolution of public goods provision from monarchical fiat – awards to court favorites and the aristocracy – to a system whereby the monarch sought the maximization of rents by offering franchises through a competitive bidding processes. (Either way, of course, the monarch maintained property rights over the provisions.) Thus the notion of competition as rivalrous bidding to obtain an exclusive franchise survived much longer in France where the monarch successfully resisted demands for popular sovereignty, yet a strong tradition of public works provision by the Crown existed. That tradition was not erased after the French Revolution, and the authoritarian regulation of the provision of particular goods lasted throughout the nineteenth century and well into the twentieth century.

The English classical notion of competition evolved as an extension of the market system with widespread private property rights. The notion of competition nurtured and came to describe entrepreneurial behavior at a different level from the experience of earlier times: not so much as a rivalry for the sole possession of a right to serve but as a contest to win the favor of consumers, all sellers having the same right to serve. It is this notion of competition that found its way into Smith's writings, possibly through Cantillon.[5]

FRANCHISE BIDDING AND IMPERFECT COMPETITION

French theory and practice as regards competition were not unknown in England, and their greatest exemplar, until Chadwick that is, was Bentham. As noted in Chapters 1 and 2, Smith adhered to a theory that could be described as the natural harmony of interests – a public good that is the summation of the harmonized interests of egoistic individual interests where there are no third-party effects. Jeremy Bentham, in contrast, whose major interest was law not economics, nevertheless developed notions that were applicable to forms of competition. His concept of an 'artificial identity of interest' meant that private and public interests did not necessarily coincide and that property rights could be altered in various ways to produce this artificial identity. From Bentham's utilitarian point of view, the contract was the most formal type of obligation: it was a means of acquiring property rights over services and was therefore a useful device in the State's hands to compel citizens to desirable social action. For Bentham, the very fact that crimes were committed refuted the harmony of interests doctrine. The problem for Bentham's statesman, therefore, was to define obligations and punishments in such a way that private interest would be brought by artificial means to coincide with public interests.

Bentham's utilitarian perspective led him to apply the artificial identity of interest concept to the most basic and formal type of obligation – the contract. A contract was a means of acquiring property rights over services and was therefore a useful device in the State's hands to compel citizens to desirable social action. We have already briefly discussed the nature of Bentham's *Panopticon* (1791 [1995]) as a blueprint for social reform – the object being a rearrangement of private interests in order to produce prison reform in the public interest. We have not, however, discussed one critical means Bentham espoused for achieving these results – contract bidding – which he thought would achieve desired social results. This idea was the kernel of Chadwick's great contributions later in the nineteenth century.

Bentham's *Panopticon* and a Theory of Contracting

The *Panopticon* (1791 [1995]) was an architectural innovation, but it was supplemented with an important administrative twist. Two major goals of Bentham's prison reform were to protect the prisoners from being mistreated and to protect society from the waste of administrators. Bentham saw the administrative alternatives as a choice between trust-management and contract-management. Under the former arrangement, a single individual or committee maintained the prison at public expense and paid into the public treasury the product of the prisoners' work. Under the latter, an individual paid the government in advance so much per convict for the right to exploit his labor in the service of the contractor's profit. Bentham favored this last arrangement because it put into action the principle of the artificial identity of interests. Under contract management, the entrepreneur's responsibility toward his prisoners became so intertwined with his own interest that he would be forced to do for his own advantage what he would not otherwise have been inclined to do for theirs, that is, to keep the prisoners healthy in order to protect his 'investment.'

Even more evidence of Bentham's administrative genius is found in his unique combination of contract management and the insurance principle. He planned to use life insurances in order to further enjoin the interest of the community with that of the contractor. Bentham proposed, first, to calculate the average mortality of prisoners in given circumstances; then to pay the entrepreneur a certain sum of money for each convict who could be expected to die during the year. Simultaneously, the entrepreneur would be required to pay back a like amount at the end of the year for each prisoner who died or escaped (Bentham 1776–82 [1962], Vol. 1: 53). In this way the entrepreneur would have an interest in extending the lives of his prisoners. The contract itself is a variable in this approach, and Bentham gave due consideration to the optimum form of contract. The nature of risk borne by the entrepreneur is altered, for example, by adding or subtracting the insurance principle. If included, the entrepreneur faces certain revenues and uncertain costs (since he must rebate according to the number of deaths); if omitted, he faces certain costs of obtaining the contract, but uncertain revenues. Nevertheless, the institutional setting with regard to property rights was the same in Bentham's theory as under that which French entrepreneurs and engineers operated for centuries: government served as the repository of certain property rights which were sold in usufruct to the highest bidder.

Chadwick and the Principle of Contract Management

Chadwick, clearly enough, was up to speed on all aspects of classical economics – of Smith, Bentham, and all of the major writers – by his early twenties. And in a massive literary outpouring, he began espousing Bentham's ideas prior to meeting the man. But an 1829 article on 'Preventive Police' by Chadwick aroused such interest in Bentham that Chadwick became the great man's amanuensis, organizer of Bentham's legal writings, and last 'secretary.' Chadwick, it should be noted, had already begun his career as sanitary reformer, lawyer, economist, and statistician, and it seems likely that Chadwick's writings had received the imprimatur of Bentham.

Chadwick's work on sanitary reform, the Poor Laws, and a rosary of social issues continued after Bentham's death (some of which will be discussed in subsequent chapters). But Chadwick went on to extend Bentham's ideas theoretically by suffusing them with utilitarian-inspired policies, one of which had, and will have, enormous implications for economics. By 1859, and as early as 1838, out of all of his policy involvements,

Chadwick had turned his attention to the evolution of a 'new' principle of competition, one based on unorthodox grounds.[6] The pervasive errors in legislation and administration in England were due, in Chadwick's view (1859c: 384), to a master defect in economic science and principle,

> or, in other words, public ignorance that there are different conditions of competition – sound and unsound; that whilst there are conditions of competition which ensure to the public the most responsible, the cheapest and best service, and which are requisite to improvements of the greatest magnitude, there are conditions of competition which create inevitable waste and insecurity of property, which raise prices and check improvement, which engender fraud and violence, and subject to the public to irresponsible monopolies of the worst sort.

Competition 'for the field' means that:

> the whole field of service should be put up on behalf of the public for competition – on the only condition on which efficiency, as well as the utmost cheapness, was practicable, namely, the possession, by one capital or by one establishment, of the entire field, which could be most efficiently and economically administered by one, with full securities towards the public for the performance of the requisite service during a given period. (Chadwick 1859c: 385)

But the regrettable fact was that, with the exception of some minor local implementations, his principle had been almost entirely neglected in England. Rather it was a Continental 'thing,' which, as Chadwick constantly reminded his readers, was not being neglected in the rest of Europe.[7] Chadwick believed that utilization of his principle would yield great economies in many areas and he supported this belief with examples from no fewer than ten product and service industries. An interesting and crucial aspect of these 'applications' is that more than half of them are drawn from industries which are by no means 'natural monopolies' in the traditional economic sense of declining average cost. Thus, an investigation of Chadwick's reasoning by source of economic inefficiency is central to an understanding of the doctrines' applicability. For convenience, we divide Chadwick's traditional market inefficiencies into two types – types that continue today in contemporary markets: (a) those whose likely source is declining average costs, that is, the 'natural monopoly;' and (b) those whose source is some form of imperfect competition due to some type of market barriers to perfect competition – externalities, information costs, heterogeneous products, and so on.

A Graphical Analysis of Natural Monopoly and Franchise Bidding

Chadwick's theory of 'contract management' and 'franchise bidding' for property rights may be made more understandable with a modern exposi-

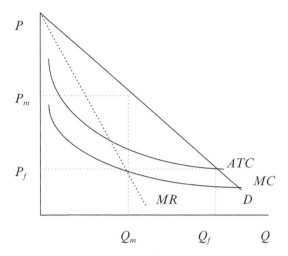

Figure 3.1   Franchise bidding

tion. As the standard static diagram of the situation (Figure 3.1) shows, conditions of natural monopoly involve a declining average cost function (*ATC*) due to economies of one sort or another (production economies, for example) with a declining marginal cost function (*MC*) below the *ATC* function at all outputs. Under the assumption that a single firm can fill out the entire demand for a good or service, a 'natural' monopoly results – that is, firms have an incentive to lower costs by increasing output through merger or acquisition and a single firm results. The usual conclusion drawn from this situation is that once achieved, the monopoly might have an incentive to restrict output and charge monopoly prices. Thus, for economic efficiency (average cost pricing), natural monopoly must be controlled in some fashion (cost-plus regulation through regulatory agencies is a common means).[8]

A contemporary interpretation of Chadwick's franchise bidding approach to the control of natural monopolies was introduced in the modern literature by Demsetz (1968).[9] Demsetz argues that even if conditions necessitate a single *ex post* supplier, monopolistic behavior will not obtain if a sufficiently large number of *ex ante* bidders vie for the right to be that single supplier. If average costs are declining, rival firms (bidders) have the incentive to increase output and lower unit costs as long as price remains above average costs.

Franchise competition, where the winning bidder is determined by the lowest per-unit output price, will produce second-best (Ramsey) economic efficiency where price is equal to average cost.[10] Representing a single-product franchise monopoly by the average cost curve ATC in Figure 3.1, franchise bidding results in the price-quantity combination Pf, Qf, where price is equal to average costs. Alternatively, the franchise contract may be granted according to the highest lump sum payment (Posner 1972). In this case, the bidder offers the franchise authority a lump sum equal to an estimate of the capitalized monopoly rents and the monopolistic solution obtains with output Qm and price Pm.[11] These monopoly rents, now in the hands of the franchise authority, may be used to further social policy either related or unrelated to the industry from which the rents were extracted or to line the pockets of bureaucrats.[12]

Water and Gas Supplies: Natural Monopolies?

Chadwick put this general contract bidding analysis of competition to work in a number of examples some would consider natural monopoly situations. Chadwick was deeply concerned with the conditions of water supply and related public health problems in the city of London. J.S. Mill was also concerned.[13] Chadwick's *Sanitary Report* of 1843 is evidence of this interest. The root of the problem, Chadwick's investigation revealed, was a natural monopoly situation accentuated by competition within the field of service; that is, the traditional form of competition. According to Chadwick's research the supplying side of the market (the 'field') was divided among:

> seven separate companies and establishments, of which six were originally competing within the field of supply, with two and three sets of pipes down many of the same streets, but which had become multiform monopolies, doling out supplies of water of inferior and often unwholesome quality, insufficient in quantity, although positively nearly three-fifths of it ran to waste during the intermittent period of service. (1859c: 387)

Though Chadwick estimated that consolidation under the principle of 'contract management' might save a full 100 000 pounds per year, constituting a fund for explorations and development of new sources of supplies, his proposed administration of London water was rejected by Parliament, owing, he claimed, to the protest of vested interests. The results of retaining traditional competition in these markets over the decade of the 1850s, Chadwick concluded, were insufficient improvements in water quality and methods of delivery, higher charges to consumers, and unsafe returns to stockholders.

Chadwick believed that a bold contrast to the London water situation could be observed in the city of Paris where municipal gas companies competed under an almost identical situation of natural monopoly. Chadwick reported that an investigation into the cost and supply conditions of several independent gas companies in Paris was directed by the government 'in behalf of the people' and charges were found to be excessive. The municipal government then undertook consolidation on the basis of Chadwick's principle to good effect. Chadwick (1859c: 388) claimed that:

> . . . the service had been, in effect, as far as circumstances permitted, put up to competition for the whole field, and the consolidation of all the establishments had been effected under the best available direction, with the result of a considerable improvement of the quality of the gas supplied, a reduction of 30 per cent. [sic] upon the previous cost to the private consumers, of 40 per cent. [sic] to the public consumers, arising from reductions of establishment charges, and an improvement of 24 per cent. [sic] in the value of the shareholders' property.

Chadwick also relied on evidence of two gas companies in northern England whose prime cost, when competing separately for the whole field of service, was three shillings per 1000 cubic feet. Implementation of his plan of competition for the whole field resulted in one establishment supplying gas at a prime cost of 1 shilling, 9 pence per 1000 cubic feet.

This principle was vigorously applied to the English railway monopoly – a national industry – and the important details of his plan and his reasoning is the subject of Chapter 4. But it is important to note at this point that in the 1860s Chadwick became the leading exponent in England of the nationalization of the railways. Chadwick's argument, of course, as in the two cases described above (urban water and gas companies), did not support government's *operation* of the railways or of supplying water or gas. (It is critical to note that water is today supplied through such private-public partnerships in many countries of the world; see Hanke and Walters 2011.) In numerous publications on the matter of nationalization, Chadwick appealed to the success of his principle in other areas of public goods supply noting that, 'it is a dogma of mine that the fact of a thing being done is cogent evidence of its possibility' (1866b: 201). Citing the government's successful implementation of a postal system by contract management as a support for nationalization, Chadwick makes clear his objections to the traditional (Marshallian) competitive principle in the railway industry:

> The chief defaults are first, those against unity of management for efficiency as well as economy; – secondly, exactions on necessities, by means of monopolies, instead of payments, merely for service, without profits; – thirdly, charges in disregard of an economical principle of increasing rations of consumption with diminishing ratios of price by means of monopolies. (1866b: 203)

Railways were thus a natural monopoly characterized by redundant competition. But he was unwilling to allow a coincidence of ownership and administration. In the best tradition of laissez-faire Chadwick argued 'that the Government is utterly incapable of any direct management of manufactures, or of anything else of an administrative character' (1866b: 202) while championing public ownership.

It would, perhaps, be useful to summarize, in preliminary fashion, the aspects of this Bentham-Chadwick principle of 'competition' under conditions of natural monopoly. Principal aspects of his version of 'competition' would involve the following characterstics.

- Competitive bidding for a franchise for the entire field of service to invoke a winning bid that would approximate average cost of production. Note that this bid would not, under natural monopoly conditions outlined in Figure 3.1, result in marginal cost pricing, that is in the opportunity cost of resources used in production;
- Government would not operate anything, but would manage contracts in the interest of society, that is, in the interest of consumers receiving the lowest possible price under the maximum of efficiency;
- Property rights would have to be altered in the transition from 'competition within the field of service' to 'competition for the field of service.' This would involve a transfer of *property rights* to supply water, gas, railways, and other industries possibly affected by scalar economies from individual entrepreneurs to the government, local or national;
- Contracts for service requirements would have to be made initially on the basis of demand and cost and revised continually, since demand and cost change over time; in any rational system, this means some form of regulation (which Chadwick admits, see below);
- Inherent to the Chadwick plan is that 'politics' plays no role in the design or awarding of contracts to serve by the contract developers or by the competitors affected. In short, 'rent-seeking' and *ex parte* proceedings in the awarding of contracts is not a subject seriously considered by Chadwick.

These issues, which remain in modern economic considerations regarding the supply of goods under natural monopoly conditions – or in the supply of public or collective goods of any kind – are inherent to the provision of goods that are not supplied in open competition (that is, within the field). But Chadwick believed that the principle of 'competition for the field of service' went far beyond the (supposed) wastes that attended natural monopoly conditions.

Does Contract Management Apply to Imperfect Competition?

Chadwick extended the principle of 'contract management' beyond natural monopoly applications (see Crain and Ekelund 1976). The extremely interesting aspects of Chadwick's discussions of these cases relate to the contemporary nature of his understanding of 'market failure.' Did the market fail in the sense that some system other than ordinary property rights would produce greater efficiency in markets such as lower prices and higher quantity or quality of service? Chadwick appears to consider two extremely important cases of such so-called failure – the existence of monopolistic (or imperfect) competition and the failure of markets due to information asymmetries. Before turning to some of these cases (an important case of so-called information asymmetry will be considered in Chapter 5) in the present chapter, it is useful to review the concept of monopolistic competition (a form of the broader concept of imperfect competition).

The sources of traditional concepts of monopolistic competition are two: a monopolistic element which may be location or product variations and/or uniqueness with substitutability, and a competitive element of a large number of sellers or these closely related products. Product or service uniqueness is the basis for a downward sloping demand curve and, assuming a 'U-shaped' cost curve applies, the typical monopolistically competitive equilibrium occurs where the long-run average cost curve (LRAC) is tangent to the demand curve. Why would this be so? So long as above normal profits (or 'rents') exist in the system, entry ensues. As entry takes place the demand curve which would yield monopolistic profits, shifts leftward and becomes tangent to the LRAC curve at point A, yielding a price of PA. This famous 'Chamberlinian' tangency solution, developed in the early 1930s and named for its inventor Edward Chamberlin (1899–1967), is, without further changes in the particular market, a stable one. One of the chief criticisms leveled at this notion over time is that it produces excess capacity in markets. And here is where some of Edwin Chadwick's observations become critical to understanding such markets.

London Cab Market 'Economies'

European capitals had made progress in the supply of many 'collective goods' or public services, but, at least in Paris, the horse-drawn cab market was not one of them. (Naturally, resistance in various services came from labor. Chadwick attributed the resistance to 'reforms' in some quarters, such as the installation of water pipes and pumps to labor pushback.) But after studying the means through which cab service was provided in Paris and London, Chadwick was ready to condemn the London system

as illustrative of the 'evils of the competition of multiplied capitals within
the field of supply, against which the opposite principle is the only effective preventive' (1859c: 393). The number of licensed cabs in London was
4500 at the time and Chadwick estimated that a cab and two horses cost
about 60*l*. Total capital engaged in the business was estimated at 270 000*l*.,
and was provided by about 1800 small owners. From this system Chadwick
argued that the 'waste' of capital should be obvious to all observers 'in full
stands or long files, waiting hour after hour, and in the numbers crawling
about the streets looking out for fares' (1859c: 393). And Chadwick set
about estimating other charges and depreciation. Consider the following
statistics he amassed (1859c: 393):

16*s.*, 4*d.* = cost of the keep of each horse per week
2*s.*, 6*d.* = depreciation of each horse stock per week
8*s.* = depreciation of the vehicle per week
4*s.* = market value of cab driver in London per week
5*s.* = stable rent per week per horse and cab
1*s.* = loss per hour with other minor items associated with unemployed cab
capital

Thus, Chadwick calculates a loss where:

on every cab stand where in foul weather, as well as fair, a dozen cabs are seen
constantly unemployed . . . capital evaporating in worse than waste, as a rate of
12s. per hour, 7l. 4s. per diem, – or at a rate of between two and three thousand
pounds per annum, to be charged on someone, i.e., the public. (1859c: 393–4)

These statistics led Chadwick to his ubiquitous conclusion concerning so
many examples of 'competition within the field' – that it created wasted
capital as it did in the supply of such items as beer and bread. With respect
to cabs, Chadwick had this to say:

It is probably a statement greatly below the fact, that at least one-third of the
cabs are, the week through, unemployed; that is to say, one-third of the invested
capital is wasted; – a service for two capitals being competed for by three, to
the inevitable destruction of one. As in other cases of competition within the
field, efforts are made by violent manifestations of discontent at the legal fare,
by mendacity and by various modes of extortion, to charge upon the public
the expense of the wasted capital . . . And yet the legal share for the commonly
wretched service of the man, horse, and vehicle is, when taken by the hour,
nearly double, and by the mile nearly treble . . . its prime cost. (1859c: 394)

Thus, Chadwick believed that although the regulated rate was double (or
triple) the prime cost, the cab drivers were pushing for higher rates from
Parliament, a condition that he believed would bring in even more com-

petitors raising, perhaps, the number of competitors to do the work.[14] The conclusion of this sort of reasoning is that excess capacities under competition were paid for by the public and had to be eliminated. Such 'wasteful competition' led, moreover, to a low moral condition amongst the cabbies, especially the obvious cruelty to the animals.[15] How could this situation be rectified? Chadwick's answer was always the same:

> In respect to this service of cabs – the analysed charges and statistics show that by a properly-conducted competition by adequate capital for the whole field – for which, in my view, the chief police or local administrative authorities ought, as servants of the public, to be made responsible – service equal to the present might be obtained at 4d. per mile; or at the present legal fare of 6d. per mile, a service approaching in condition to that of private carriages, might be insured out of the mere waste which now occurs. (1859c: 396)

Technology could become a chief element in the process of monitoring because Chadwick knew that a machine that measured time and distance covered in cabs had been invented and could be used to ensure honest charges. (Such machinery had been introduced in Paris but was, as one might expect, destroyed by 'conspiracies of the whole body of the drivers.') Economies through consolidation and contract for the whole field would also inure, according to Chadwick, to the care for the animals and for the benefit of the moral condition of the drivers. Centralization of facilities would lead to monetary economies for the company and for the laborers and animal tenders. Sanitation and uniformity would be hallmarks of the unified supply of service under 'competition for the field.'

Excess capacity was not the only rationale for employing competition for the field in Chadwick's view, as we will see in Chapter 5. But certain relevant issues regarding the scheme applied to cabs are noteworthy. Chadwick's theoretical rationale for consolidation due to excess capacity in the London cab service might have been respected for over a century. The Chamberlinian tangency solution (named for economist Edward Chamberlin) tells us why that is so. When demands differ, as when closely related products or services are differentiated by some element (appearance, quality, or location), the demand curve facing the firm is negatively sloped and the equilibrium yields a price that covers average cost of supplying cab service demanders. The competitive element produces (in the simplest interpretation of Chamberlin) a tangency solution wherein price is equal to average cost, but not at the lowest average cost. Thus, both Chadwick and Chamberlin identified some excess capacity or inefficiency under monopolistically competitive conditions. But, as Chadwick recognized, the so-called surplus of cab drivers were not driven out of business by excess capacity so that long-term average cost was being covered. Cab prices to consumers reflected average cost – but, Chadwick believed, a cost that was inflated due to excess capacity and inefficiencies since scalar economies were not being taken advantage of.

Contemporary economic theory throws a completely different light upon the notion of excess capacity. That time has economic value has been recognized for centuries, but that notion was formally developed and integrated into economic theory by Gary Becker (1965). Unoccupied capacity is, indeed, valued by consumers and cannot be considered 'wasted' resources, per se. For example, unoccupied cabs lower the full cost of service by reducing waiting time and hence, the time cost to the rider (Demsetz 1959; DeVany 1970). This means that the unused capacity of the Chadwick-Chamberlin tangency solution is not without value. Cab queues have value for those waiting for transport, so that excess capacity has utility– a value calculable on the basis of time costs foregone. Full utilization of horses and cabs yielding no excess capacity would, in all probability, reduce utility to patrons beyond the additional cost of providing the cab system within the field of service. We will visit yet other examples given by Chadwick for implementing contract bidding in the provision of other goods and services (see Chapters 4 and 5, for example), some produced under conditions of various forms of imperfect competition. Consider however, the means by which Chadwick would develop contracts under both natural monopoly and imperfect competition, and regulate them for the public good.

CONTRACTING FOR GOODS AND SERVICES: IS IT SIMPLE REGULATION?

The theoretical basis for 'contract bidding' is a rather simple matter and is readily understandable. Not so simple are the prerequisites and conditions for achieving economically efficient results, both temporally and intertemporally. Inefficiencies will creep in because, in the words of a modern observer, 'of the difficulty of devising suitable contracts' (Demsetz 1968: 57). The nature of the contracting process and of contract specification is at the core of avoiding monopoly rents and allocative inefficiencies. Chadwick was not unaware of these problems and in the present section we look at Chadwick's institutional views on contract specification and on the regulation he thought it made necessary. Though his views on these matters are somewhat sketchy, we will show that: (1) a reasonable approach to contract management in practical cases requires some form of regulation; and (2) that such institutional arrangements were not limited to natural monopolies.

In the many cases he examines, Chadwick becomes obscure when facing the question of setting up a contract through which 'rivalrous competition' could possibly work its wonders. In the case of cabs, for example, Chadwick argued for 'superior public administration' to supplant the existing system of licensing and regulation of fares by Parliament, while failing to specify the contract terms which would bring about the desired reforms in cab service. Presumably he envisioned a role in this area for a public commission to contract with 'large capital' firms supplying cab service to all demanders at specified minimum prices (which of course required prior knowledge of demand). And throughout, Chadwick assumes an elastic supply of bidders.

Chadwick's primary emphasis is on minimum price bids for given quantities of goods or services (again requiring a priori knowledge of demand). In the case of a single supplier of the field for improved sewage facilities, Chadwick even poses the hypothetical contract: 'At what rate will you [competitors] undertake to abolish the cesspools of all sorts . . .?' (1859c: 403). Similarly, in discussing the sanitary and health-producing effects, warming and ventilation of hospitals, the emphasis is on minimum price and on contracting for guaranteed results. Chadwick even produced statistics to show that the 'Paris system' of contracting for these services produced lower charges and reduced death rates. In this case, 'the contract administrators concern themselves only with these results, leaving the contractor to his own devices as to the means and their management by his own servants' (1859c: 406–7).

Chadwick of course saw 'waste' everywhere – in areas that could not conceivably have been 'natural monopolies' in the manner described above (see Figure 3.1). On the question of retail food manufacture and distribution, for example, he believed that the wastes of competition within the field justified entry regulation through contract management. Such a device, Chadwick notes, was being used in the urban areas of Paris, but not in the *banlieues* (suburbs). A study was instituted by the suburban bakers which demonstrated that the quality of bread was lower and the price higher in the unregulated market. The suburban market, moreover, was characterized by a higher average number of bankruptcies and greater entry to and exit from the market. They were, in short, ready to submit to regulation and maximum price restrictions. Location monopoly and ruinous competition in the London beer market demanded similar remedies in his logic (1859c: 415–17), a very broad generalization of the principle from actual natural monopoly situations.[16]

Specifications of quality, quantity, price, or some combination thereof required, at a minimum, some prepatory statistical analysis of cost and demand. The form of the contract and the type of monopoly regulated has

profound effects upon efficiency, as we shall see. The institutional framework which Chadwick envisioned for contract management is another
matter. The only institution which could practically institute this device
in the public interest was government. Nationalization and consolidation
were part of Chadwick's proposed solution. The government would be
required to fulfill specific roles:

> For the application of the principle of competition for the field, to recognized
> subject matters of administration such as I have described, I presuppose, quali-
> fications of high administrative intelligence and integrity and public zeal, to
> plot out the most advantageous fields for competition, to conduct with judicial
> impartiality the competitions for their occupation, and to enforce the rigid per-
> formance of the contracts on behalf of the public. I presuppose also the ability
> to analyse closely the cost of service, so as to guard against concealed emolu-
> ments, which are sources of corruption, and firmness to withstand the imputa-
> tions of vulgar competitors, and to make those direct liberal allowances of due
> market rates of profits which are preservatives against the use of surreptitious
> means to obtain them. (1859c: 408)

Chadwick, then, envisions nothing less than a regulatory commission (in
the case of Omnibus regulation he calls it a 'Council of Surveillance') to
act as agent for the public. Regulatory functions would include a wide
array of activities including: (a) statistical cost estimation; (b) enforcement and policing; and (c) supervising contract negotiations and terms.
Chadwick envisioned an administrative body charged with calculating
costs on 'socially desired' quantities of goods and services and ensuring
that successful bidders covered them with compensatory rates of return.
Policing of the rates of successful bidders over the contract period and
legal enforcement against surreptitious suppliers would be required of the
body. In the case of contracts awarded to multiple companies the body
must have the means of calculating the optimum size firm utilizing some
cost criterion in order to determine the optimum number of firms. The role
of the market, in most cases, is simply to price-compete for the field or for
a specified (presumably by contract) portion of the field. When bidding for
a portion of the field is conducted, special limitations would presumably
be built into the contract itself. The latter would require estimations of
demand as well as costs *by location*.

  The point here is that monopoly (or 'temporary monopoly' or competitive disequilibrium), in Chadwick's view, demanded and justified commis-
sion-style regulation of everything by price or rates. Such regulation is
entirely reminiscent of federal and regional regulation in the United States
as it was practiced in both twentieth and twenty-first centuries. Federal
and State regulatory agencies practiced (and continue in many areas
to practice) regulation in all of the dimensions identified by Chadwick

– utilities, medicine, power, transportation, alcohol production and distribution, and in a myriad of other areas. Some such regulation is practiced by 'certificates of need' or by licensing, requiring permits under open-ended or closed competitive conditions. Here, consequently, is the real modernity of Chadwick's proposal, and naturally it is question-begging. Is franchising or contract management superior or equivalent to traditional cost-plus regulation and what are the relative effects on consumer welfare? Is regulation of any kind necessary at all? On what grounds could rational arguments be made for or against standing forms of regulation, contract bidding, deregulation, or no regulation at all? Unfortunately, the answers to these questions are not simple and insights can only be gained through careful case studies (see Chapters 4 through 8 of this book). Before tackling these issues, however, some insights are to be gleaned from a discussion of the possible theoretical problems with the application of the Bentham-Chadwick principle.

A PRELIMINARY EVALUATION OF THE CHADWICK PRINCIPLE

A spirited debate emerged in the latter part of the twentieth century as to whether or not the supply of such things as utility services, cable television, or other services could be made through Chadwick's practice of contract management (without giving credit to Chadwick). The chief advocate was economist Harold Demsetz (1968), who argued that the principle meant that conditions of natural monopoly (scalar economies) did not necessarily imply that monopoly price and quantity would result, and further, that contract bidding could replace common forms of regulation, ostensibly cost-plus forms of regulation. But, as noted above, Chadwick anticipated, correctly we believe, an elaborate 'contract enforcement' body, composed of civil servants, as a necessary accouterment of the scheme. (Striking is Chadwick's faith that there would exist individuals of 'high administrative intelligence and integrity and public zeal' to manage contracts when he did not, in general, have faith in government's ability to 'run' enterprises.) Most importantly, readers will have already recognized that the fundamental rational choice of a means of providing collective or public goods, however those are identified and defined, requires some choice of the most effective and efficient institution to supply them. That in turn will depend on the particular costs and benefits that apply to specific institutional structures, remembering that no institution creates perpetual efficiency.

Many problems are attached to any form of government regulation – problems that will become apparent as we examine specific cases put forth by Chadwick in the nineteenth century. These problems are equally applicable to contemporary forms of regulation. We believe it useful to consider some of these issues before we take a close look at Chadwick's proposals for franchising to promote economic and social welfare.

Franchising and Traditional Regulation

In most forms of contract management competitive bidders set rates. But this system does not avoid regulatory commission concern for the aggregate earnings problem, legal limitations on entry over the contract period, or policing the rates determined at the awarding of the contract(s). That prices are not commission-directed but determined by contract competition does not mean that price control is exercised by the enforcement body over the contract period. Chadwick believed that the efficiencies covered by contract management justify what can only be termed 'commission regulation.' The longer the term of the initial contract, the more likely that demand and cost conditions will change creating either a necessity to re-open bidding or some contingency(ies) built into the initial contract to deal with cost or demand changes. Obviously all contingencies cannot be built into any contract. That means that 'negotiations' between awardees and regulators or contract managers will likely be necessary over time (consider defense contracting as only one example; how does one handle cost overruns that would bankrupt contract winners?) In other words, though it may well be that 'the best prices can be secured if reliance is placed on the collection of bids, rather than on cost-plus price regulation by commissions,' as argued by contemporary observers (Demsetz 1968: 56, n. 3), that fact does not mean that a Chadwickian scheme of contract management removes the necessity of commission regulation. In any practical example, contract design, specification, and enforcement could easily create more subtle and complex difficulties for commissions than cost-plus pricing.

Contract Terms and Economic Efficiency

The time-length of contracts is a key to some problems with Chadwick's scheme. Consider a contractual situation in which community-owned physical faculties are let out for limited production intervals. The workings of a firm producing under such circumstances would roughly correspond in a theoretical sense to conditions characterizing short-run optimality. In particular, private decisions concerning the relative employments of capital and labor – given a specified output – would minimize production costs only over the period guaranteed by contract. Should long-run optimality require an adjustment in the capital-labor ratio, a disparity would arise between the production costs obtained under profit maximization and the minimum costs possible to society. One would suspect, given the limited production horizon, that the firm would tend to be biased toward the utilization of labor (upsetting the optimum capital/labor ratio). Hence, in the absence of some commission 'responsibility' for long-run investment planning, contract competition could lead to non-optimal costs of production. The requisite body of enforcers and planners necessary to remedy the capital-labor bias would be very similar to the regulators that we find under traditional regulation. (Note also that the variable 'contract length' directly affects the willingness of bidding entrepreneurs to employ capital that may or may not be salable or transferrable at market rates if the entrepreneur fails to secure a new contract when it comes up for re-bid.)

Yet another issue raised regarding the contracting process described in the nineteenth century by Chadwick concerns the nature of the possible advantages that the initial winning firm or firms might have. Would the implanting of fixed or sunk capital and the idiosyncratic human capital advantages (to a particular firm or firms) create a measurable advantage for these firms? Certain contemporary writers (Goldberg 1976; Williamson 1976) believe that the costs associated with the franchise bidding proposal in the area of contract establishment make the proposal, as a substitute for cost-plus regulation, practically unworkable. Williamson believes that the problem primarily lies in the inability of the franchise mechanism to efficiently generate plausible long-term contracts due to the existence of incumbent advantage, which eliminates the possibility of parity between the bids of the incumbent firm and the new competitors. A discussion of these factors would take us too far afield at this point, but it is important to understand that the nature of the contract (long-term contract, recurrent short-term contract, or once-and-for-all contract) and the problem of incumbent advantages to the initial firm or firms will affect the operation of Chadwick's proposal of franchise bidding. These concepts will be addressed in Chapter 9.

Contract Management, Property Rights, and Competitive Market Capitalism

Chadwick's advocacy of contract management contains some hidden assumptions and prescriptions. As Stigler (1971) and Peltzman (1976) initially argued (followed by legions of regulatory economists), regulation is acquired by industry or by interest groups and operates as a transfer of wealth from one group to another through the democratic political process. Chadwick assumes that the contracting body and the administration of it are accomplished by individuals of the highest ethics and intelligence. But at other points he recognizes that interest groups (industry groups in the case of water; cabbies in the case of technological subversion) affect results. In other words, there is simply no reason why interest groups would be any less important or active under conditions of contract management as with a regulatory agency.

Even more disturbing, the principle of contract management raises important questions for the institutions of an economic system. Here a contrast between Chadwick and his good friend John Stuart Mill is interesting. Mill, in part under the influence of Bentham and Chadwick, was also a supporter of government interventions. As early as 1832, Mill was justifying legislative interventions squarely and clearly on grounds of the 'free rider principle' (Mill 1832). There are crucial differences, however, between Mill and Chadwick. Though Mill lauded Chadwick's efforts at sanitary reform (as in the case of London water), Mill did not support the extent or the form of all of the interventions proposed by Chadwick. Chadwick saw 'externalities' everywhere, but Mill only to a much lesser extent. Chadwick wished to implement interventions with market forces and incentives to industry, as did Mill, but with crucial alterations in the system uncountenanced by Mill, that is, massive governmentally-enforced consolidation and contractual assignment of exclusive rights to produce and sell. Mill was skeptical about the extent of Chadwick's proposals and of the political and economic effects which would be generated by an implementation of the principle of contract management. After reading Chadwick's 1859 (see 1859c) essay Mill wrote to Chadwick: 'I have gone through your proof . . . But I do not well see where your principle is to stop or at what place you would draw the line of demarcation between it and conflicting principles' (Letter, Mill to Chadwick, 26 January 1859, in Mill 1972). Chadwick answered Mill's question in the essay itself (1859c: 408) 'To the questions sometimes put me, where I would stop the application of my principle, I am at present only prepared to answer, "where waste stops".'

The problem, as we have seen in the examples of the present chapter, is that 'waste' in Chadwick's lexicon could mean the waste due to the presence of natural monopoly – where scalar economies encouraged merger and the emergence of a single firm charging monopoly price and selling monopoly output. But Chadwick did not limit his principle to such cases. He argued that waste could have many sources – market failures of various kinds that might be made more efficient by government implementation of contract bidding for an exclusive right to serve. The source of these 'failures' could be market externalities, information asymmetries or simply competitive disequilibrium of some kind. Recall that Chadwick applied his theory to markets for baked goods, beer, cabs and cabriolets, and (as we will see in detail) funeral markets and cemeteries. Such markets may be competitive in the traditional sense of course, but simply in disequilibrium. Would this or any other of Chadwick's cases justify a transfer of property rights from free entrepreneurs to the government? That is, it is one thing to argue, as Mill did in the nineteenth century, and as Milton Friedman did in the twentieth century, that incentives and competition be built into socio-economic governmental interventions. It is something quite different to maintain, with Chadwick, that the efficacy of a controlled competitive bidding process in all of these situations justifies the removal of rights to private ownership.

CONCLUSIONS

This very modern issue in the world's developed countries is the essence of Chadwick's great intellect and it is the subject of this book. How are rational institutional structures chosen for the regulation or control of industry in the interests of societal welfare? What is the economic basis for such a choice? How do 'politics' and interest groups affect regulation and the social control of industry? Naturally, a rational institutional choice for industry regulation demands some kind of clear assessment of the costs and benefits of industry control for the 'public good' taking both short- and long-term factors into account. This required careful statistical assessment – assessments as Chadwick made for practically all of his proposals. And therein lies the kernel of Chadwick's genius. He sought – however unsuccessfully or unconvincingly in some cases – to classify instances of possible market failure, whether failure is through natural monopoly or other means. No economist of his century or even in large swaths of the next got closer to the issues that vex, intrigue, and challenge economists of today who are interested in how the social control of industry is related to consumer welfare and economic growth.

NOTES

1. We shall see that, under conditions of decreasing average cost, the scheme will not pass the full test of economic efficiency, where price equals marginal cost.
2. In no way does this discussion seek to denigrate Adam Smith's contributions and additions to this model.
3. This discussion is based on Ekelund and Hébert (1981).
4. The England of this time had experienced a significant decline in mercantile practices by the Crown, and the emergence of a thriving merchant class engaged in competitive practices with open individual property rights (see Ekelund and Tollison 1981; 1997).

5. Smith seemed to have been aware (1776 [1937]: 714) of the potential of engaging 'undertakers' by contract to provide certain public works.

6. The following discussion is extracted in part from Crain and Ekelund (1976).

7. Chadwick marshaled cases and statistics – to the point of redundancy – from France, Belgium, the German States, Prussia, and other nations to prove his point.

8. Note that economic efficiency; that is, $p = mc$, does not obtain under any average cost solution so that any kind of regulated system that brings price to average cost is a 'second-best' solution.

9. While traditional analysis of natural monopoly focuses on the case of declining average cost, subadditivity requires only that the entire market output be most efficiently produced by one firm (Baumol et al. 1982). Therefore, even in the absence of declining average costs single firm production can be most efficient. For an analysis of Chadwick's franchise scheme in the presence of increasing costs, see Dnes (1994).

10. Lester Telser's (1969) criticism of Demsetz notes that franchise bidding does not ensure economic efficiency because zero economic profits do not imply marginal cost pricing. However, marginal cost pricing under conditions of natural monopoly will require government subsidies as the monopolist will realize economic losses. If such subsidies and non-linear pricing are ruled out, then average cost pricing is a second-best optimal (Baumol and Bradford 1970). Multiproduct natural monopolies must choose price and product structures, a decision which under franchising will be made by some type of administrating regulatory commission. As is evidenced by regulation in telecommunications markets, such decisions are often driven by politics and self-interest rather than by economic efficiency.

11. The franchise schemes used in the funeral markets of both France and Germany involved regulated prices. In Germany franchises were granted to a single person at a 'certain fixed scale of prices.' In France, all interments were performed by joint contractors at 'regulated prices' (Chadwick 1843: 117). This same approach was used in cable television markets before the 1984 Cable Act and has been reinstituted by the 1992 Cable Act. Under such a regulatory regime, price and output should fall between the monopoly and franchise price-output combinations if the regulation is effective. In cable markets, the combination of rate regulation and franchise monopoly has been shown to be marginally effective at keeping rates below monopoly levels (Mayo and Otsuka 1991; Rubinovitz 1993).

12. The classic case of such extractions is cable television. There is no evidence that rents attained by franchise authorities through franchise fees or franchise requirements are specific only to the cable television industry. See Commanor and Mitchell (1971) and Beil et al. (1993).

13. See J.S. Mill, 'The Regulation of the London Water Supply' (1851 [1967]). Though Mill considered use of the Chadwick principle, he rejected it due to a distrust of joint stock companies and recommended, instead, a centralized Board of Commissioners. See Schwartz (1966).

14. Chadwick notes, however, that a reduction in the fare level in 1852 created an increase in the number of cabs in the metropolis from 3297 (ostensibly in 1852) to 4507 in 1857. Given allowances for population growth and other variables, it is hard to believe that entry would have taken place under sustained losses in the cab trade.

15. Chadwick went to police records for penal statistics from 1853 and 1854 related to 'coach and cabmen,' finding recurring crimes such as 'Offences against the Hackney Carriage Act,' larcenies, assault, assaults on the police, cruelty to animals, drunkenness, 'furious driving,' and so on committed by these destitute cabmen, ascribing it to this excess capacity or wasteful competition.

16. This case will be discussed at greater length in Chapter 5 where other potential forms of 'market failure' in the absence of scalar economies are discussed. At this point, however, the reader might ponder how openly competitive conditions – with rapid response to changes in cost and demand conditions – might fare in a cost-benefit comparison with the contracting solution.

4. Railways: the national franchising alternative

INTRODUCTION

The principle of contract management, which was a central anchor of Chadwick's attempt to 'regulate' monopolies or non-performing markets, was a broad-based idea. It could be used at all levels of provision, local, regional, or national. The present chapter analyzes Chadwick's well-developed contribution to a new technology that was reaching markets worldwide in the 1830s and following decades of the nineteenth century – railways. Naturally this technology had stark implications for economic analysis.[1] It developed into integrated systems, competed with other forms of technology (for example, canal and roadway transportation), and raised problems for economic analysis which had not been emphasized before: the nature of cost conditions, price discrimination, market structure, the meaning of competition and, most importantly, the importance of monopoly and the appropriate governmental response. Edwin Chadwick responded to all of these issues.

Naturally, the emergence of railway technology brought on engineering problems as well as new inventions, but Chadwick introduced a different style of analysis to railway economics. There was, of course, a perpetual desire for statistics, but beyond this Chadwick exhibited little interest in the technical or engineering side of railway operations. Rather, he beamed his interests on the sociological, political and, especially, the economic aspects of the field, or in other words, on railway policy. As such, he sought to apply his economic theory of 'contracting' to a national industry.

THE ESTABLISHMENT AND PROVISION OF EARLY ENGLISH RAILWAYS

Transport service between Liverpool and Manchester introduced the railway to England. The industry expanded rapidly by 1849, but not without growing pains.[2] Parliament passed 866 acts authorizing railway construction: later in the century (by 1880) over 6625 miles of track had been laid and over 50 000 men were permanently employed by the companies. Rail investments and installations were, like their American and French counterparts, beset by periodic credit crunches where sources of funds dried up, causing temporary slowdowns in construction. These developments were cyclic rather than linear in nature. As traffic and speeds increased in the early days, accident rates varied directly, causing much loss of life, capital, and revenue.[3] Contributing to the disorganization was the tendency of the companies toward autonomy. Rail managers, as early as the late 1830s, made it clear to Parliament that their track was not to be regarded as a public thoroughfare like state-built roadways. There had been some organization in this direction consisting of the acquisition of feeder lines by the main trunk lines. These combinations left the large trunk lines to compete with each other, resulting in a fragmented system consisting of non-interconnected lines, many of different road gauges, presenting a problem not unlike that of the alternative typewriter keyboards several generations later (Liebowitz and Margolis 1990). A long-distance traveler was frequently required to change train lines and even depots to get to his or her destination. The first move toward consolidation of the companies into a single network occurred when Parliament passed an act standardizing the gauges of tracks to be constructed.[4] Final monopolization was completed with the passage of the Railway Clearing Act in 1850 which allowed the pooling of accounts and provided for the exchange of rolling stock at junctions.

It was this kind of system that Chadwick and observers from other nations with similar problems placed under attack. He attributed three major faults to the railways:

> The chief defaults are first, those against unity of management for efficiency as well as economy; – secondly, exactions on necessities, by means of monopolies, instead of payments, merely for service, without profits; – thirdly, charges in disregard of an economical principle of increasing ratios of consumption with diminishing ratios of price by means of monopolies. (Chadwick 1866b: 203)

Thus, managerial inefficiencies, the existence of monopoly and monopoly pricing (through legalized pooling; that is, through cartels sanctioned by the government), and monopoly inhibition of economics of scale were the essential problems. Although Chadwick utilized these criticisms to support nationalization in 1866, he founded them upon an empirical study of costs, fares, and profits which he conducted using his 1859 paper on 'Competition for the Field' (Chadwick 1859c). As evidence for the inefficiency of the British system when compared to railway transport organization on the Continent, Chadwick offered the statistics which we have abbreviated and reproduced as Table 4.1.

Table 4.1   *Comparison of British and continental railways*

	England 1857	France 1854	Belgium 1856	Prussia 1857	Austria 1857	Germany 1857
Population per statute sq. mile	304	168	337	138	143	–
Aver. cost of railways per mile (£)	39 275	25 668	16 391	14 486	18 465	13 232
Aver. working expenses per mile (£)	1564	1191	1259	1248	1239	898
Aver. earnings per mile (£)	3161	2706	2158	1983	2686	1417
Aver. fares per mile:						
1st class (*d.*)	2.01	1.55	1.33	1.4	1.4	–
2nd class (*d.*)	1.41	1.16	1.0	1.15	1.1	–
3rd class (*d.*)	0.87	0.84	0.65	0.77	0.83	–
Aver. payment (percent) to original shareholders	⎰ 3.88 ⎱ 4.20	6.58	5.48	7.44	6.75	5.52

Source: Chadwick (1866b: 203).

As one of the foremost anecdotal empirical investigators of the day, Chadwick urged analyses of the facts concerning British railway supply as an absolute prerequisite to public policy.[5] These 'laboriously prepared statistical tables,' moreover, were to illuminate certain economic principles as sound or unsound. Clearly the facts of the table revealed some of the defaults which bothered him later in the next decade. Average capital costs (presumably average fixed costs) and average operating costs were indeed higher on British rails than those of five European countries. Additionally, fares were higher in all classes of transport in England and price discrimination was practiced consistently. Though the data revealed that price discrimination was also practiced in other rail systems, the *degree* of discrimination was greater in England, and the most elastic group of demanders – the third class passengers – in all countries had roughly the same charge. Percentage proportions of net receipts to total capital expenditures were also lower under the English system.

Chadwick provided several other criticisms which were bases for the three serious problems which he observed in British railway management. For instance, the lack of unity is the direct cause of duplication of capital (when two lines compete for the same traffic), scheduling problems (that is, having to change depots when changing trains), and the high search costs from having to acquire the fare schedules of several companies. Price discrimination and monopoly, that is, a 'disregard' of the law of demand, was the cause of low load factors (percentage of available seats occupied) on the trains.

One of Chadwick's most fascinating arguments is an outgrowth of the third criticism (the monopolists' quantity restriction). Chadwick practically equates monopoly pricing with treason, since it hinders the economic progress of the nation. He argues that since transportation costs were such a high percentage of the total cost of goods, lower fares would lower the costs of many goods and open up new markets for the rest of industry. Not only did the economic organization of the British rail system thwart industrial progress; the English companies failed to accept and use new technology to improve the quality and comfort of railway travel. This last is attributed to the indifference of railway directors and the unwillingness of the managers to accept responsibility for the new technology.

It is a mistake to argue that Chadwick was a defender of government operation or management of anything. He had no faith whatsoever that the government could operate the railways and he believed that all railway problems could be solved by the application of his principle of contract management and competition for the field of service: as he put the matter, 'the best plan would be to let the railways to farmers [entrepreneurs] . . . who should pay a certain fixed or variable rent to the shareholders, and retain the surplus rents,' with the result that 'the shareholders would be secure of their dividends, and the public of good accommodation' (1866b: 200). The details of the manner in which this plan was to be implemented are a bit sketchy, however. Chadwick clearly argued for the benefits of amalgamation and consolidation: 'purchase of the railways by the State would be beneficial to all parties, and . . . if the Government were to incur for a time an extra expense of two or three millions, until the net income were replaced, the loss would be amply repaid by the great improvements it might be the means of attaining' (1865a: 100). Demand elasticity estimates and underutilized capital on private lines, moreover, justified these benefits. He noted that:

> The extensive collateral as well as direct services obtainable from the separate establishments which I have brought under notice will be of importance, as showing the greater value of these means of communication to the public at

large than to any private company, and consequently suggesting the means for a part purchase of existing interest, or for compensation to the shareholders. (1865a: 104)

The government would not run the lines, and it would not be necessary that it be responsible for maintenance or for actual construction associated with new investment:

> I see no reason to alter the opinion . . . that it was not necessary that what is usually understood as the Government should undertake either the mainte- nance of the old, or the construction of new works; that it might constitute a responsible department to put them up for competition, to construct them, and form them on conditions of direct public responsibility. (1865a: 107)

What would be the charge for such a board? In practice, along with the application of contract management, the governmentally constituted board would have to: (1) take control of part or all railway capital, though not manage it; (2) modify it so that it would be a completely interlocking system; and (3) determine optimal investment and the introduction of innovations in railways, and let out these activities to private entrepre- neurs. Abstracting, for the moment, from any problems associated with this plan, and given that there are a large number of bidders and high collusion costs among them, the outcome would be to lower fares substan- tially, to guarantee a return to investors, and to provide the most modern and best service possible *without* government *operation* of the rails at a national level.

Return, from a purely analytical perspective, to the discussion of Chapter 3 and to Figure 3.1 in order to understand the results Chadwick posited for his scheme of national operation of the railways. According to Chadwick, railway operation and consolidation could be achieved through a bidding process and operation by the (or possibly a number) of franchisees after bidding is complete. How would the bidding go? If monopoly is the initial condition, price would settle at Pm and quantity (of travel or freight carriage) at Qm. Clearly Chadwick saw this as the situ- ation afflicting the British railways in the late 1850s and 1860s. Note that average cost is decreasing at service outputs greater than Qm, meaning that bidders could expect price to be greater than average cost up to output Qf. Thus, the franchised quantity would be greater – according to Chadwick, a good deal greater – than that under the contemporary monopoly service output. Average costs would determine how low bidders would go (given of course their knowledge of average revenues read off the demand curve). A competitive bidding process would, under specified conditions, yield a 'competitive' solution.[6] The monopoly rents that formerly went to the monopolist (under monopoly conditions) would then accrue to the franchise authority ('society'), to be disbursed in some manner – plowed back into the industry or disbursed in some (possibly opportunistic?) manner.

ISSUES SURROUNDING CHADWICK'S PROPOSAL FOR THE RAILS

The unique aspect of Chadwick's plan of franchise bidding for the operation of the railway, is operation separated from ownership (which would lie in the hands of society – government). His plan requires actual competitive bidding rather than the special pleading or sub rosa dealings for franchises or licenses which we observe in modern-day transportation, communications, or banking. Service and rates are fixed by contract in his system rather than on an ad hoc basis as in the 'adversary system' of cost-plus regulation so common in the United States and other countries. If – some would say a big 'if' – strict conditions are met where bidders are non-collusive and property rights are public rather than private, Chadwick's system is not only possible in a formal sense, but is an interesting and important alternative to open competition, orthodox commission regulation, or nationalization of ownership and control. (All of these systems, as we see later in this chapter, were proposed and/or advocated by British, Continental, and US economists at the time.) However, there are some practical difficulties with implementing Chadwick's plan for the railways which immediately present themselves. We limit ourselves to discussing only four of them at this point: (1) the question of innovation and the introduction of new technology; (2) the issue of parallel tracks and the nature of cost; (3) the 'load factor' and excess capacity; and (4) the costs of unifying the railways.

Advancing Rail Technology

Rail technology was moving rapidly during the period of Chadwick's investigations. One of Chadwick's complaints against the railways was that they did not innovate in order to improve the quality of their service. He charged that the cause of this is the 'directors, who give only occasional attention to the work.' They 'must necessarily leave [innovation decisions] to the subordinate executive officers, who have rarely any interest in making any change or trying any improvement. If it fails in execution, these officers are blamed for want of judgment, and if it succeeds they get nothing for their trouble' (1865a: 91). Lack of incentive or 'incentive incompatibility,' then, is the cause of the lack of innovation. Suppose that Chadwick's plan was instituted. In this case 'the Government should stand in the position of a landlord of the railways, and leave the details of executive management to the working tenants' (1865a: 101). Under this system, it would be the government's responsibility as 'landlord' to make the decisions pertaining to innovation. Here the government might own fixed capital and be responsible for maintaining and enlarging it; or it might direct responsibilities for innovation via contract to successful bidders.[7] Under either system, Chadwick's belief that a private joint stock company manager's unwillingness to optimally apply innovation can be transferred, *mutatis mutandis*, to civil servants and politicians if, for instance, the rail contract management team were to be put under an elected commission. (Mill believed as we will see later in the chapter, that incentive compatibility could be attenuated by linking rewards to the performance of private managers.) The civil servants would be in the same position as the hired manager when neither would be able to reap the rewards of successful innovation but both are responsible for failure. A politician would be in a slightly different position. He could reap the rewards of innovation (if successful), in that the reports on those successes would make good campaign material. (The changes would probably take place shortly before elections so as to minimize the effect of a failure and prove to the voting public that the person is doing his job.) In sum, it does not matter whether the innovation decisions are made by a civil servant or politicians, the application of contract management might produce sporadic changes in investment at best, especially since the long-run 'competitive' solution (as shown in Figure 3.1) is enforced through contract over some *fixed* period. Under ordinary conditions of competition with free entry, cost-reduction and/or utility-enhancement are introduced through a process of competition.

Collusive Agreements on British Rails

Chadwick clearly believed the railways were a 'natural monopoly' or at least characterized by decreasing costs, but he curiously ignored the phenomenon of predatory pricing. Predatory pricing occurred when two railways competed for the same traffic and each company tried to drive the other out of business. Chadwick noted that this was not in fact the case in England:

> It is most important to observe in this and other such examples [parallel track], that they are examples of traffic divided between two competitors, neither running under the best conditions for a productive result . . . It is further to be noted from such instances how many more are hindered from travelling by higher fares than would be anticipated. (1865a: 85)

From observation, Chadwick asserted that monopoly prices exist even though there is not a pure monopoly over the traffic. In order for this to occur, the competing lines must be colluding, and their agreement must be enforceable or at least ignored by the courts to prevent a collapse of the agreement and the competitors lowering their fares. Thus, in the case of the competing railway companies, the government was at fault for ignoring tacit collusive agreements.

The fact that collusive agreements were effectively ignored has a serious implication for the downfall of the application of 'contract management' to the English railway industry. Collusion on the part of potential bidders must be impossible in order for the system to reach a non-monopoly price. With collusive agreements enforceable in the courts it seems likely that some agreement could be worked out between the bidders, since there are higher potential returns to collusion. Any such agreement would serve to keep fares high and defeat the purpose of implementing the Chadwick principle.

Load Factors and Excess Capacity

Chadwick clearly objected to the excess capacity that he observed on trains. He commented that, 'I have myself been assured, by railway officers in the more populous districts, to whom I have spoken, that they would have no difficulty in carrying regularly a three or four-fold traffic, with little additional expense' (1865a: 91). While this may be true of freight traffic, passenger traffic loads may be much different. To say that additional passengers *could* be carried where capacity exists and that they *should* be carried are two different things. The full price of a service may be defined as the fare plus the value of the time waiting for that service. Thus, excess capacity has a value in that it reduces the waiting time. That is, although there may not be a train leaving exactly when the traveler wishes to go, the traveler can be assured a seat on the train of his choice without having to show up hours before departure. Thus, if the trains were filled as Chadwick wanted, the effect would be to raise the full price of train service and therefore to reduce the demand for the service. Chadwick also failed to realize that by filling up the trains, the extra crowding in depots and on the train serves to alter the quality of the service, and thus the demand for the service is affected.

Mergers and Consolidations

One aspect of Chadwick's argument for nationalization and franchise is particularly puzzling. Chadwick quoted Sir Rowland Hill, approvingly, that if in the process of unifying 'the Government were to incur for a time an extra expense of two or three millions, until the net income were replaced, the loss would be amply repaid by the great improvements' (1865a: 100).

If the unification of the railway was as profitable as Chadwick claimed, why did the many railway companies remain independent? It seems highly improbable that Chadwick and his followers were the only ones capable of perceiving the great benefits of unification. Surely one of the railway directors would have recognized that the railway was the ideal industry for amalgamation. Railways could then be run on the basis of a multiple-plant monopolist so as to minimize marginal cost (Patinkin 1947). However, multi-plant monopoly was not the result. Chadwick notes that 'For the most part, they have been aggregations of defective sectional manage-ment to defective sectional management, which are almost as expensively independent and jarring as before, without the system, and efficiency, and economies of general unity of direction' (1865a: 107).

If the mergers that did occur failed, and if the railways were not unified by the market mechanism, then the merger costs must be prohibitive. That is, the costs of effecting the merger must be greater than the present value of the benefits to be gained. This would appear, at first glance, to be fatal to Chadwick's argument that unification by government would be economically efficient. In calling for the unification of the railways, in other words, Chadwick expected the government to achieve the merger within the market, but in order for this to be possible, the government must be possessed of some special quality that enables it to lower the merger costs. Otherwise, the project would not be profitable. This criti-cism is not fatal, however, given Chadwick's maxim, which referred, not to profitability in an objective sense, but rather the maximization of social benefit (of which consumers' surplus was a part). With reference to Figure 3.1, Chadwick's proposal was that society capture the 'benefit' (utility or welfare produced) under the demand curve subject to an average cost constraint. Additionally, the social benefits associated with reduced cost of the transport inputs could be obtained. Clearly, however, the benefits, including those captured under the demand curve, can only be estimated. Chadwick's investigations led him to believe that the benefits of govern-ment amalgamation with cost-based pricing exceeded all merger and system average costs.

In the end, Chadwick's argument rests upon an empirical judgment or calculation of subjective benefit. Chadwick's arguments are persuasive, but they do not present a conclusive case for nationalization. Reliance on subjective estimates of benefits and the likelihood of collusion, coupled with the problem of innovation, which inure to the proposal, raise ques-tions on the practicability of nationalization of railways. But Chadwick was unique in his approach to national railway development. His pro-posal was not simply nationalization and operation by government. Other nations and other economists of the period over which Chadwick wrote took a variety of different approaches to the issue. Specifically, economists from England, France, and the United States sponsored a number of positions on the important issue of railways and their regulation (or non-regulation). It is highly instructive to consider some of the other major economic proposals for the railways of the period.

WILLIAM GALT AND BRITISH RAIL NATIONALIZATION

Outright nationalization of the railways with leasing and private management, or management by a government board *without* competitive bidding, or a pre-specified contract, were some alternatives considered in England. Consolidation and operation of the rails was urged by some writers well known to Chadwick. One English writer in particular – William Galt – published (anonymously in 1843 with a later attributed version in 1865) a book entitled *Railway Reform, Its Expediency and Practicability Considered.* In it, Galt presents an appealing proposal for nationalization and supports his case with clear and plentiful statistics. Among other advances, Galt: (1) documents with supporting data the practice of third-degree discrimination on 26 English rail lines for 1842; (2) shows that experiments with lowered rates on one British line reveal that owing to a universal law of demand and decreasing costs, nationalization and declining marginal costs would produce great social utility for travelers and consumers at one-third of then-current transport rates; and (3) demonstrates statistically that the government purchase of rail property would be feasible (and even profitable) to stockholders (by 1845, almost one-half of the railways in Great Britain were operating below a competitive rate of return).[8]

Galt, in 1843, had great faith in a government board possessed of 'expertise' to manage the railways. 'Under what system would the railways be managed?' he asked, asserting that:

> I believe the best system would be that which would approach nearest to that of our own Post Office. One individual of rank and talent, and a member of the cabinet, to have the sole management, responsible of course to the government and the country for the due performance of his duty; or perhaps, what would be better as the Board of Trade was lately constituted, the Present in the House of Peers, and the Vice-President in the House of Commons. (Galt 1843: 57)

Government management would be accomplished by outright purchase of the lines from existing stockholders 'at the high rate' of £106, 3 percent consols for each £100 worth of railway property.

Table 4.2   Galt's estimates of takeover costs on British railways

Creditor, £		Debtor, £	
By amount of net receipts	2 946 450	To interest on *£66 311 000* stock, at 3 percent	2 051 000
By reduction in annual expenditure by the consolidation of 48 establishments into one	300 000	To amount paid by Post Office	120 000
By gain to revenue through the Post Office, by increased facilities for the conveyance of mails	150 000	To increased expenditure in carrying department, and other charges	200 000
	3 396 450	To reduction in gross amount of receipts	1 000 000
By balance	25 450	To balance	25 450
			3 396 450

Source: Galt (1843: 56).

Cost economies from sharply falling marginal cost owing to high fixed investment, coupled with a lesser fall in total receipts accompanying a reduction in fares by 70 percent, would produce sufficient revenue to cover the interest on consols. In fact, Galt's estimates, reproduced in Table 4.2, make the government a net creditor after purchase in the amount of £25 450. Clearly, Galt's case that the government would end up a net creditor hinges entirely on the empirical adequacy of his cost and revenue estimations, and they have been questioned.[9]

Although Chadwick was much impressed by Galt's arguments and quotes him approvingly on the matter of consolidation, nationalization, and the proposed benefits of lower rates, the two did not agree on the matter of the *management* of the railways. Chadwick thought the government or its agents incapable of managing anything, whereas Galt's view of nationalization included a governmentally constituted board of governance. These matters came to a head in 1867 when Galt provided testimony for the Royal Commission investigating the railways, advocating government purchase of railways and the leasing of them to companies under specified conditions of operation with no 'Board' specified. Galt only drew the limited support of two commissioners, Hon. W. Monsell and Sir Rowland Hill (Hawke 1970: 337, n. 8). Two years earlier Galt apparently opposed Chadwick's administrative arrangement (bidding for rights with a lump sum payment) since, according to Chadwick (1865a: 106), Galt was advocating a managing board 'elected by the railway companies from amongst their own directors, with the addition of Government representatives.' Chadwick, of course, took strong exception and made the argument, similar to George Stigler's modern version (1971), that an identity of interest must develop between the governors and the governed. (How he would avoid this problem under his own plan is left unsaid.) Indeed, it is difficult to envision any sort of administrative body as immune from such influences, unless some kind of incentive system could be designed unlinking administrative rewards from industry interests.[10] But Galt was a strong supporter of nationalization, and of price, output, and capital management by a constituted board regulating the rails in the interests of societal welfare. Chadwick believed otherwise, supporting nationalization, but with private enterprise managing the system through a franchise bidding scheme.

CHADWICK VS J.S. MILL ON MARKET INTERVENTION IN RAILWAYS

The greatest British economist of his age, John Stuart Mill, had a high regard for Chadwick's abilities, and the two were close friends. With common roots in Benthamism, it seems clear that some of Mill's ideas on economic and social reform were influenced by Chadwick. Mill certainly never missed an opportunity to advance his friend's career. He read and 'corrected' practically all of Chadwick's papers (no mean task, since Chadwick rarely avoided awkward constructions in his writings). In April of 1842, Chadwick sent Mill a draft of his Poor Law Report and it is at this point (or possibly earlier) that Mill was introduced to Chadwick's view of competition. Though complaining of Chadwick's lack of compositional skills and poor grammar, Mill wrote to Chadwick: 'I have read through your report slowly and carefully. I do not find a single erroneous or questionable position in it, while there is the strength and largeness of practical views which are characteristic of all you do' (Mill 1963, Vol. II: 516).[11] In any case, Mill's views on public goods supply and regulation expressed in the first (1848) edition of the *Principles* reflect, to some extent, Chadwick's principle.

While Mill distrusted centralization, he did believe that intervention was necessary in the case of natural monopoly. An advocate of government ownership of waterworks (production and distribution) and gas companies, Mill urged *municipal* purchase and administration of these companies where possible. As Pedro Schwartz (1966: 71–83) has shown with respect to Mill's views on the regulation of the London water supply, Mill was quite concerned that a centralized board not be given power to consolidate water services. Chadwick had urged that water distribution, drainage, and interment systems (see Chapter 5 on the latter issue) be consolidated under a board of health (consisting of a board of commissioners) which would utilize competition for the field. Mill, in this case, not only rejected Chadwick's proposal for giving ultimate power to a centralized board but also considered and then rejected the *form* of the regulation proposed by Chadwick, choosing municipal ownership and operation as his ideal solution instead. A distrust of joint-stock companies seems to have been at the base of Mill's objection to the use of Chadwick's principle in the case of London water, as Schwartz suggested.[12] Clearly, Mill distrusted centralization.[13]

Interestingly, however, Mill's views as to both the level and the form of regulation may have changed when he considered the issue of English railways and what to do about them, if anything. Though it was possible to place ownership of public goods such as waterworks or gas companies at the local or municipal level, the same was not true of the railways. Discussing the railway's (assumed) natural monopoly at two points in *Principles*, Mill offered the following comments:

> It is much better to treat [the services of a natural monopoly] at once as a public function, and if it be not such as the government itself could beneficially undertake, it should be made over entire to the company or association which will perform it on the best terms for the public. In the case of railways, for example, no one can desire to see the enormous waste of capital and land (not to speak of increased nuisance) involved in the construction of a second railway to connect the same places already united by an existing one . . . Only one line ought to be permitted, but the control over that line never ought to be parted with by the State, unless on a temporary concession, as in France: and the vested right which Parliament has allowed to be acquired by the existing companies, like all other proprietary rights which are opposed to public utility, is morally valid only as a claim to compensation. (Mill 1848b [1965], Vol. 2: 142)

The quotation may imply that Mill was an advocate of government nationalization (but not operation) of railways. Again, this might be suggested in Book V of the *Principles* where Mill notes: 'It is perhaps necessary to remark, that the state may be the proprietor of canals or railways without itself working them and that they will almost always be better worked by means of a company, renting the railway or canal for a limited period from the state' (Mill 1848b [1965], Vol. 3: 956). Such statements certainly appear to indicate approval of at least part of Chadwick's proposed arrangement. But scrutiny of other remarks made by Mill appears to cast government as less of a nationalizer and provider of capital (and consolidator), ideas at the heart of Chadwick's vision, and more of a traditional franchise-issuer and cost-plus rate regulator. Mill argues that the government should subject a natural monopoly:

> To reasonable conditions for the general advantage, or to retain such power
> over it, that the profits of the monopoly may at least be obtained for the public.
> This applies to the case of a road, a canal, or a railway . . . To make the conces-
> sion for a limited time is generally justifiable, on the principle which justifies
> patents for inventions: but the state should either reserve to itself a reversionary
> property in such public works, or should retain, and freely exercise, the right
> of fixing a maximum of fares and charges, and, from time to time, varying that
> maximum. (Mill 1848b [1965], Vol. 3: 956)

It might appear, then, that Mill espoused nothing more than the system of
rail regulation which the United States adopted in 1887 (one was already
in place in France in the 1840s and 1850s), and one which was only slightly
more stringent than the legislative restrictions imposed on British lines in
the 1840s and 1850s.[14]

Truthfully, however, Mill could never quite make up his mind about
the railway issue. He was, as most observers have pointed out, extremely
distrustful of centralization, believing that the ideal was the greatest dissemination of power consistent with efficiency. But Chadwick believed
that effective and efficient control of the railways could hardly be obtained
without centralization. (Recall, also, that rate and other controls could
be asserted by government – as in the United States – *without government
centralization or ownership.*) Two of Mill's later views are relevant here.
In 1864 Mill wrote to Chadwick concerning centralization and railways:

> About the economical advantage, touched upon in your letter, of a consolida-
> tion of railways, you are not likely to find any help in the French economists.
> They are, nearly all of them, more hostile to consolidation and to government
> action than I am; and I am more so than you. (Letter, Mill to Chadwick, 28
> October 1864; in Mill 1972)

But by 1869 Mill was suggesting a guarded, experimental approach to the
question of nationalization, a shift which coincided with sharply increased
public criticism of railway operations around 1867. Thus in 1868 a movement to nationalize the telegraph system and the railways was still active.
The Electric Telegraph Bill, introduced in Parliament in 1868 and adopted
in July of that year, authorized the Postmaster General to acquire, maintain, and operate the telegraph system. Mill's opinions on these matters
were expressed in a letter to A.M. Francis:

> I took no part in the discussion about the purchase of the Telegraphs because
> it was a mere experiment of which I do not foresee the result. I should object
> to the purchase of the railways until the smaller measure shall have approved
> its policy by its success. And in no case does it seem to me advisable that the
> Government should work the railways. If it became proprietor of them it ought
> to lease them to private companies. (Letter, Mill to A.M. Francis, 8 May 1869;
> in Mill 1972)

Mill, it seems, would have approved railway nationalization under general government, contingent upon successful government operation of a smaller industry. The important point is that Mill seriously flirted with Chadwick's principle of competition 'for the field' as a possibly efficient form of regulation, *given* that nationalization took place. Chadwick's idea, then, probably influenced Mill's view on the proper form of railway regulation, one which sought to integrate incentives with public assurances of cheap and efficient service. But Mill was infinitely more wary of the abuses of centralized power than Chadwick, whose litany of market failures demanding authoritative interventions was a long one indeed. It does appear, however, that Mill was attracted to the 'market features' of the Chadwick plan in the special case of railways, features which would make the interventions of general government more palatable and more efficient.

THE FRENCH SYSTEM OF RAILWAY PROVISION

We discussed, in Chapter 3, the prescience of the French (including the engineer Bernard de Belidor, and in practice, reaching back to medieval times) in bidding schemes for the execution of national defense and public works projects. Chadwick was, as mentioned in earlier chapters, enthralled with the system he *believed* to be in place in European nations, especially France. This system of 'bidding' for exclusive rights to serve by a single company or by multiple companies was actually in use in France in a number of urban industries, including funeral and interment supply (see Chapter 5, for example). However this was not the case with the 'industrial organization' of the railways over the 1840s and 1850s. From 1823 onwards, French railways were licensed by the State. Eventually this led to consolidation, so that by the early 1850s there were six large companies that served the national market. In the literature of the day, these companies were referred to as 'private,' a term which, it turns out, provokes mischief and misunderstanding. Americans have a tendency to equate 'private' with 'competitive,' which in the case of French railways is completely inappropriate.

When Mill mentioned to Chadwick that the French economists were less supportive of centralization or nationalization by the government than he ever was, he was undoubtedly thinking of some of the French 'liberals' such as Joseph Garnier, who were most reluctant to turn the railways over to government ownership and management. Socialists believed that nationalization with government management would maximize the utility of the railways. Extreme liberals such as Gustave de Molinari were strong advocates of a free market, that is, a free entry solution in virtually *all* industries and services. (Molinari teetered at the brink of anarchism at some points.) Chadwick, ostensibly very familiar with French practice, curiously found (what he believed to be) a clear influence in the economist-engineer Jules Dupuit (1804–1866).

Chadwick (1865a) probably read Dupuit's essay 'On Tolls and Transport Charges' (1849 [1962]) or 'On Utility and Its Measure' (1853a [1933]) where Dupuit initiated the use of demand and revenue functions. Chadwick curiously does not discuss utility maximization and price discrimination, featured prominently in these essays, and instead cites, with many compliments, Dupuit's works in his discussion of the effect of railway companies' pricing policies on the level of traffic, and he implies that Dupuit advocated government ownership or regulation of the railways in order to promote maximum welfare. Though it is correct that Dupuit discussed the total utility provided by railways under alternative institutional arrangements, including government ownership and/or regulation, it is by no means clear that Dupuit believed that government was the only redress for the welfare loss created by railway monopoly. In fact, Dupuit vehemently attacked the effects of government regulations of railways then existing (1853) in France, concluding that competition, which he correctly understood as the absence of entry control, while not perfect, was infinitely superior to government ownership or control over private monopoly. For Dupuit it was the French government – often involved in special pleadings and support from railway companies – that created the *de jure* monopoly that then existed on French railways (Ekelund and Hébert 2012). The rate regulation to which the railways had to submit was disastrous in terms of the efficiency and welfare-production of the railways, with rates being too high for some railways and too low for others. This of course gave supra-normal profits to some and losses to others, requiring government subsidies.

The whole question of 'natural monopoly' due to the impossibility of competition in cases of high investment (parallel tracks) raised by Chadwick and others was denied by Dupuit. A critical case in point is the unnecessary duplication of facilities, or the so-called 'problem' of two companies operating between Paris and Versailles (on opposite sides of the Seine), noticed by Dupuit in 'Voies de Communication [Transportation],' which purportedly leads to (or defines) natural monopoly (see Dupuit 1853b, in Breton and Klotz, Vol. I: 451–2).[15] Here, Dupuit sets up a hypothetical situation in which a railway company earns a sufficiently high rate of return to attract a competitor. Further, he admits that capital redundancies and material losses occur with open competition but argues that such losses are endemic and necessary to the competitive process and to competitive results (price-cost margins close to unity). Dupuit thus supported the *actual possibility* of a functional, competitive railway system. Having considered the 'sunk-cost' argument of redundant tracks, he rejected it as an impediment to competition.[16] Such redundancies ('wastes') are indeed common costs to society in a variety of fields wherever competition inevitably puts some suppliers out of business. Nevertheless, Dupuit argued that these costs are dwarfed by the welfare losses in 'public utility' that inure to government monopoly, or government-managed 'private' companies. He preferred transport means open to competition, which, in his scheme of the possible, definitely included railways.

Dupuit understood that competition takes place not only in a static context, but in a dynamic, spatial, and multi-dimensional context as well. His prescient analysis may be found in a number of his writings, including his 1849 article on the influence of tolls on the utility of transportation (Dupuit 2009, in Breton and Klotz, Vol. I: 243–308). In this and other essays, and in 'Voies de Communication' (1853b), Dupuit laid out his spatial theory involving competition between railways, canals, and highways. Citing actual examples of spatial competition between Tours, Châteauroux, and Orléans, Dupuit pioneered a spatial-competitive model that led him to condemn, unequivocally, the setting of fixed tolls per mile on the railways, that is, the favored practice of the 'company monopolies' (Dupuit 2009, in Breton and Klotz, Vol. I: 301–8). In this important analysis, Dupuit argued that his non-proportional tariff principles – based on demand, utility, and full price (money plus time) would become increasingly significant as the railway network in France developed further, because the lines would interconnect and cross each other in all directions to form an intricate pattern of indirect routes. In such circumstances, he said, the railways could be run only with reduced rates, not with proportional ones (Dupuit 2009, in Breton and Klotz, Vol. I: 307). Proportional tolls, in fact, denied French railways the opportunity to meet the competition from highways and canals, much to the detriment of the rails, consumers, and the general welfare.

Dupuit's approach to inter-modal competition was *dynamic* because technology was continuously changing competitive margins, modifying the nature and form of transport competition. Dupuit not only debunked the conception of natural monopoly – in rails and, presumably, in other industries with high capital requirements – but argued that 'company monopolies,' *de jure* railway monopolies created by the state cannot be regulated to maximize consumers' utility. He also recognized that technology, when left to competitive forces, had the power to reduce prices and expand social welfare.[17]

Chadwick's (apparently) keen attention to Dupuit appears to have missed these critical points. Further, Chadwick failed to recognize (or did not understand) the utilitarian case Dupuit made for price discrimination under either private or public ownership. Indeed, one of the factors bothering Chadwick concerning the private ownership and operation of the railways was that they engaged in price discrimination. As Chadwick put it:

> The common railway administration, under erroneous legislation, goes beyond payments for services to systematic and pernicious exactions on necessities. There is . . . a large and wide economic distinction . . . between charges which have relation solely to services rendered, and charges which are founded . . . on the view and estimate of the necessities, and on the power of exaction under monopolies. (1865a: 78)

It is important to recognize that both Chadwick and Dupuit proceeded from utilitarian principles, although Dupuit did so in a far more precise and formal sense. One might even say that he operationalized the Benthamite form of utilitarianism with modern microeconomics (Ekelund and Hébert 1999). But since Chadwick was interested in promoting the economy of the country and was a reader of Dupuit, he might have made some comment on Dupuit's important and original discussion of the price-discriminating monopolist. While it seems clear that Dupuit at least opened up the real possibility of a competitive system of railway supply (with no entry restrictions), he also established the fact that certain types of monopoly pricing systems could approximate competitive results. Specifically, he noted the price-discriminating monopolist could increase both output and total utility of the industry by using price discrimination. It was aggregate welfare that Dupuit wanted to maximize, and (to him) it should not have mattered whether or not the railways were price discriminating in either public or private monopoly cases, since (as Dupuit had shown in the 1840s) discrimination can result in an expansion of both producers' and consumers' surplus. That is to say that, given monopoly, it should not matter who reaped the gain in utility of the expanded service, that is, either the rail company gaining additional producers' surplus (economic profits) through price discrimination, or the people gaining extra consumers' surplus from a low uniform rate.

Chadwick, unable or unwilling to view the problem in this manner, chose to interpret Dupuit as requiring government intervention, whereas it did not appear to be the preferred or even the second-best solution of the railway problem to the French writer. (Dupuit, like Chadwick, did not look at the government's operation of anything as supportive of the general welfare!) Thus, Chadwick's focus upon governmental consolidation of the British lines probably owes much to the influence of Galt (and Bentham, though he did not live to see the British development of the railways). A superficial reading of Dupuit's writings merely served to support his belief that a uniform cost-based rate could be devised by a bidding scheme imposed by government (which was not Dupuit's position at all).

AN AMERICAN PERSPECTIVE ON RAIL MANAGEMENT

The US situation with respect to the railways was markedly different.[18] The 'free enterprise' system enshrined in the American psyche extended to most industries (with post-Civil War protectionism always an exception). The railways, with distinct spatial-technological characteristics leading to high fixed costs, were initially provided as they were in most major countries of the world. Land and right-of-way grants and other subventions to 'special interests' characterized the early development of railways from the 1830s onward. The spirit of non-intervention meant that the serious debate over whether to regulate (or nationalize) the railways was several decades behind the melee that occurred with Chadwick and Galt in England. Open entry and decreasing costs led to certain inherent instabilities amongst the rail cartels, however, just as they did in England. These features precipitated serious railway crises in 1857–59, 1873–77 and in 1884–85, the latter being a clear prelude to the Act to Regulate Commerce in 1887 (which created the Interstate Commerce Commission, or ICC), the signal intervention by the federal government into private markets. Interestingly, when faced with ownership of the railways, regulation of routes and rates, or outright open entry competition, the middle-ground was chosen, remaining the chosen form of intervention in many industries to this day.[19]

There were clearly advocates for all forms of rail regulation, except for Chadwick's unique proposal, particularly when crises occurred. Many observers believed the railways were a natural monopoly, a situation demanding nationalization or some form of regulation. An important exception was Arthur Twining Hadley (1856–1930), a freelance writer on railway subjects, a tutor of Greek logic and Roman law at Yale University and, ultimately, the University's president for over 20 years (1899–1921). Hadley was not yet born when Chadwick had begun his investigations, but the former wrote presciently on railway economics during Chadwick's lifetime and his views, like Dupuit's, form an important counterpoise to the Chadwick plan.

The question of 'what to do about the railways' was on the minds of consumers, politicians, and economists of the pre-1887 period. Railway problems of the 1870s and 1880s very probably led Hadley to an analysis of railway questions. The issue: were the railways 'natural monopolies' in that monopoly and monopoly pricing was inevitable? In common with virtually all other writers on railway questions, Hadley thought railways to be characterized by decreasing costs due to the high component of overhead (fixed) costs. But unlike so many of the others he did not believe them to be natural monopolies. If the latter were the case, one would expect to observe much merger activity and a dearth of new entrants. Neither was observed, however, since railway costs were not perpetually declining. The rails were 'particular monopolies' (Hadley 1885: 63) with particular short-run problems due to high fixed costs and limited ability to discriminate. Competition in these circumstances would cause oscillating rates between those based on short-run variable costs and the monopoly rate. Although some consolidation took place (Hadley 1886) as a result of declining costs, Hadley argued that the *non-regulated* market solution was to allow pooling through cartelization.[20]

Private pools (cartels) among railway operators and competitors had the effect of creating stability in the menu of railway rates. But Hadley believed (1885: 76–7) that private cartels tended to breakdown since cheating by any member of the cartel would increase the cheater's quantity demanded and profits. The railways had recourse to other forms of agreements, some which could lead to monopolized rates and reductions in consumer welfare. But, Hadley argued that the market for rail services was *contestable*, that is, open to free entry. The effectiveness of rivalrous competition, in short, may have *no relation to market structure.*

In fact, as a consequence of cartel breakdown the railways *demanded* federal regulation in the United States in the 1880s, and Hadley was one of the earliest observers to recognize this seeming anomaly. In other words, the railways captured regulation to *legalize* pooling with federal policing and enforcement mechanisms. Hadley was worried that the industry's 'capture' of regulation might not produce rate stability, owing to the prohibition against pooling contained in the provisions of the Act, but he underestimated the ability of the rivals, with the approbation of the ICC, to quote differential rates which in effect pooled traffic. He also thought that the ICC or any similar regulation would necessarily create massive allocative distortions, a prediction which, unfortunately, was largely borne out.[21] A 'protective stance' toward the US railways began early (Spann and Erickson 1970) and continued until the ICC was abolished in 1995. Hadley's position was that allocative distortions were inherent to, and a consequence of, the Act.

CONCLUSION: PROPERTY RIGHTS AND INSTITUTIONS MATTER

It should be obvious from our brief examination of both government nationalizers (Galt) and market-oriented economists of the period (Dupuit in France, Hadley in the United States) that Chadwick's economic plan for the railways was unique.

His was not an institutional structure that permitted open entry (at least over a contract period) or one that simply supported government nationalization and operation of the railways, or even one of cost-price regulation of privately owned but publically regulated operation. Chadwick believed that society's welfare, both short and long term, would be maximized by outright purchase of the English railways from stockholders, integrating them into a whole system, sectioning them into regions and putting them up for competitive bid with quantity, price, and other details specified. The railways would, however, be operated by the leaseholders.

We have highlighted Chadwick's plan in the present chapter by contrasting it to other possible institutional arrangements – those suggested by fellow English writer William Galt, who advocated outright nationalization and cost-plus regulation of the railways; by French and American writers Jules Dupuit and A.T. Hadley, who argued that, despite recurring problems, open entry and free competition would maximize the welfare produced by the railways; and by J.S. Mill who never could quite make up his mind concerning Chadwick's plan versus other institutional arrangements. The quest of all of these writers was to determine an institutional and property rights structure that maximizes societal welfare – represented technically as the area between the demand curve for rail services and the average cost of production (as in Figure 3.1).

Consider the openly competitive solution first. As both Dupuit and Hadley recognized, this solution contained the kind of historical 'instabilities' that had existed on both French and US lines. Importantly, such competition had not actually been 'tried' in France or other European countries where, from the beginning subventions, subsidies, and rates were regulated by statute by the French government. Dupuit at least admitted the possibility that open competition which, undeniably, created duplication and redundant capital, was a viable system for maximizing the sum of consumers and producers welfare (that is, utility and profits). Such a system supported the most rapid technological innovations and reactions to the emergence of either rail competition or competition from other modes (canals, road transportation). There were costs to competition – short-term pricing that was above cost and possible instabilities – but these costs were swamped by those associated with inflexible and politically driven rates. The government had made an inefficient mess of the railways in France and, according to the American Hadley, was about to about to do the same (and ultimately did do the same) in the United States. Hadley, however, believed that the pooling of traffic, with free entry, was the solution. Why? Because pools (cartels) have a tendency to breakdown through cheating and because *potential* competition makes the railway market contestable (so long as government does not prohibit entry). Rates would vacillate between average variable costs and the monopoly rate, but in general open competition would be preferable to any other institutional arrangement. Both of these writers stressed that government ownership and/or regulation of any sort would be bound to create 'rent-seeking' on the part of the regulated, as well as cost inflation and incentive incompatibilities.[22] Government owned or regulated railways would tend to 'capture' the regulators – the end result of the twentieth century US system according to most modern observers.

In truth, Chadwick, and most certainly his friend J.S. Mill, were aware of some of these problems. But Chadwick believed that his franchise bidding proposal would help eliminate some problems since government would (eventually) own the railways but not take any part in actually operating them. Clearly Chadwick did not believe that the private market, open entry (unregulated) solution would be optimal or preferable to direction by a board of experts. While Chadwick provided no data to support the case for the costs of capital duplication, that cost was one that overwhelmed the benefits emphasized by writers such as Dupuit and Hadley of open competition. Also, since Chadwick did not believe that the government was capable of running anything through direct administrative control – due to problems of 'capture' and opportunistic behavior of regulators – an institutional system of government nationalization with traditional cost-plus regulation was not a system to guarantee maximization of societal welfare.

Therein lies the uniqueness of Chadwick's system: he believed that 'management through contract' would avoid, through a body possessed of expertise, the problems of an open market, or of a nationalized system using traditional regulatory methods. The Chadwick system was one of contract design to achieve specific goals: (a) to reign in monopoly pricing (including price discrimination); (b) to bring price – presumably some 'average price' – in line with average cost of provision so as to increase the 'load factor' for both passengers and freight; (c) to modify the railways of England so as to create an interlocking system; and (d) to determine optimal investment and the introduction of innovations in railways, and let out these activities to private entrepreneurs, ostensibly to be introduced over a contract period, by opening up the bidding at appropriate intervals, or by separating invention and innovation functions for rails from simple managerial functions (all conducted by private enterprise).

The fundamental issue is not how to achieve 'nirvana' in any and all of these proposals, Chadwick's included. Nirvana would include a perfect maximization of social welfare (the sum of consumers' and producers' surplus) at all points in time. Although we will examine the various proposals in detail in the concluding chapter of this book, we have already seen that the 'competitive' or the 'nationalization with cost-plus regulatory' solutions would clearly contain problems. The point here is that Chadwick believed that his franchise bidding proposal was superior to these alternatives because it left management, if not ownership, to private enterprise. Yet there are practical difficulties and at least potential problems associated with his solution to the social provision of the railway as well.

Chadwick's solution seems to call for ideal conditions in the sense that not only must collusion of bidding firms be impossible, but the government agency directing the railways or any other public good must also be free from *ex parte* dealings with industry and problems of expertise as well. The problems of contract management vary with the technical and competitive characteristics of the industry or utility, as we will see, and must be developed in the context of a case study. It is unlikely that the institution of a Chadwick plan by itself would eliminate the source of institutional inefficiencies. But if constraints facing contract managers could be altered in such a manner that rewards were independent of industry interests, the Chadwick plan for goods or services afflicted with market failure of one kind or another could have some appeal. (Certainly the plan or variants of it have already been implemented, successfully, in international settings, including national defense contracting in the United States and elsewhere.) Again, the principle issue is not whether the Chadwick plan *could* be implemented. Rather, the central matter is how well a particular institutional arrangement would promote societal welfare in contrast to alternatives. On which side did the maximization of welfare lie – with the problems created within an openly competitive system (duplication, cycles of provision, and so on) or with government abrogation of property rights with a contract-letting board of experts guiding a privately managed system? Societies may well be forced to make future choices between inefficient and expensive solutions to market failures and alternative arrangements, including alternative property rights structures. This situation may be of particular import in the provision of local or regional services of various kinds, one of which we examine in Chapter 5.

NOTES

1. It is perhaps not too much to argue that the invention of the railway helped lead thinkers to what may be called 'neoclassical' economics. The writings of Jules Dupuit, Charles Ellet, Dionysius Lardner, Emile Cheysson, and many others bear out this assessment. Consider only the concept of marginalism – the centerpiece of neoclassical economics. The central pricing problems of a railway clearly revolve around the question 'should a passenger or a unit of freight be carried when free capacity exists?' The answer clearly leads to the issue of marginal cost and marginal revenue as well as to the opportunity cost of the freight or the passenger in getting from A to B.
2. The present discussion draws on Ekelund and Price (1979).
3. Accident rates are reported in Lardner's *Railway Economy* (1850 [1968]).
4. Today such standardization would be termed 'internalization of a network externality.' Such an externality occurs when the additional use of a device or technology increases economic efficiency, lowers cost, and increases utility of all users. An additional use of a cell phone or the social network by one individual increases the utility of other phone or network users.
5. Chadwick proudly belonged to the so-called 'school of facts,' which utilized induction from facts, rather than to the Ricardian 'hypothesists.' He also (in 1885) confided to a friend that 'John Stuart Mill always deferred to me on any questions I had examined because as he said, I always got my information first hand, whilst he could only get it second hand or from books' (Chadwick quoted in Lewis, 1952: 15). Mill differed with Chadwick on a number of policy issues, including Chadwick's view of 'competition for the field' (see Chapter 3), but he often displayed frank admiration for Chadwick's abilities.
6. Remember that such a solution is only an *approximation* of a competitive solution when average costs are declining throughout the relevant range of output. Price would not equal marginal cost under these conditions.
7. Naturally, *if* franchise winners and bidders provided capital (under unlimited franchise periods), incentives would exist to incorporate and develop new cost-reducing technologies. But the amount of capital in place and incentives to innovate would depend on the terms of the contract, specifically on its length.
8. Galt collected and presented very valuable data on virtually all of the railways of Great Britain for the early 1840s in the text of, and in a large appendix to, *Railway Reform* (1843: 77–106). His performance in the collection, assimilation, and use of railway data to illustrate economic conditions should earn him regard, alongside Dionysius Lardner, Charles Ellet, and the French engineers of the École des Ponts et Chaussees, as one of the first great students of empirical-oriented transportation economics (see Ekelund 1971; Spengler 1969).
9. While comparatively little is known concerning Galt, G.R. Hawke's generally excellent *Railways and Economic Growth in England and Wales* (1970) devotes a good deal of attention to Galt. We believe, however, that Hawke misinterprets Galt when he questions Galt's views on price elasticities under national rates and when he states that:

    > Galt's reorganization scheme was to be compatible with his belief that railways were maximizing profits [before nationalization] and were to cover their costs after reorganization, the low level of railway profits in the 1860s implies that the reorganization was to be accompanied by considerable economies in costs and Galt was unable to specify where these would occur. (Hawke 1970: 338)

    Though Hawke's interpretation may hinge on the fact that he uses the 1865 edition of Galt's *Railway Reform* (we have used the 1843 version, which Hawke only mentions as an early 'pamphlet'), it is clear that Galt was very careful in his statements about costs and elasticities. He admits that 'it would be absurd to attempt forming anything like an estimate of the profit and loss on each railway, that would result from a reduction of

70 percent on their average scale of charges,' although he provides empirical examples of lines which have experimented with raising and lowering rates (Galt 1843: 44, 55). As Table 4.2 in the text shows, Galt counted on gross receipts *declining* by one million pounds after nationalization, giving wide latitude for error. The economies represented by net receipts were the result of costs economies which Galt treated in great detail. An empirical study of the London and Birmingham Railway for 1842 convinced Galt of the tremendous cost economies of increased loads, due to high overhead costs (operating costs would increase only by 25 percent). Translating these estimates into the cost and revenue estimates for all lines of the United Kingdom provided Galt with the estimates of Table 4.2 (Galt 1843: 28–44 *et passim*). Most private managers were solely interested in profits and did not, in any case, conduct rate experiments, because of demand uncertainty. The latter inhibited progress and social utility, even though lower rates might provide higher returns to private stockholders. In any case, Galt urged governmental experimentation with costs and returns on a limited number of rail lines before complete nationalization (Galt 1843: 67–71). In short, Galt held a healthy skepticism concerning the empirical support and validity of his proposal, along with careful support and clear presentation of the facts as he knew them. For these reasons, it seems to us, Hawke has not provided a balanced assessment of Galt's proposal for nationalization.

10.   Depending on the interpretation one takes from a statement by Galt, it may be that Galt was won over to a Chadwick type proposal, either independently or under Chadwick's influence, by 1867. In Chadwick's 'Address' to the National Association for the Promotion of Social Science (1867d), he quotes a dialogue between Commissioner Lowe and Mr Galt on the matter of railway organization. When questioned by Lowe on the exact objection raised by Chadwick to Galt's earlier version of nationalization, namely, that an identity of interest would build up between MPs and railway directors, Galt replied, 'If you give no option, if you make it binding that you shall let the contract to whosoever gives the most money, there is no option left in the power of Government' (Chadwick 1867d: 596). Thus, Chadwick's plan might have been (at least) an acceptable alternative to Galt.

11.   Both Mill and (probably) Chadwick himself may have first learned of 'contract management' from Bentham or from their active intellectual intercourse with French savants and practitioners. Bentham used a similar idea in 1791 in the *Panopticon*, related to prison reform (Halévy 1928: 84–5). For his part, Chadwick himself claimed priority for the idea with his examination of the sanitary conditions of town populations in 1838 (1859c: 384–5). Given Bentham's popularity, however, it seems reasonable that the concept was floating around British writers for some time.

12.   Though Mill's 'ideal' solution to the London water problem was municipal ownership and operation, he advocated that the work be entrusted to a commissioner, appointed by the government and answerable to Parliament (Schwartz 1966: 81). A portion of Mill's letter to the Committee of the Metropolitan Sanitation Association is reprinted in Harris (1959: 604–11).

13.   Mill underwent a metamorphosis of thought on the issue of administrative centralization. His evolution is shown in his policy position on the Poor Laws. Though he favored centralization in the original law of 1834, his view was later substantially altered, probably under the influence of Alexis de Tocqueville (who Mill introduced to English readers). Specifically Mill came to believe that increased legislation was required for social progress but that laws were best administered by local authorities who, ideally, would be possessed of expertise and would act as a vehicle for 'educating' the public.

14.   The railways faced maximum rate regulation imposed upon them by parliamentary legislation in England. But as Galt points out, these maximum rates were so high that actual rates were consistently below them even in the less elastic markets.

15.   The Paris-Versailles railways merged in 1855 under government rules and regulations, including entry control, after initially being given government permission to build separate facilities.

16.   The decreasing cost argument is not the only one used to argue for 'natural monopoly.'

A de facto monopoly argument is better focused on the fixed vs sunk cost distinction. The modern focus on market 'contestability' involves the degree of sunk (that is, non-recoverable) costs associated with particular productions. Those with high degrees of non-recoverable costs would, according to some definitions, be 'natural monopolies.' Critics note that, in reality, many costs of entry (advertising for example) are non-recoverable and 'sunk.' The so-called 'network externalities' argument for government interventions is not necessarily an argument for government interventions. For example, cases such as the alleged superiority of the Dvorak (typewriter) keyboard over the standard QWERTY keyboard have turned out to be bogus. Liebowitz and Margolis (1990) argue that inasmuch as a superior technology would have enabled market entry, the dominance of the QWERTY keyboard was not a 'natural monopoly.'

17. See Ekelund and Hébert (1999; 2012).
18. The present section includes portions of Cross and Ekelund (1980).
19. The ICC's role and scope mushroomed throughout the twentieth century to include interstate trucking (1935), water carriers (1940), interstate pipelines (1906–77) and regulations on interstate telephones (1910–34). Parallel regulation in antitrust was largely a product of the Progressive fervor that overtook the US in the decades surrounding the turn of the century. The mid-course of rate and scope of service regulations continued throughout the century. The Federal Communications Commission (FCC) was established in 1934 to regulate interstate telephone and broadcasting (after which came cable television in 1968 and 1992). The Federal Power Commission (FPC), established in 1935, was assigned the responsibility of regulating wholesale electricity in that year and natural gas pipelines in 1938. Regulation of the field price of natural gas sold in interstate commerce was assigned to the FPC in 1954. The Federal Maritime Commission brought ocean shipping under control in 1936 and, in 1938, the Civil Aeronautics Board (CAB) regulated price and entry into airline markets. While certain regulations have been lifted or modified in the post-1970s, cost-price and entry-scope regulation have been the chosen course of 'social control' in the United States.
20. Indeed, Hadley developed a theory of cartel formation long before Stigler ('A Theory of Oligopoly' 1964). According to Hadley, cartel agreements 'may take any one of four forms; (1) Agreement to maintain rates; (2) To divide the field; (3) To divide the traffic; (4) To divide the earnings. The last three are commonly known as pools' (1885: 74). Cartel violations (usually carried out in secret) are a constant threat to the stability of rates and, Hadley continued, 'It is for the interest of all that rates in general should be maintained; but it is for the interest of each concern to secure business for itself by not quite maintaining them. This constitutes a great temptation to depart from schedule prices' (1885: 75).
21. When motor and air transportation became viable competitors for railways, they were brought under the umbrella of the ICC, creating a massive cartel in transportation and massive resource misallocations, reducing the social welfare of these industries.
22. Consider Hadley's remarks on 'profit regulation' or limitation as a means of public control of the rails. Limiting profits on 'utilities' were characterized as leading to intransigence in management, that is, cost increases and not rate reductions follow profit restrictions (1896: 166–7). (Hadley thus anticipated the x-inefficiency problem in regulation.) Managers of public corporations or publicly regulated business would maximize their own present value rather than that of the firm (1896: 179). Not the least of the problems of commission regulation, according to Hadley (1885: 144–5), was the inherent tendency for such bureaucracies to expand.

5. Urban externalities: funeral and burial markets

INTRODUCTION

Traditional economic theory gives a central role to 'economies of large scale production' or 'natural monopoly,' somehow defined, as a *possible* rationale for government regulation. Such economies were at the root of Chadwick's advocacy of franchise bidding for railways as shown in Chapter 4. While a separate tradition relating to other explanations for market failure always existed, that tradition swirled around philosophical theories of externalities in a Benthamite world or governmental interventions in the Pigouvian tax-bounty framework.[1] In modern times, the Coasian revolution relating to social costs, and its offshoots in the works of such economists as Alchian and Demsetz (1972), Demsetz (1968; 2011), and Williamson (1979; 1985), have raised the *possibility* of market solutions (as opposed to government solutions) to so-called externality problems. (For example, private solutions to providing information may function when asymmetric information problems arise in private markets.) While for the most part contemporary economists have embraced a 'comparative institutional framework' for evaluating so-called market failures, scientific analyses evaluating particular failures often give way to political exigencies, and not to sound, sometimes even to unsound, economic logic or empirical support. Environmental externalities, treatment of endangered species, cable regulation, and legal protection of the medical and legal professions are perhaps good examples of how self-interested politicians react to particular interests. Chadwick, as we argued in Chapter 4, observed these impediments to maximum social welfare before the middle of the nineteenth century. Lacking faith in government's ability to make positive contributions to social welfare, Chadwick proposed that governments take rights to supply goods and services – railways in Chapter 4 – but to let operations out to private enterprise. National, geographically dispersed industries were candidates for this scheme, but Chadwick's franchising device was directed especially to local problems.

Chadwick is of course most famous for his work on (and advocacy of) urban sanitation reform. His *Sanitary Report*, published in 1842,[2] is most certainly one of the two or three most important social and economic policy documents of nineteenth-century England. But totally neglected, at least among economists, is the separately published second part of the *Report* on sanitation dealing with the 'business of death.' In this astonishing essay on *Interments in Towns*, published in 1843 as a supplement to the formal 1842 report and containing thirteen data appendices, Chadwick presents what is surely the first comprehensive study of the funeral-burial industry and one of the very first thorough studies of *any* industry in the history of economic and social studies.[3] In this report Chadwick sought to establish a base for government intervention in the business of death and the nationalization of cemeteries.[4] His belief that untoward market incentives and conditions could be harnessed for the public welfare through franchise bidding led him to advocate the socialization of property rights in a market not thought to be characterized by scale economies.[5] In doing so, he developed: (a) a particular rationale for government intervention in markets; and (b) a unique theoretical scheme for supplying public goods that mimed 'competitive efficiency.'

Here we analyze Chadwick's study and regulatory rationales based on the evidence he presents. We show that the whole conception of regulatory rationales based on *assumed market failures* antedated modern analysis by more than 125 years! Externalities and information costs support alternative forms of government intervention, including franchise bidding and outright socialization, as compared to open competition. These arguments actually provide the foundation for many forms of actual and proposed contemporary regulations in the funeral industry and in many other industries at the federal and lower levels in the United States.[6]

Contemporary societies must often choose between a range of possible solutions, none of which maximize welfare. Chadwick's views on market failure in an industry which at first appears to be of relatively simple form are even more relevant in these modern contexts. We will show that Chadwick clearly understood how franchising rights to serve could and likely would take on the form of monopoly redistribution. While nominally espousing a quasi-competitive institutional solution to the provision of goods, Chadwick portrayed the actual operation of goods supply as often fraught with political opportunism and transactions costs, especially information costs. His idea that a franchising scheme could be made efficient (welfare-maximizing) in England through superior 'machinery for public control and instruction' (Lewis 1952: 246) was one alternative in nineteenth-century England, as it is today in developed nations. A critical contemporary lesson drawn from a study of Chadwick's treatment of the funeral industry is that rationales for regulation should be studied carefully by economists quite apart from questions of political exigency.

EXTERNALITIES IN THE BURIAL MARKET

Chadwick, in carrying 'practical' Benthamite utilitarianism to new limits, was predisposed to find relevant externalities under every bush and tree. But as one of the most able descriptive statisticians of his time, Chadwick never proceeded without facts.[7] His report on sanitation was crammed full of empirical support on the conditions of the laboring classes vis-à-vis such matters as drainage, sewerage, and disease, for example. Chadwick brought that same eye for detail into his inquiry concerning death and burial.

Issues relating to death and burial were in Chadwick's view, and in reality, inextricably bound up with questions of poverty, sanitation, and ignorance – in short, with all of the evils he thought were created by increases in population and urbanization at the apogee of the Industrial Revolution.[8] These externalities were created by the prevailing death-related services, and Chadwick marshaled testimony from physicians, undertakers, insurance agents, scholars, town registrars, and his own data to prove it. Traditions and general social and economic conditions were in part to blame, but (in Chadwick's view at least) several types of market failure explained the desperate conditions of the poor vis-à-vis the certainty and occurrence of death.

In barest outline, his argument was that two interrelated factors – the location of urban burial grounds and, more importantly, the existence of competitive conditions in the market for funerals – created health externalities for families and for the population at large. As the size and density of urban areas grew, the extent of the first externality gained importance. Crowding and monopoly conditions along with unsanitary burial traditions exacerbated the second by delaying interments. Competitive markets, in his view, failed to address the burial *externality* question while monopoly in funeral markets (created by search and information costs as *market failure*) was the primary explanation for injuries to the health and well-being of survivors. Both urban gravesites and home funerals created health and sanitation externalities, but the explanation for each was different.

Externalities Produced in the Graveyard

Chadwick concluded, with the aid of some of the most macabre testimony and evidence in the literature, that the health of towns was severely threatened by urban gravesites, including parish graveyards, gravesites of Protestant 'dissenters,' and private grounds. Chadwick argued that 'emanations' and 'miasma' from such sites close to the dwellings of the living is the prime explanation for the externality:

> That inasmuch as there appear to be no cases in which the emanations from human remains in an advanced stage of decomposition are not of a deleterious nature, so there is no case in which the liability to danger should be incurred either by interment (or by entombment in vaults, which is the most dangerous) amidst the dwellings of the living . . . That all interments in towns, where bodies decompose, contribute to the mass of atmospheric impurity which is injurious to the public health. (1843: 31)

As the population of London, and other cities, grew in the early nineteenth century, as expected the number of dead increased apace. Space to bury these bodies did not grow however, and intramural cemeteries were quickly filled well beyond capacity. While private cemeteries were developing on the outskirts of the metropolis, the prices were beyond the means of many people in the poorer classes. Compared to the German experience, where the number of interments averaged 110 bodies per acre each year, London's 218 acres of burial grounds were required to absorb 20 000 adults and nearly 30 000 youths and children each year.[9] The parish graveyards were so full that no sooner was a body interred than it was disturbed to admit another – entering ten bodies where one had been buried before (Lewis 1952: 67). Bunhill Fields cemetery contained over 100 000 bodies in four acres and continued to inter thousands annually. Here and in other intramural cemeteries the poor were buried in pits and graves – often left open until the coffins rose to the surface. With no formal burial registry, empty space was found by prodding the ground with iron staves. When the graveyards became overfilled, bodies were collapsed into pieces so that they would fit the space. These bodies, which rose to the surface through only a thin layer of dirt, were often simply wheeled off to the bone house.

Not only were the sites of such graveyards obscene, but the odors which filled the air around them were pandemic and scurrilous. So viscous and execrable were the escaping gases that if conditions were right, the emanations could be detected up to five miles away (Chadwick 1843: 131). To Chadwick, these emanations were the breath of death. Much like 'dissecting room fever,' which had been known to strike down medical students and doctors, Chadwick believed that the putrid effluvium of decomposing human remains created health problems among the living.[10] Chadwick's evidence suggests that the private graveyards, usually owned by undertakers, were the most crowded. Some of these private yards interred more than 2300 bodies per acre per year.[11] Appealing to scientific evidence and practices in other countries where interment was controlled to a much greater extent, Chadwick estimates that 444 acres plus land to separate the gravesites from surrounding homes was needed for the city of London.[12]

Moral and 'Taste' Externalities

The sanitary externality was certainly critical to the population. However, Chadwick identified what might be termed a 'moral' or 'taste' externality associated with London burials.[13] He notes that 'Neglected and misman-aged burial grounds superadd to the indefinite terrors of dissolution, the revolting image of festering heaps, disturbed and scattered bones, the prospect of a charnel house and its associations of desecration and insult' (1843: 142).[14] Equally appalling were the disturbances occurring during processions within the city. Urban traffic made burial processions through the busy town less impressive. Other testimony implied that the sanitary problems of intramural interment were dubious and that 'Christian impres-siveness' was of far greater importance. Chadwick argued that unlike the national cemeteries in Russia, Germany, and France, the London graves-ites were crowded together in the 'busy, noisy, unclean, and almost grass-less churchyards' (1843: 144). Chadwick was also critical of the disparity between the burials of the poorer and richer classes in England. Creation of a national cemetery would ensure that all persons receive a respectable burial. The most humble artisans would be buried along with those in the highest social classes.

'MARKET FAILURE' IN THE ENGLISH FUNERAL BUSINESS

If burial sites were suboptimal and created health externalities, funeral practices *circa* the early 1840s in England were disastrous. Home funer-als, and the protracted delays in the funerals of the lower and (especially) the middle classes of society, were the primary source of health and other problems to individuals in urban areas. Chadwick admirably summarized the reasons for delayed interment:

> The causes which influence this practice [long delayed home funerals] amongst the greatest number of the population appear to be, first, the expense of funerals – next, the delay in making arrangements for the funeral, – the natural reluctance to part with the remains of the deceased, and occasionally a feeling of apprehension, sometimes expressed on the part of survivors, against premature interment. (1843: 46)

The chief reason for funeral delays (estimated at between 5 and 12 days) was economic, with exorbitant expenses associated due to the actual conduct of the funeral.[15]

Abysmal living conditions of the working poor contributed to the hazardous situation as well. One room dwellings, where individuals were born, lived, and died, were common in London and manufacturing districts. A study by Mr Weld, Secretary of the Statistical Society, as to the condition of the working classes residing in the ward of St George's (Hanover Square) was revealing. The culture for disease-spreading externalities, especially during times of epidemics, was ripe. Weld's elaborate data was likely representative of urban areas generally in England at the time (see, for example, the table in Chadwick 1843: 31). Weld calculated that 1465 families resided in 2175 rooms with 2510 beds total. He found that (even in a season that was not 'unhealthy,' such as summer) 839 individuals out of 5945 were ill and that only one family in 11 had a third room in which to place a corpse.

Chadwick marshaled mountains of evidence to demonstrate a connection between survivors' health and home funeral services. For the externality to exist: (a) the family member (or other person) would have to be placed in direct or indirect contact with the corpse; and (b) the transmission of disease must be possible from the deceased person to the living. Proximity to the corpse was not only possible but likely in laboring-class homes, given Weld's evidence. But evidence on disease transmission came from one Mr Leonard, surgeon and medical officer of the parish of St Martin-in-the-Fields, who studied death-to-life transmission of 'fever,' typhus, and other diseases from 1840 to 1843 (Chadwick 1843: 32–4). One excerpt from the doctor's testimony relating to scarlet fever transmission is typical. Chadwick (1843: 33) asked the doctor about the consequences of body retention of a workhouse inmate:

> Upon the 9th of March, 1840, M was taken to the Fever Hospital. He died there, and without my knowledge the body was brought back to his own room. The usual practice, in such cases, is to receive them into a lock-up-room, set apart for that purpose in the workhouse. I find that upon the 12th his stepson was taken ill. He was removed immediately to the Fever Hospital. Upon the 18th the barber who shaved the corpse was taken ill, and died in the Fever Hospital, and upon the 27th another stepson was taken ill, and removed also.

Chadwick used prodigious amounts of data from dozens of physicians, medical officers, and undertakers to secure the point. These grievous 'externalities' from death were an addition to the usual misery inflicted on families by the death of a loved one.[16]

Are Information Costs the Source of the Externality?

Given the facts surrounding funeral practices and the transmission of disease, especially contagious disease, the primary cause of delayed funerals was to be found, according to Chadwick, in an inefficient and non-competitive funeral market.[17] Chadwick viewed market failure as the primary source of the sanitation externality.[18] The chain of causation is clear: market failure caused the high price of funerals, the high price of funerals caused delay, and delay caused a sanitation externality.

Chadwick characterized survivors – not only of the lowest laboring poor but also of middle class – as completely at the mercy of unscrupulous undertakers. The widows of lawyers, army, or navy officers, and those of the gentry of limited means are often thrown into penury by the expenses of funerals where 'those who have a direct interest' (Chadwick 1843: 51) call the shots regarding the 'proper' ceremony for their particular class. Even bishops and estate executors hold no power against the unscrupulous undertaker![19] Chadwick actually suggests collusion among undertaking establishments 'in maintaining a system of profuse expenditure' (Chadwick 1843: 51) but information and search costs on the part of survivors (and custom, to a degree) are the principal sources of monopoly in the funeral market.[20] Chadwick makes the argument clear throughout his report.

The kernel of Chadwick's analysis, to which he repeatedly returns, is that information and search costs are the primary explanation for market failure in the funeral market. Chadwick's following statements are illustrative:

> The circumstances of the death do not admit of any effective competition or any precedent examination of the charges of the different undertakers, or any comparison and consideration of their supplies; there is no time to change them for others that are less expensive, and more in conformity to the taste and circumstances of the parties . . . The survivors, however, are seldom in a state to perform any office of every-day life; and they are at the mercy of the first comer. (1843: 52)

There are *many* potential 'monopolists' or imperfect competitors in the funeral market at all times. Profiteers, who may be acquaintances of the survivors, head servants, or even physicians, become 'finders' for actual undertakers and take a monopoly profit from their contacts due to the high information costs. Chadwick says:

> The supplies of the funeral goods and services, are, therefore, a multiform monopoly, not apparently on the parts of the chief undertakers, or original and real preparers of the funeral materials and services, but of second or third parties living in the immediate neighbourhood – persons who assume the business of an undertaker, and who obtain the first orders. (1843: 52)

Chadwick supports this view with testimony from officers of Burial Societies (more on these below), ministers, medical personnel, and others

(1843: 111–13). Market failure, according to Chadwick (1843: 111), is created by *high information costs*:

> [T]here appear to be no grounds to expect the extensive spontaneous adoption of improved regulations by the labouring classes without aid *ab extra*. The labour of communicating information to them, to be attended to at the time it is wanted, would be immense. Their sources of information on the occurrence of such events are either poor neighbours, as ignorant as themselves, or persons who are interested in misleading them and profiting by their ignorance, to continue expensive and mischievous practices.

It is important to note that however unscrupulous undertakers and their agents might be, custom and the 'demonstration effect' also play a role in monopoly creation. Chadwick argues that custom, grief, and fear of the loss of social standing prevent the widow or other survivors from complaining *ex post* about severe or extortionate charges. Further, no individual could break through these customs because all objections to them 'are exposed to the calumny that proper respect to the deceased is begrudged' (Chadwick 1843: 52). The private individual is simply helpless against these practices, an argument which exactly parallels that for contemporary regulation of the funeral industry.

Insurance as Moral Hazard

Death is, of course, an obvious certainty for everyone in all classes in all times. Just as contemporaries put away for funerals, the laboring poor and middle class in mid-nineteenth-century London did the same in the provision of a decent burial for themselves, and to prevent a burden on loved ones when that inevitable day arrived. The insurers (often undertakers themselves or 'publicans' who ran 'public houses') were called Burial Societies. In such friendly societies or clubs, dues are paid either as an insurance premium, chiefly, but not exclusively, to provide interment. But Chadwick used data and interviews to pronounce such insurance an outright fraud. Undertakers were often the organizers and sponsors of such schemes – not the poor themselves. The arrangements were evidence only of the intensity of people's feelings on the subject of funerals and interment, 'of their ignorance and their extensive need of information and trustworthy guidance' (Chadwick 1843: 57).

Subscriptions were often excessive from an actuarial perspective (Chadwick offered 'proof') but the evils were more than purely monetary. Publicans – barkeeps – were also sponsors or beneficiaries of burial insurance, sometimes offering a weekly allowance for beer in return for the dues.[21] All age groups, according to Chadwick's calculations, paid more than the actuarial value of the policies. But an even greater evil attended such policies – monetary incentives created deviations from acceptable behavior. We now call this phenomenon *moral hazard*. Chadwick drew an example from burial clubs in Manchester. Infanticide was the result of the problems created by costly information and moral hazard. The actual cost of burying a child was 1*l.* to 30*s.*, but the death benefits in Manchester were 3*l.* to 5*l.* Children, especially female children, were put at risk by multiple registrations in burial clubs. Testimony from a Mr Gardner, clerk of the Manchester Union, was clear regarding deaths by starvation of seven children in a particular family.[22] Poisonings, willful starvation, and maltreatment were common according to sordid evidence from many English locales. Children were insured in as many as 19 clubs and societies, although, according to Chadwick:

> . . . the better constituted societies have perceived the evil of insurances, carried to the extent of entirely removing responsibilities, or creating bounties, to the promotion of the event insured against, and have endeavoured to abate the evil, as far as they could, by the adoption of a condition, that no payment should be made where a party was found to have been a member or to have insured in another club. (1843: 67)

Some of these societies adopted rules which alleviated moral hazard (and adverse selection) as much as insurance companies adopted the common rule against payment for suicide. 'Yet,' says Chadwick, 'frauds are occasionally committed by persons who much know that they have not long to live' (1843: 68), yet another form of moral hazard attributable to insurance.

Insurance up to but not exceeding the amount of insurable interest was the rule in the higher order of life insurance, and Chadwick thought that the principle – stated legislatively during the reign of George III – should be applied to burial insurance as well. Importantly, however, Chadwick thought that a collateral means of preventing infanticide was to *lower the expense* of funerals and, by consequence, 'the temptations to crime constituted by the apparent expedience of the insurance of the payment of large sums to meet that expence [sic]' (1843: 69). Untoward incentives could be addressed by changing rules and regulations affecting markets.

Economics and Empirics of the Funeral Market

In order to model the funeral market Chadwick appealed to data from the city of London. Surveys from the provinces convinced him that, on average, London data was fairly typical. On a three-year average there were 114 deaths per day. But consulting the official London post office directory revealed that in 1843 there were no less than 730 undertakers to conduct the 114 funerals or between 6 and 7 undertakers each.[23] To this were added those 'occasional undertakers' (not listed in the directory) who might perform 1 or 2 funerals per year and other agents who contract out to furnishing undertakers.

Chadwick's point (1843: 53–4) is that, even for those 275 undertakers who specialize in the business:

> [T]he cost of their own maintenance, must, if the business be equally distributed, be charged on little more than two funerals a-week. If the business be not equally distributed, and a minority have (as will have been perceived) a much larger share of the funerals than the rest, the majority will be the more severely driven, as they are in fact, to charge their expenses on a much smaller number of funerals. When the additional number of tradesmen of mixed occupations is brought as waiters for the chances of employment, the number of burials distributed amongst them all is reduced to 10 funerals to every master in 11 weeks, or less than one a-week.

Analytically, the problem allegedly facing undertakers in London is shown in Figure 5.1. As the figure suggests, each undertaker, certainly the 'marginal' undertaker, finds himself on the decreasing portion of the average cost curve at some point such as A. The optimal or 'competitive' supply of funerals would be at point Q in Figure 5.1.

The mass of undertakers were not wealthy because of their inability to enjoy scale economies. 'Agents' – such as servants and even medical men – took in high sums (10–50$l.$) according to the scale expense and profit of the funeral. These were the profiteers.[24] The actual average cost of funerals was calculated by Chadwick from samples of undertakers' bills for London (see Table 5.1). Chadwick thought such charges an underestimate of the actual *total* expenses with actual interment expenses at probably one million pounds per year.[25]

Economic conditions of at least quasi-monopoly (those described in relation to Figure 5.1) were responsible for the massive waste. Testimony from Mr Wild, a successful undertaker, suggested that the actual costs of funerals apart from the side payments to agents could be substantially reduced to the poorer classes without any lapse in decoration or propriety. Vast cost savings could be obtained by fewer bearers (with burial at a governmentally provided cemetery with lowered cost of conveyance) and a reduced number of paid mourners who required 'fittings' and proper attire. Suggesting economics of scale in coffin building, Wild argued that the price of coffins appropriate to the laboring or middle classes might be 'supplied on a large scale' for about 50 percent less than the current average expense. For the classes of tradespeople and mechanics (London estimates) Wild presented Chadwick with the following statistics shown in Table 5.2. Cost reductions of up to and in some cases more than 50 percent

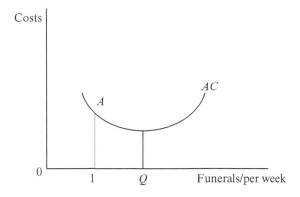

Figure 5.1   Cost conditions – London undertakers

over actual expenses (see Table 5.1) are reported in Table 5.2. The statistics in Table 5.2 for conveyance would be greatly reduced, Wild thought, if mourners for several funerals could be carried in one carriage. Bearers (carriers of the coffin to the place of burial) could be sharply reduced, moreover, if a hearse was used in place of 'walking funerals.' Before such economies could be achieved, however, new institutional arrangements and constraints would have to be placed on the overall 'business of death' – on funeral and graveyard provision. Chadwick argues that his report will present grounds which appear to sustain the position that '. . . all the solemnity of sepulture may be increased, and solemnity given where none is now obtained, concurrently with a great reduction of expenses to all classes' (1843: 77).

THE CHADWICK PLAN

Chadwick found the solution to the funeral and burial problems he posed in a comparative institutional study of practices in America, Germany, and France (Habenstein and Lamers 1955). He focused on city practices in Boston, Berlin, and Paris where there was, in each case, more government involvement in the death business than in England. However, in each of these cities, a different institutional arrangement for funerals and burials prevailed. Boston was distinguished by a governmentally appointed Board of Health which both nominated a Superintendent of Burial Grounds (usually a medical doctor) and also *licensed* undertakers. Licenses were revocable at any time depending on the judgment of the Board of Health. Chadwick adds:

Table 5.1 *Estimates of actual expenses for funerals of different classes in London, 1839*

	Tradespeople								Mechanics							
	Adults				Children				Adults				Children			
	From		To		From		To		From		To		From		To	
	£	s.	£	s.	£	s.	£	s.	£	s.	£	s.	£	s.	£	s.
Coffin	1	5	4	4	0	15	1	10	0	17	1	5	0	10	0	15
Fittings, &c	0	15	2	0	0	10	1	0	0	10	0	15	0	5	0	10
Sundries	–	–	–	–	–	–	–	–	–	–	–	1	–	–	–	–
Conveyance	1	1	4	4	1	1	2	2	0	17	1	1	0	10	1	1
Totals	3	1	10	8	2	6	4	12	2	4	3	1	1	5	2	6

Source: Chadwick (1843: 109).

Table 5.2 Estimates of cost savings from large scale production for funerals of laboring classes

Class	Total number of funerals of each class that have taken place in the metropolis in the year 1839	Number of children under 10 years of age	Present average expenses of each funeral of each class, inclusive of burial dues				Total expenses of all the funerals of each persons of each class, inclusive of children	Annual expense of funerals in England and Wales
			Adults		Children			
			£	s.	£	s.	£	£
Gentry, &c	2253	529	100	0	30	0	188270	1735040
Tradesmen, 1st class	5757	2761	50	0	14	0	250792	2370379
Tradesmen, 2nd class and undescribed	7682	3703	27	10	1	15	103728	–
Artisans, &c	25930	13885	5	0	1	10	81053	766074
Paupers	3655	593	13s.				2761	–
			Total expense for the metropolis . . . ⇒				626604	

Proximate estimate of the expense for the total number of funerals in one year, England and Wales ⇒ 4871493

Source: Chadwick (1843: 70).

113

> The bills of the undertaker are made out on a blank form, furnished by the public superintendent of interment, to whom all bills are submitted, and by whom they are audited and allowed, before they are presented for payment to the relations or friends of the deceased. Previous to interment, the undertaker must obtain from the physician who last attended the deceased, a certificate specifying the profession, age, time of illness, and cause of death of the deceased. This certificate is presented to the superintendent of funerals. An abstract of these certificates, signed by the superintendent of funerals, is printed every week in the public journals of the city. (1843: 116)

Costs for the 'highest class of tradesmen' in Boston were only about $50 (or 10*l*. English). A mahogany coffin was only about 3*l*. 5*s*. (about $15). These arrangements, it would appear, met with Chadwick's approval as far as regulating the trade or at least reducing or eliminating externalities due to infection.

Chadwick's brief survey of the funeral and burial markets in the German states revealed much government involvement. Burial was in fact governmentally provided in a number of cities. The funeral market was also nationalized to a degree, suggests Chadwick, in Frankfurt. With a little more information from the city of Berlin, Chadwick describes the form of contract management which he first formalized. In Berlin, one contractor was chosen to be responsible for 'funeral materials and services for the public at certain fixed scales of prices' (Chadwick 1843: 117). Charges were far lower than the English equivalents (an artisan's funeral that would cost 4*l*. English was no more than 15*s*. in German equivalent). Moreover, Chadwick had information that 'the contractors' profits on the extensive supplies required are deemed too high,' and that the Berlin city government was going to 'find it necessary to protect the poorer classes by a contract at a lower rate' (1843: 117).

The *Service des Pompes Funèbres* in Paris

The primary example of urban franchising for the public good in the matter of funerals and interments was in Paris. Chadwick in fact used this case as his prototype for all models of franchise bidding (later discussed in the context of economies of scale). Parisian interments were made the subject of the 'fisc' of the city, that is, a subject for city revenue. All interments of a wide range of quality classes were paid for under one contract to secure services and supplies to the private individual. The contract was between one individual (representing a number of joint contractors) and the city of Paris. Nine classes of service from funerals of the 'greatest pomp' down to *service ordinaire* were established by the city. One chief contractor representing joint contractors then bid a scale of prices. All comers were to be served at these prices, and the *Service des Pompes Funèbres* (the title of the winning contracting agent and his apparatus) agreed to bury, gratis, 'upwards of 7000 destitute persons, or nearly one-third of all who die in the city' (Chadwick 1843: 117). Table 5.3 shows the quality scales and the prices of nine funeral classes offered in two years, 1839 and 1841, and the quantities sold.

All this was, Chadwick argued, of great benefit to survivors who could be sure of charges and that they were protected by 'market regulated' rates. The nine classes contained widely disparate qualities of service at the time of death.[26] But the interesting feature of the Parisian arrangement was the disposition of the 'private' contractors' annual income. Converting receipts of the *Service des Pompes Funèbres* into English pounds for the year 1841, Chadwick figured a gross income of 80000*l.* on the number of burials in Paris. The contractor, out of this sum, pays the salaries of *public officials appointed chiefly by the municipality*. These are the 'fixed salaries of the staff of officers, which consists of a chief inspector of funeral cere-monies, of 27 other directors besides, 78 bearers, one inspector of cemeter-ies and four keepers' (Chadwick 1843: 118). These public officials are part of the regulatory apparatus, with the possible exception of the bearers, and it is important to note that these arrangements of contract bidding were not noted in Chadwick's 1859 (see 1859c) account of the Parisian case. In 1841 this amounted to 5862*l.*

Rent-seeking by municipal officials riddled this scheme. In 1841 the contractor kept 30 hearses and 76 carriages along with suites of minor attendants burying, as noted above, 7000 paupers per year as specified in the contract.[27] Chadwick notes that '. . . the last contractor paid annually to the municipality 17,000*l.*, which sum was chiefly devoted to ecclesi-astical objects. The large profits which he realized led to considerable competition, and a new contract was recently sealed for nine years, secur-ing for public purposes an annual income of 28,000*l.*' (1843: 119). The rent-seeking did not stop here. The municipal government of Paris took in about 20000*l.* per year from the sale of tombs and the tax on interments (20 francs for each adult and 10 francs for children under seven years of age). One-fourth of this revenue (about 4000*l.*) was devoted to hospitals. One is left to wonder where the non-earmarked revenue went.[28] The important point to be made with respect to the Parisian system was that it was *not* a 'competitive result' – as described at least by Chadwick's prin-ciple of competition for the field. In the Parisian variant the municipality simply collected rents, including a lump-sum transfer, from an industry. These transfers from consumers and funeral suppliers are more akin to monarchical rent-seeking ('Colbertism') than to Chadwick's idealized 'competitive' solution.

Table 5.3 *Price, quality, and quantity of funeral services in Paris, 1839 and 1841*

Class	1st	2nd	3rd	4th	5th	6th	7th	8th	9th	Total of the nine classes	Service ordinaire	General total
Religious funeral service	24	19	11	8	5 10s.	2	1	0 16s.	11s.			
Anniversary religious service	26	20	12	9	6	3	–	–	–			
Undertaker's material and service	95	83	49	23	14 10s.	5	3	1 11s.	4			
Total expenses	145	122	72	40	26	10	4	2 7s.	15s.			
Number 1839	23	52	138	256	828	1457	2523	141	530	5948	14087	20035
Number 1841	30	47	188	201	816	1655	2377	78	715	6107	14185	20292

Source: Chadwick (1843: 118).

Extrapolation of the essentials of this system to the population of urban centers in England was a clear path in Chadwick's argument. Comparing the total population of Paris and the average annual number of deaths there (900 000/28 000 or 30 000), Chadwick calculated that 1 in 30 Parisians died annually, a number far higher than in all but the least sanitary working towns in England (for example, Manchester or in the Whitechapel section of London). The London average was 1 death per 42 inhabitants per year, a lower mortality rate by one-fourth than in Paris. Chadwick linked (in a lengthy discussion) the higher death rates to lower sanitary conditions of the laboring population in Paris than even in the large urban centers of England.

Open competition or 'competition within the field' for London funerals was far more expensive, according to Chadwick, than in Paris even given the appalling sanitary conditions there. (Chadwick liked practically nothing about Paris other than the franchising scheme.)[29] London funerals (based on Chadwick's estimated 730 undertakers per 114 daily funerals) cost 626 000*l*. in 1843 and would have cost only 166 000*l*. if the European system, specifically that of Paris, had been used (1843: 53; 1859c: 389–90). An enormous saving (about 460 000*l*. per year) could be secured through the government's acquisition of property rights with a 'leasing arrangement' to contractor(s). Lower, contractually regulated prices would also eliminate the sanitation externality that higher prices caused in the matter of home funerals of the laboring classes. The cost savings and efficiency from eliminating monopoly, the welfare increase on the part of survivors, and the elimination of a negative sanitation externality combined to justify property rights alterations in the funeral market. Comparative statistics and comparative institutions, in particular between Paris and London, led Chadwick to advocate similar regulatory arrangements at local levels of English government.[30] The English, however, were to prove far more recalcitrant in their acceptance of Continental solutions.

Chadwick Goes to Parliament: The Short-Lived Interments Act of 1850

If Chadwick's report of 1843 did not exactly fall 'stillborn from the press,' it might be fairly described as having met effective opposition. As Chadwick anticipated, and as reformers of any era anticipate, plans for socialization and centralization of any industry will elicit the investment of opposition. Chadwick's report drew the hatred of the 'Dissenters,' the cemetery companies, the undertakers (at least those not represented in Chadwick's study), and most especially churchmen, who stood to lose a significant portion of yearly revenues if churchyards were closed (see Lewis 1952: 82). Chadwick's plan was labeled a 'bill of plunder, sacrileges, injustice and wrong' (Finer

1952: 388) and Chadwick was considered 'nothing better than [a] socialist' by the Secretary to the Treasury. While parliamentary opponents and representatives of opposing special interests railed that board-managed cemeteries, monopolized burials, and socialized and regulated funeral prices would not work, Chadwick pushed on undeterred throughout the 1840s.

A cholera epidemic struck London and other metropolitan areas in 1849 and it was the ill wind that Chadwick needed to revive his plan in Parliament. Chadwick's persistence, aided by crisis and fear, led to the passage of the Metropolitan Interments Act on 5 August, 1850. Chadwick's plan for the nationalization of the entire funeral industry in England, accompanied by urban-level socialization of property rights and franchise bidding, first prohibited burial inside the Metropolitan areas. (London was to be the first city socialized.) The Board of Health (directed by Chadwick himself) would direct the purchase and management of public cemeteries to replace intramural grounds. These public cemeteries would be laid out at some distance from the Metropolitan boundary.[31] Residential development in the area surrounding the cemetery would be restricted.[32] All burials would be administered by one system placed under a Government Commission of five members appointed by the Home Secretary. The plan made burial anywhere but in the public cemeteries unlawful in order to ensure the success of the national cemeteries and to completely eliminate the sanitary and moral externalities. The burial restraint was restricted to the Burial District, or the Metropolis, and burials outside of the Burial District *could* be conducted by private arrangements. However, Chadwick wanted nothing less than complete monopoly within the Metropolis (Finer 1952: 382–3 and 413).

Significant opposition had to be mitigated. In order not to create 'undue burdens' on the parishioners, each parish would be granted a plot of land equal to its burial space within the city. In addition, clergymen would be appointed to perform the full service according to the liturgy, and compensation would be paid to clergy and private cemetery companies who lost burial fees in consequence of closing their graveyards. The more able undertakers would ostensibly participate in bidding for a portion of the government franchise – the others simply were to go out of business without compensation. The most peculiar addition to the plan was included to mollify parliamentary and Treasury opposition: finances required to purchase the grounds would be secured by *private loan* and paid out of the public undertakers' fees. No Treasury funds would be needed, except to make up for any unexpected shortfalls in annual revenues. This financing scheme proved useful in securing the passage of the Act, but its inclusion ultimately crippled it.

The first step in implementing the Interments Act was the purchase of eight cemeteries, including the Brompton and Nunhead cemeteries which were served compulsory purchase notices first – only one of which was suitable for interments. The Board desired to purchase all eight at one time and estimated the expense at 251 000*l*. The Treasury argued that the cemeteries could be purchased for no less than 750 000*l*. and would not grant the Board permission to enter negotiations. After a long and heated battle, Chadwick managed to convince the Treasury to let the Board proceed as planned and purchase the cemeteries.

Chadwick thus acquired the permission needed to build his national cemetery and began to seek funding for the purchase of sites for cemeteries. Chadwick's certainty with regard to financing was met with instant astonishment when the Guardian Insurance Company refused to finance the purchase of the first cemeteries. The company cited the Board's limited life of only five years, as well as the failure of the Act to specify how liabilities would be transferred after termination, as an insufficient period of time to secure the loan.

Chadwick failed again in his attempt to secure private funding after the Treasury refused to fund the purchase. The Treasury was reluctant to finance the purchase due to political unrest within the agency and the fact that the monopoly was restricted to the Metropolis and would face competition from cemeteries *outside* the Burial District. One such cemetery in particular, the Necropolis, was viewed as a significant threat to the financial viability of Chadwick's plan. Under the direction of Sir Richard Bethell, the Necropolis Company proposed evading the monopoly cemeteries by opening a cemetery on the fringe of the Burial District where it would be free from Chadwick's interventionist schemes. The Treasury thought that delays in the purchase of cemeteries and in the beginning of the Board's work would only allow more of these unregulated cemeteries to be opened (Finer 1852: 413).[33] Parliamentary rent-seeking, an institutionalized distrust of 'socialist solutions,' and the powerful lobby of private interests (disenfranchised undertakers and cemetery entrepreneurs), combined to forever end the ill-fated plan. In June 1852 a Bill to repeal the Interments Act of 1850 passed Parliament. Cemeteries, the worst of which could still be regulated under a Metropolitan Burials Bill, went back to parochial control and undertakers were again free to compete for the supply of urban funerals.

COMPARATIVE INSTITUTIONS

Chadwick's case study for franchise bidding in the funeral market gives modern economists plenty to think about, and these considerations hark back to the kind of comparisons that must be made in the case of railways. There is no questioning Chadwick's originality in the economic study of agency, incentives, and market functioning, although the general approach was clearly Benthamite in origin. His handling of moral hazard (in addition to the franchise bidding apparatus) is an important case in point. But Chadwick's early case study of the market for death must be evaluated on the evidence he presents and on the basis of economic theory. Three interrelated issues within his context have clear overtones for contemporary studies of like kinds. Did monopoly or relevant externalities exist in the nineteenth-century funeral-burial market? If monopoly or 'monopoly elements' existed in these markets, would regulation of the kind suggested by Chadwick be the most efficient response in terms of addressing the problem? What criteria may be used or might have been used to determine the appropriate efficiency or welfare response in Chadwick's time (or, for that matter, in our own)?

Monopoly and its Source

Chadwick's case for monopoly in the mid-nineteenth-century funeral market might be easily dismissed but for the fervor and originality of his study. Monopoly on the *supply side* of the market over the period, suggested by a very selective sample of undertakers in Chadwick's study, was most unlikely. If significant long-term economies of large scale existed, mergers would be expected. Rather, Chadwick describes a market with huge (and growing) numbers of suppliers – over 700 in 1841. (We have seen other estimates in the range of 2000 to 3000.) It is important to note, moreover, that the cost curve he described (shown in Figure 5.1) was a *short-run cost curve* exhibiting no decreasing (or increasing cost) 'natural monopoly' conditions. The motive for competitive activity was strong for funeral suppliers (those who sold funeral services exclusively in particular) who could lower costs by increasing production and sales. As Chadwick describes the market, 'finders,' such as friends of the family, certain 'medical men,' servants, or agents of the funeral director, were necessary to increase sales. The typical London funeral director had clear incentives to employ finders, engage in personal sales activities, or use some form of advertising. Did existing city statutes forbid advertising of funeral services? Was there a 'secret cartel' of suppliers not mentioned by Chadwick? Surely, his beagle-like investigative style would have produced such information if it existed. But a successful cartel of over 700 independent members would not have lasted long anyway (Stigler 1964) without prohibitive collusive and enforcement costs.

However, an interesting feature of the market is described by Chadwick, one that is shared in some funeral markets today. Funeral services in more than half the cases reported by Chadwick for London were only *one* product supplied in a multi-product firm which most often sold 'complementary' services. In small and/or remote rural areas of the United States today it is not uncommon for funeral firms to supply only a few funerals per year. County coroners or other medical personnel are often owners of these small firms. High transactions costs to survivors in terms of waiting time or distance from urban markets help explain these firms.[34] It is not at all apparent that such multi-product firms are inefficient when the *full* price to survivors is considered. Though Chadwick does not provide details concerning the particular markets of the part-timers in the London funeral market, their existence even in such large numbers is not so surprising. Thus it appears unbelievable that the process of market entry and exit which would occur under conditions described by the cost curve in Figure 5.1 would not tend to regulate quantities, qualities, and rates in the London market in an efficient manner.[35] The source of monopoly, if it existed, must be found elsewhere.

If we take Chadwick's evidence at face value, we are tempted to say that the data (compare Tables 5.1 and 5.2) reveal that price *was* above cost in the market. If monopoly exactions were being taken by the finders or middlemen, other conditions simulating monopoly might have existed in the marketplace. Chadwick's position is clear on the matter: monopoly conditions exist or were at least simulated by dint of high transactions and search costs. If he is to be believed, conditions were so lax in London concerning funeral arrangements and charges that the poor were at the absolute mercy of the rent-seeking middlemen when faced with a death in the family. A downstream monopoly agent (the middleman) created the monopoly market. Although ancient laws concerning the issuance of death certificates were in place since the plague period of the sixteenth century, no one was willing to provide information to survivors at the time of death.[36] They were forced to get information from friends and neighbors as poorly informed as themselves, says Chadwick. Although a proposed ordinance set a maximum period for warm weather interments, moreover, the law (which was considered but did not pass in 1842) had no enforcement provisions.[37]

In this regard, Chadwick interviewed medical and religious 'authorities' for his 1843 report who argued that the poor did not get adequate information and that they could receive it from a government agency. Chadwick notes that:

> The appointment of a responsible agency, which would be respected, to convey the information of what may be deemed requisite for the protection of the living

and exercise influence to initiate a change of practice, appears to all the practical witnesses examined to be a preferable course, as being the most suitable to the temper of the people, and as being the least expensive, as well as the most efficient. (1843: 111)

As part of the plan, then, the government was to provide information concerning the availability and pricing of funeral services to the poor. But why there was insufficient information to the poor at a time when information was of such high value to both individuals *and firms supplying funerals* is not clearly answered. The witnesses, who were 'medical men,' curates, and some undertakers clearly advocated an 'officer of the public health' or some public health apparatus appointed from the 'first class of physicians' to administer publicly provided information. All stood to gain from such a system, however. Parish burials produced a regular income of burial 'dues' and other gratuities to prelates, the demand for physicians' services would increase, and funeral directors would (ostensibly) get the public to subsidize advertising of their services. Moreover, it is unclear why reputations of funeral arrangers or of service providers did not develop among the poor. The high information cost argument is, at the very least, questionable.[38] Even if high information costs did pertain to the market, the question of the nature of the externality created by 'monopoly prices' remains. Certainly a high information cost of exchange, in and of itself, is no argument for government intervention. Information costs attend *all* exchanges for goods and services. Individuals acquire information up to the point where the marginal cost equals the marginal benefit of such information. Whether government is the least cost provider is another matter. Is, for example, a regulated system of posting all known defects on used cars as cost efficient as private and independent monitoring devices and for-profit agencies?[39] Ethical arguments also often masked open rent-seeking in markets where information provision through advertising was forbidden (funeral markets are and have always been a ripe candidate for such arbitrary regulations that are legitimized legally). It is well known in medical, legal, and other markets that advertising restrictions have cartelizing and rent-seeking purposes (Benham 1972; Haas-Wilson 1986).

The question of the dual-source 'sanitation externality' remains. Save for the case of epidemics and of provable connections between holding bodies over in household dwellings and disease transmission, most damage (perhaps of both the biological and psychological kinds) was internalized by the families of the deceased.[40] In the case of graveyards, moreover, it is difficult to see how a relevant externality existed. Would not the property values surrounding a cemetery adjust in compensating fashion in the presence of real and significant externalities? Technological developments such as the widespread use of embalming were soon to eliminate this kind of externality even if it did exit.

Chadwick (selectively?) ignored good evidence that the private provision of cemeteries *could* avoid all of the ills and externalities he described. While he took great pains to describe the regulation of funerals in Boston, he failed to mention the enormous success of private entrepreneurs there and elsewhere in providing sanitary and decorous burial places. Boston was experiencing the same problems with rapidly growing populations and miasmic graveyards as London. A committee was appointed to study the issue but no public action was taken. Dr Bigelow, the Chair of the Boston Committee, was so disgusted with the city's inaction that he assembled a group of investors and established a rural cemetery. This cemetery, Mount Auburn, founded in 1831, was the very model for well-managed private rural cemeteries in the United States and in Europe. Within 20 years, the concept of the rural cemetery had spread across the United States (French 1975: 85).

Chadwick's unwavering position on the necessity of nationalized cemeteries to correct the externalities in burial markets was founded more on impatience than market failure, if the American experience is a useful comparison. There is little reason to believe that market-driven private graveyards would not have eliminated much of the sanitary and moral externalities from intramural interment in London.[41] There is even evidence (which Chadwick ignores) that the problem was being attacked in England. In 1843 John C. Loudon, arguably the most important landscape artist in Britain, published a book entitled *On the Laying Out, Planting, and Managing of Cemeteries*. Even earlier, in 1662 John Evelyn advocated an end to city burials and the development of rural garden cemeteries. Chadwick's 1843 report (and his tone of urgency) ignored the fact that rural cemeteries in London, such as Abney Park, were already providing a market solution to the interment 'externality.' Testimony in the report even suggested that sanitary problems were 'dubious,' and that many poor had already begun to seek interment at rural cemeteries. Chadwick, it appears, may have been overzealous in his assault on the burial industry. His approach further suggests that he wanted to extend his regulatory authority beyond market failure in a misguided attempt to mimic a long-run competitive solution through strict and detailed regulations. It is distinctly unclear, when all of Chadwick's evidence is appraised, that a case has been made for governmental intervention on the basis of information costs and/or externalities.

The matter of using franchise bidding to solve problems of monopoly or of natural monopoly is even today open to much debate. If the funeral supply case actually demanded government intervention, use of the Parisian system in urban markets was only one of a very wide range of possible alternatives such as traditional cost-plus regulation, licensing, or alterations in liability placement. Chadwick's competition for the field envisioned perhaps the most radical form of intervention in the private market for it required a socialization of property rights. While nominally holding to the principle that government could not effectively run anything, Chadwick nevertheless envisioned an enlightened 'board' of investigators and regulators that would oversee the urban funeral market. He tried to push it forward in the Interments Act of 1850. If it was to be anything like his description of the Parisian *Service des Pompes Funèbres*, publicly appointed officials would be paid by the winning contractor from the contractor's revenues. In his 1859 essay on the subject of franchising Chadwick notes that he presupposes:

> [Q]ualifications of high administrative intelligence and integrity and public zeal, to plot out the most advantageous fields for competition, to conduct with judicial impartiality the competitions for their occupation, and to enforce the rigid performance of the contracts in behalf of the public. I presuppose also the ability to analyze closely the cost of service, so as to guard against concealed emoluments, which are sources of corruption, and firmness to withstand the imputations of vulgar competitors. (1859c: 408)

Practical implementation of such a plan for *either* natural monopoly markets or markets with 'monopoly elements' would require nothing less than a regulatory commission composed of saintly lawgivers.[42] (Chadwick himself would have run the franchising-nationalization process through the Board of Health if his plan had succeeded.) While there are suggestions that the size of bureaucracy and the amount of redistribution would be considerably less in the case of England, any bureaucracy would be open to *ex parte* proceedings and opportunistic behavior.

The problem of opportunistic behavior on the part of self-interested regulators is only one part of a contemporary and familiar critique of franchise bidding as a means of supplying goods and services. Other problems attend the implementation of the proposal and, in modern contexts; such problems have been critically analyzed. Incentives to reduce costs through instituting optimal capital-labor implantations over the contract period, cost changes, demand changes, uncertainty, 'incumbent advantages' at re-contract time, and other difficulties have attended virtually all attempts to practically implement the plan (Williamson 1976). Contract design so as to minimize and monitor opportunistic behavior is a fundamental problem which gives way to the conclusion that, for all practical purposes, franchise bidding *à la* Chadwick is but another form of traditional cost-plus regulation, but with *the socialization of property rights.* Opportunistic behavior on the part of regulators is another matter.[43]

Chadwick in his 1843 study of funeral markets in Paris suggests another distinct rationale for local-level regulation (in this case of funeral services). The city of Paris used the mechanism of the *Service des Pompes Funèbres* as a 'cash cow.' That is, it extracted revenues from funeral contractors and ultimately from funeral service consumers in order to redistribute income to city coffers. The nature of some of these redistributions (a portion was ceded to 'hospitals') is irrelevant. These kinds of franchise fees are identical to those charged in locally franchised markets in the United States today, especially for local cable TV (Hazlett 1991). Monopoly elements exist in these markets largely because municipalities have resisted the introduction of overlapping competition (Beil et al. 1993).

CONCLUSION

Chadwick's plan to collectivize property rights in both national and local markets, despite some rather obvious problems, must be evaluated through the prism of alternative plans to regulate enterprise, and to models of open competition as well. The real world is not, unfortunately, as neat and tidy as economic models. The results of Chadwick's proposal to socialize property rights and to let out temporary rights to create goods or services is a radical solution but it must, in any objective analysis, be set beside and evaluated against all alternative solutions. The world does not permit strict optimality as much as the economist (and society) might like it to. Alternative institutional structures must be evaluated on the basis of the net benefit they create, recognizing that perfection is not possible. In this light Chadwick's utilitarian-based alternative deserves serious consideration along with those produced by standard regulatory solutions and outright laissez-faire. These will be considered in more detail in our final chapter. However, Chadwick's incredibly perspicacious views on labor, sociology, crime, and sanitation will precede a comparative analysis of social and public goods provision, market failure, and utilitarian policymaking.

NOTES

1. Marshall's contemporary Henry Sidgwick based a 'philosophical' concept of externalities on Benthamite utilitarianism, a perspective that might have influenced Pigou's famous foray into welfare economics.
2. This famous study carries the official title *Report to Her Majesty's Principal Secretary*

of State for the Home Department, from the Poor Law Commissioners, on an Inquiry into the Sanitary Condition of the Labouring Population of Great Britain (1842a).

3. The full title of the 1843 supplement was *A Supplementary Report on the Results of a Special Inquiry into the Practice of Interment in Towns made at the Request of Her Majesty's Principal Secretary of State for the Home Department.*

4. This was not the only urban industry for which the franchise bidding solution was ultimately proposed. In 1859 Chadwick was advocating take-over of bars, beer, and milk sales using similar logic but without the mass of evidence he adduced in the case of the funeral market.

5. Penultimate property rights of an individual or survivors in land is a difficult legal issue, one which we do not consider in detail here. Chadwick appended a brief exposition of the English law with respect to perpetuities in public burial grounds (1843: 269–71). Rights, it seems, are a balancing act between those of the dead and those of the living. The Consistory Court of London held that 'The time must come when *'ipsae periere ruinae*,' when the posthumous remains must mingle with, and compose a part of, that soil in which they have been deposited.' While the time may be disputed (100 years? 200 years?), the legal doctrine was that 'the common cemetery is not *res unius aetatis*, the property of one generation now departed, but is, likewise, the common property of the living, and of generations yet unborn, and is subject only to temporary appropriations' (Chadwick 1843: 270).

6. For decades consumer groups (and other interests) have sought the imposition of federal regulations on the funeral industry (Consumer Reports 1980; Young 1994). (All states regulate funeral directors but with varying degrees of stringency.) Congress, over many years, has held hearings into funeral and funeral-related industries (see, for example, Committee on the Judiciary 1964). The Federal Trade Commission has responded with hearings, studies of their own, and commissioned reports (FTC 1978; Market Facts 1988). FTC regulations may be reviewed at: http://www.ftc.gov/bcp/edu/pubs/consumer/products/pro19.shtm.

7. Apocryphally perhaps, John Stuart Mill once said that Chadwick had personally counted the number of rats in all of the London prisons. Mill, according to his own testimony, always deferred to Chadwick on matters of fact.

8. Some of the material presented here relating to Chadwick and the London funeral industry replicates that reported in Ekelund and Ford (1997).

9. Chadwick's statistics suggest that in London the practice was to bury an average of 219 bodies per acre, and sometimes as many as 891 (1843: 133).

10. Chadwick provided extensive testimony alleging the 'fact' of fatalities from 'inhalations' from surgeons and physicians (see 1843: 8, 11, and 23 *et passim*).

11. Evidence from other sources suggests that Chadwick's assault on private graveyards was unfounded and that these cemeteries were far better than the parochial grounds.

12. As was common in Chadwick's assessment of market conditions, he considered a number of factors which affected the number of bodies per acre and the distance from the city the cemetery needed to be. These factors included the size of the city, the number to be buried, the type of soil, the type of vegetation, the direction of the wind, the number of bodies per grave, the wood of which the coffin is made, and many other details.

13. His 'meddlesome preferences' with regard to 'lewdness' and 'drunkenness' are also noted in his later paper (1859c). These kinds of 'externalities' at least from the perspective of the economist, are irrelevant, although some economists believe that they should be put on a par with all other arguments for market failure (Dnes 1994, for example).

14. Ghoulish testimony (from Mr Blackburn) highlighted these concerns:

I have no facts to communicate relating to the physical effects produced by the present crowded state of the old grave-yards, but I am sure the moral sensibilities of many delicate minds must sicken to witness the heaped soil, saturated and blackened with human remains and fragments of the dead, exposed to the rude insults of ignorant and brutal spectators. (Chadwick 1843: 134)

15. Chadwick supported his view that expense was the primary cause of delayed inter-
     ments with a good deal of testimony from undertakers, officials of 'burial societies,' and
     coroners. One Mr Wild, a prominent undertaker, noted that funerals took:

>   from five to twelve days [to be completed]. This arises from the difficulty of procuring
>   the means of making arrangements with the undertaker, and the difficulty of getting
>   mourners to attend the funeral. They have a great number to attend, neighbours,
>   fellow-workmen, as well as relations. The mourners with them vary from five to eight
>   couple; it is always an agreement for five couple at the least. (Chadwick 1843: 47)

     All testified that the source of the problem was the inability to get the money together
     for a funeral. Dreadful cases of abandoned corpses were also cited. Note that the
     problem did not occur in the upper and upper-middle classes. These corpses were early
     placed in either lead or in double coffins, and the delay was of less consequence.
16. Chadwick notes that long retention of the body had very evil social effects, using a
     minister's testimony as support. Primarily these effects consisted of a 'hardening' of the
     lower classes (which must always be kept in line) toward the fear of death. Chadwick
     approvingly cites the testimony of a clergyman that:

>   when respect for the dead, that, for the human form in its most awful stage, is gone,
>   the whole mass of social sympathies must be weakened – perhaps blighted and
>   destroyed. At any rate, it removes that wholesome fear of death which is the last hold
>   upon a hardened conscience . . . the heart which vice has deadened to every appeal of
>   religion is at last rendered callous to the natural instinct of fear. (Chadwick 1843: 46)

     The demoralization of society is thus equated with a lessened hold of religion on the
     lower classes through reduction of the 'natural' instinct of fear. These sentiments are
     of course very close to those registered by Marxian doctrine and by religious zealots
     throughout the ages. Promises of 'fire and brimstone' in an afterlife are a mighty force
     to keep the poor and ignorant in line in this life.
17. Funeral 'traditions' (at this particular place and time) are an alternative hypothesis
     explaining delay in burial and the display and cost of the funeral, but we do not develop
     this argument here. Clearly tradition dictated the 'pomp and circumstance' of the
     funeral with one's station in life (see Chadwick 1843: 50–51) and the 'fashions in funer-
     als established by the wealthier classes' must be strongly considered when planning a
     funeral.
18. The externality attending survivors was, from evidence in Chadwick's view, by far
     greater than those foisted on urban populations from improper burial or proximity to
     graveyards. As he maintained:

>   . . . the miasma from the remains of the dead in grave-yards can only reach the
>   living in a state of diffusion and dilution; and that large proportions of it prob-
>   ably escape without producing any immediately appreciable evil. The practice,
>   however, of the retention of the remains in the one room of the living brings the
>   effluvium to bear directly upon the survivors when it is most dangerous, when they
>   are usually exhausted bodily by watching, and depressed mentally by anxiety and
>   grief – circumstances which it is well known greatly increase the danger of contagion.
>   (Chadwick 1843: 42)

     Chadwick may well have been the earliest observer to connect stress with disease.
19. Chadwick notes that even the exhortations of a bishop in resisting 'extortionate' charges
     for services in a court of law had no impact on the monopoly. Other factors leading to
     the high price of funerals were cited. Since many funerals of the higher and upper-mid-
     dle classes were paid for out of trust funds, there was little or no resistance to the high
     prices of undertakers. Further, close examination of undertakers' bills after the funeral

would be met by social approbation (presumably from the undertaker) that the survivor might have begrudged the deceased a 'decent funeral' (see Chadwick 1842a: 52).

20.   The argument for collusion is most dubious. With 600–700 undertakers competing for funerals in London, policing costs would be prohibitive in maintaining a cartel. Monopoly on the supply side in this market is only an assertion, one that Dnes (1994: 534) appears to accept as plausible.

21.   The announcement of a death was often the signal for a coming carousal. How are the insurance proceeds used, queried Chadwick of the secretary of one of the better organized societies? The secretary's answer:

> The family provide themselves with drink, and the friends coming also drink. I have known this to be to such excess, that the undertaker's men, who always take whatever drink is given them, are frequently unfit to perform their duty, and have reeled in carrying the coffin. At these times it is very distressing. The men who stand as mutes at the door, as they stand out in the cold, are supposed to require most drink, and receive it most liberally. I have seen these men reel about the road, and after the burial we have been obliged to put these mutes and their staves into the interior of the hearse and drive them home, as they were incapable of walking. After the return from the funeral, the mourners commonly have drink again at the house. This drinking at the funeral is a very great evil. (Chadwick 1843: 60)

22.   While speaking of a particular case, Gardner noted that the child of a laboring family 'had been entered in at least ten burial clubs; and its parents had six other children, who only lived from nine to eighteen months respectively. They had received 20*l*. from several burial clubs for one of these children, and expected to receive at least as much on account of this child.' Testimony was given in a criminal proceeding from an acquaintance that 'she was a fine fat child shortly after her birth' but that she soon became quite thin and did not get a sufficiency of food. In spite of the testimony the case was dismissed by the jury due to a lack of evidence due to the exact cause of death (see the testimony, Chadwick 1843: 64–5).

23.   These statistics were briefly summarized in Chadwick's later essay (1859c). Of the 730 undertakers, only 275 were 'official.' All the others listed denoted complementary occupations as well. Thus, there were '258 "undertakers and carpenters", 34 "undertakers and upholsterers", 56 "undertakers and cabinet-makers", 51 "undertakers and builders", 25 "undertakers and appraisers", 19 "undertakers and auctioneers", 7 "undertakers and house-agents", 3 'undertakers and fancy cabinet-makers", 2 "undertakers and packing-case makers"' (Chadwick 1843: 53), making a total of 730 listed. Many more, it would seem, were unlisted.

24.   These 'medical men' were of a lower order of physician, akin to the 'ambulance chasers' of the legal profession (Chadwick 1843: 54).

25.   Burial fees from the poorest class were about 15*s*., out of which the average traditional 'take' of the clergyman (called 'Soul Scot') was about 3*s*. (the average take on all funerals for clerics was estimated at 6*s*. 2*d*. from data reported by Chadwick 1843: Appendix 13: 273).

26.   A sample of the services one could obtain is as follows:

> The first class of funerals are of great pomp: they include bearers, crosses, plumes, eighteen mourning coaches and attendants, grand mass at church, 120 lbs. of wax tapers, an anniversary service, and material of mourning cloth; and also the attendance of Monsieur le Cure, two vicars, twenty-one priests, six singers and ten chorister boys, and two instrumental performers, at a cost of 145*l*., for a funeral superior in magnificence perhaps to any private funeral in England. The charge for the service and materials of the ninth class, in which there is the attendance of a vicar and a priest, and of a bass singer or chorister for the mass, is about 15*s*. of English money. In the *service ordinaire* there is less religious service, and that is performed gratuitously. The only charge made is the price of the coffin, which is five or seven francs,

according to the size: the coffin is covered by a pall, and carried on a plain hearse, drawn by two black horses. This funeral is conducted by a superintendent and four assistants, exclusive of the driver. (Chadwick 1843: 118)

27. Taking the number of annual funerals in Paris at 28 000, the average number of funerals conducted daily was 76.7. Each hearse would be used about two-and-a-half times per day unless subcontractors were used. Actually, those who died in public hospitals and who were not claimed by friends (part of the 7000 *gratis* funerals provided by the contractor) were used for medical purposes and 'merely enclosed in a coarse cloth and deposited in the ground, without any funereal rites.' The pressure on the capital stock of the contractor was thus less than suggested by the total number of dead in Paris per year.

28. The similarity between Parisian municipal regulation of the funeral market and the modern urban regulation of cable TV can hardly be missed. One of the chief criticisms of local cable regulation is that the monopoly at the local level is maintained in the interest of city government revenues (Beil et al. 1993; Hazlett 1991).

29. Chadwick's was clearly selective in ignoring some positive aspects of the French burial system. He might have noted that a model urban cemetery (admittedly for the upper classes) was established in Paris as early as 1804 (French 1975: 85–6). Père Lachaise cemetery, established in Paris that year, was the first and most important European 'garden' cemetery serving as an example for upper-class cemeteries in Europe throughout the nineteenth century. It remains a tourist attraction to this day, housing the remains of many renowned statesmen and artists, including Oscar Wilde, composer Frederic Chopin and, until recently, rocker Jim Morrison (an added expense of special guards had to be employed to protect his grave from souvenir seekers, and Morrison's remains were moved).

30. Interestingly, Chadwick did not distinguish between the possible problems that might be encountered at the local versus the national (or federal) level of government. As we saw in Chapter 4, he envisioned nationwide sector-related contracting in the case of railways (Chadwick 1859c; 1866b).

31. Chadwick suggested that, ideally, these rural public cemeteries would be located close to a river or stream so that transportation costs (and the lack of solemnity) of urban 'processions' could be minimized or avoided. Bodies for burial could simply be floated down the river.

32. With the rapid population growth in London, some earlier suburban graveyards were surrounded by residential development not long after they were started. Chadwick argued for a type of zoning around the cemeteries to prevent the same development problems in the vicinity of the national cemeteries. Despite Chadwick's criticism of these early suburban gravesites, their existence does suggest that private and joint-stock burial companies had begun an attempt to alleviate the problems of intramural burial.

33. The Necropolis Company failed to find suitable land and never buried a single body. Despite its failure to develop, the Necropolis Company had played a significant role in keeping Chadwick's nationalized funeral system out of the business of death.

34. High information costs also appear to explain recommended reforms of contemporary funeral markets. Typically, funeral 'packages' have been bundled with the coffin separated from 'all other charges' – some of which are used and some not. Reform has most often taken the form of recommendations for 'unbundling' with a list of charges presented to customers (see Darmstadter 1983, for example). A similar tack has been taken in cable television regulation. After unbundling, however, higher prices for *à la carte* service are a distinct possibility.

35. Yet another explanation for a less than minimum low-cost position on a *long-run* average cost curve is that unused capacity may itself have a value. In his 1859 essay (see 1859c), for example, Chadwick defends regulation of the London cabriolet market by observed unused capacity (hacks lined up at points around the city). Since time has a clear value in full price considerations, the unused capacity may well economize on time costs.

36. In response to plagues the Privy Council issued orders (in 1595) to justices to see to it that church ministers or 'substantial householders' viewed the bodies before they were buried. Further they were to determine the cause of death and to keep a tally which would register deaths. Chadwick reports that 'It is supposed that this scheme of registration gave rise to the bills of mortality' which were preserved annually from the year 1603. Unfortunately, argues Chadwick, the system degenerated after the times of plague to simple rent-seeking at the local level (the office of 'searcher' was given to old women who half-heartedly performed their duties for a few shillings and liquor). The quality of information given the ministers as warrant for interment was unreliable (if not bogus) under this system (see Chadwick 1843: 113 for details).

37. The proposed ordinance to forbid all delay of interments beyond a certain number of hours would 'in the shape proposed, and without other securities, run counter to the feelings of the population, and standing as a self-executing law it would have but little operation' (Chadwick 1843: 85). Additionally, according to Chadwick, the 'closeness' of the rooms in which the poor die and the warmth of these rooms meant that the problems were as (or more) severe in winter.

38. The practice of 'precontracting,' which has become so popular today, was available to the poor at that time by Chadwick's own evidence. It is possible that some 'burial societies,' especially those sponsored by undertakers themselves, provided service descriptions and future prices in Chadwick's time? Unfortunately we have found no evidence on this point.

39. For example, from the perspective of law and economics, is the costly system of acquiring FDA approval for drugs as cost efficient as using liability arrangements or private certification agents?

40. Note that the externality did *not* exist for the upper classes where lead coffins (or double coffins) were most often used to house the dead.

41. The market solutions to funeral externalities in the United States as well as the developing private solutions in England suggest that detailed controls are not desirable. If the net gains from regulation are only temporary then policymakers must be alert to the fact that competition may become viable and entail no cost penalty. Schmalensee argues that under such circumstances the administrators of the controls cannot be relied upon to 'call attention to the desirability of its own demise' (1979: 7). The availability of good substitutes for the monopolist's output reduces the potential benefits from detailed controls. Although Chadwick was open to some competition from private cemeteries at first, he eventually settled on the complete monopolization of the industry due to fears that competition would decrease the demand for the monopolistic output (Finer 1952: 414). Thus, the potential and actual benefits from the monopolization of the burial industry may not justify the detailed intervention proposed by Chadwick.

42. In an interesting extension of his desire to regulate (actually to socialize) competitive markets, Chadwick argued for entry regulation through contract management in the market for bread in Paris. Regulation (ostensibly by franchise bidding) took place in the urban Parisian market for bread, but not in the suburbs (*banlieues*) of the city. The suburban bakers (using a 'study') claimed that the unregulated market produced higher prices and lower quality in addition to greater entry and exit from the industry. This waste justified (in the opinion of the incumbent suburban bakers) regulation and price restrictions. This 'wasteful' competition, in other words, justified cartelization of a competitive business. These arguments are familiar in the case of local restrictions in the building trades, in restaurants, and in zoning laws. Competitive markets do not always work in the ways desired by incumbent suppliers.

43. Socialization of property rights and franchise bidding are not the same institutional structures as the contemporary meaning of 'privatization.' The later term is much broader in potential meanings – from completely unregulated private property rights to completely specified input services and government ownership of the capital stock. Between these two extremes exist an infinite number of possibilities.

PART III

Law, sociology, and economics

6. Chadwick on labor, education, and the business cycle

INTRODUCTION

In 1950 R.A. Lewis analyzed Edwin Chadwick's reaction to the railway laborer's situation, writing that, 'The episode exhibits his best qualities as a man and as a reformer – his sense of public duty, his courage, his contempt for the power of wealth, his sympathy for an exploited class' (Lewis 1950: 107). While this is only partly correct, attributing as it does a strictly humanitarian motive to Chadwick, there can be little doubt of his deep and analytical concern for the nineteenth-century laborer.[1] Nor can there be doubt as to the extent of Chadwick's knowledge concerning the conditions of the wage classes, the importance of education and human capital, technology, and the impact of these on the business cycle. Chadwick's long romance with the empirical led him to gather, first hand, information concerning many aspects of the living and working conditions of the English workforce – more than any observer up to his time. Chadwick's *Report on the Sanitary Condition of the Labouring Population of Great Britain* (1842a) is sufficient evidence of the dimensions of his knowledge, as is his expertise on the labor conditions of railway workers (1846).

Lewis' article was an attempt to correct the record so far as Chadwick's reputation on the wage classes was concerned. Historically, Chadwick's image had been that of a repressor of the laboring population, an attitude that had developed principally from Chadwick's work on the Poor Law Act of 1834 and the ensuing turmoil during his tenure as Secretary to the Poor Law Commission. To counteract the perceived bias, Lewis presents and discusses the substance of Chadwick's pamphlet entitled *Papers Read Before the Statistical Society of Manchester, on the Demoralization and Injuries Occasioned by the Want of Proper Regulations of Labourers Engaged in the Construction and Working of Railways* (which Chadwick had printed at his own expense in 1846). Chadwick's study recommended deep parliamentary reforms of the treatment by private entrepreneurs of railway labor. These reforms only gained partial success in Parliament, essentially by changing liability for fatal accidents.[2]

The work of Lewis on Chadwick's dealings with rail workers

unfortunately does not describe Chadwick's *economic* analysis of labor and the critically related matters of education and technology. Neither does it connect these contributions to Chadwick's macroeconomic theory of the business cycle. In this chapter we show that Chadwick addressed critical propositions regarding the issues of human capital and education, technology, and business cycles within an analysis of labor and labor's condition. In doing so, he went far beyond the received classical views on these matters. Chadwick's analysis was, as always, analytically inventive and, in some quarters quite atypical of the classical theorists that were part of his intellectual environment. Chadwick's views, more importantly, provide one part of his remedy for poverty among laborers and the destitute.

LABOR AS A UTILITARIAN ISSUE

A critical and central issue facing classical economics related to the position of labor, both in English society and in economic analysis. Certain mercantilists either took an extremely dim view of human nature or succumbed to the interests of the moneyed merchant class when dealing with the poor. There was a 'utility in poverty' according to some writers: if the laboring poor received wages in excess of the barest subsistence, they would be lazy and slothful; if they received less, they would not survive. Thus there was some 'optimum' level of poverty. No one, perhaps, was more severe in this view than Bernard de Mandeville (who was an economic liberal in other respects). Arguing that the children of the poor and orphans should not be given an education because it would 'ruin' them, he opined:

> Reading, Writing and Arithmetick [sic] are very necessary to those whose Business requires such qualifications, but where People's livelihood has no dependence on these Arts, they are very pernicious to the Poor . . . Going to School in comparison to Working is Idleness, and the longer Boys continue in this easy sort of Life, the more unfit they'll be . . . for downright Labour, both as to Strength and Inclination. (Mandeville 1723 [1924]: 311)

This bleak assessment of progress for the poor and laboring classes found its way into both classical economics and into the politics of the day. Poor relief administered at the parish level was considered by some to be a disaster. For many writers the poor, barely considered human in some quarters, were cogs in the whole classical mechanism explaining how economic growth and progress took place. Capitalists invested in circulating capital (that is, wages for the workers), increasing short-term wages. But wages were dissipated in increased population (the Malthusian proposition), increasing labor supply and bringing wages back to that 'optimal subsistence' (see Ekelund 1976). Within this depressing assessment, it was allowed that some would save, raising their prospects. Others would be at or below the margin of starvation requiring society's help through Poor Law relief. The back story of Poor Law reform, the hot political issue of the 1820s and 1830s, contained these elements. Should social relief be 'indoor' in workhouses, or 'outdoor,' administered by government functionaries? Should workhouses be accommodating in uplifting the poor (through education, sanitary housing, and so on) or should they be places of horror to discourage the poor from malingering? All these issues and many more were facing Poor Law reformers, including Chadwick.

Chadwick sometimes fell back into the mercantile view of labor, but ultimately adopted a very different perspective on the possibilities for the laboring and the 'undeserving' poor. Consider his utilitarian perspective in the context of Poor Law reform. Chadwick enunciated 'the general propositions or principle, that a man will seek that condition which is most pleasurable to him' (1836: 490) which is an explicit acceptance of the utilitarian philosophy. But – a large 'but' – in addition to this hedonistic law, Chadwick held the belief that man's character is strongly affected by environmental influences. Referring to laborers engaged in railway construction, Chadwick writes: 'Many of the men are reckless, but what is the cause? No man cares for them; they labour like degraded brutes; they feed and lodge like savages; they are enveloped in vice as with an atmosphere; the sensual only is present' (1846: 49). And as additional proof of Chadwick's views on the relative importance of genes and environment, he argued that 'I do not deny the force of hereditary conditions and habits which countenance such superficial generalisations, but I have seen those conditions and habits may be much sooner and more effectually altered, than is commonly supposed' (1856b: 77). Combining these propositions, Chadwick (using modern terminology) viewed behavior as being a utility maximization process subject to environmental and (as we shall see) institutional constraints. Environmental constraints – improvements to sanitation – include the physical and social surroundings of labor, whereas institutional constraints refer to the legal structure. Chadwick's understanding of these environmental constraints facing labor provided him with a large stock of information on the overall condition of labor. At times in his writings, a hint of the mercantilist contempt for the wage classes arose, but he most clearly believed that altered constraints were the key to social mobility and at least the potential for success of the laboring and poor classes.[3] Indeed he strongly criticized this inherited mercantile attitude in others as a great evil:

There is yet a strong body of the disciples of Mandeville whose sentiment, 'If a horse knew as much as a man, I should not like to be his rider' is more constantly seen to govern their actions than avowed in their discourse. The sentiment is as false as it is base, The Mandevillians have brutalized millions of human beings, and brought them to a state in which they are ready to rush on to the injury of themselves, and the destruction of all around them. (Chadwick 1831b: 246–7)[4]

Why is Chadwick's Position Important?

The dehumanization of labor espoused in received English thought – enshrined in a historical class system, remnants of which exist to the present day – may seem academic. However, it is critical to understanding some of Chadwick's unique social, political, and economic positions amongst his peers. Chadwick speaks to the basic nature of human beings, whereas the mercantile writers and most of Britain's upper classes thought of the poor as base animals, a belief that of course led to policy. We will see that Chadwick was not alone in his more exulted opinion of human nature, and shared it with a number of contemporaries (notably John Stuart Mill). But the critical issue is, given the expressed equality of all humans, how far would or should society go in ameliorating the environment that shaped the ultimate condition of the laboring poor and destitute. (This is of course a debate that frames policy and debate in many countries of the world today.) It appears that Chadwick believed that the wage classes were intrinsically no different from middle-class English society. In fact, at times, Chadwick allowed admiration to infiltrate his writings concerning the state of the laborer. Referring to the manufacturing distress in the textile industry caused by the American Civil War Chadwick writes: 'The wage classes . . . have it is said, borne their privations nobly, and I would be far from detracting their praise; for I well know to how many unfavorable circumstances they have been subjected' (1856b: 78). Chadwick approvingly quotes Robert Rawlinson (an engineer to the Bridgewater Trust, who Chadwick cites extensively in his works on Railway Reform) as to the character of the laborers: 'If proper means are taken to provide for the spiritual, temporal, and bodily comfort and welfare of the men, they will become as orderly and well-behaved as any other portion of the community' (Chadwick 1846: 39). The phrase 'if proper means are "taken"' is in essence the solution Chadwick was to put forth for the relief of the laborers. That is, the state of the workers was not due to any inherited failure or character but rather to a *mélange* of environmental constraints. Thus, the solution was to develop social, economic, and political institutions to bring out the bourgeois characteristics in the lower classes. Chadwick was not unique in espousing an enlightenment view of man, but he stood alone in the nature and extent of policies to improve the lowest in society.

Chadwick and His Contemporaries on the Nature of Labor

Chadwick and the coterie of classical writers that faced the issues of labor, subsistence, and poverty were all primarily 'utilitarian' in their views, as many have observed (Coats 1971: 150). But that, as suggested above, is not the central issue and here, we believe, Chadwick's stance is different. Could environmental constraints be changed or lifted to permit improvements in their condition? Put another way, could mobility in income distribution be achieved through social and public policies? (These issues and their solutions are, of course, an ongoing and central question in virtually all contemporary societies, advanced and developing.)

Consider the interesting opinions of classical writer John Ramsey McCulloch. McCulloch in one instance defends the lower classes, attributing to them the same basic sentiments as the upper classes and yet in another, he attributes *class differences* to natural differences. Speaking in favor of the lower classes, McCulloch writes (1824: 334):

> The poor have ... the same understanding, the same penetration, and the same regard to consequences as those who are rich. It is indeed a contradiction and an absurdity to pretend, that if the labourers are capable of earning, by an ordinary degree of application, more than is sufficient to support them, they alone, of all the various classes of society, will spend the surplus in riot and debauchery. They have the same common sense, they are actuated by the same passions, feelings, and principles as other men.

In contrast to the above, however, McCulloch (1830: 26) used divine ordination to proffer an explanation for a mercantile view of the class structure in England:

> The distinction of rich and poor, is not as some shallow sophists would seem to suppose, artificial, but real; it is as much a part of the order of Providence as the distinction of the sexes. It depends on the differences of the mental and physical powers and dispositions of different individuals and of the different circumstances under which they happen to be placed.

Thus a classical observer as sagacious as McCulloch could not bring himself to argue that environmental factors could be used to positively alter inherited differences between rich and poor, blaming the distinction on 'divine Providence.'

The very font of English classical economics contains this view. In the *Wealth of Nations*, Adam Smith went on record as denying the mercantile myth about the low state of the laborer. Admitting that there are instances of laborers striving to attain merely a subsistence level of income (that is, a social subsistence, not necessarily a biological one), and consuming leisure once that subsistence is met, Smith avers that this is the exception and not the rule. Smith writes, in an argument with a unique twist, that:

> Some workmen, indeed, when they can earn in four days what will maintain them through the week, will be idle the other three. This, however, is by no means the case with the greater part. Workmen, on the contrary, when they are liberally paid by the piece, are very apt to over-work themselves, and to ruin their health and constitution in a few years. (1776 [1937]: 81–2)

Smith goes further and denounces the mercantilist notion that workers must be paid as little as possible in order to maintain their productivity: '[The notion] . . . that men in general should work better when they are ill fed than when they are well fed, when they are disheartened than when they are in good spirits, when they are frequently sick than when they are generally in good health, seems not very probable' (1776 [1937]: 82–3). Smith does not offer an explanation for the persistence of this argument amongst the upper classes.[5]

Chadwick and Mill

A corollary to Chadwick's rejection of the mercantilist attitude toward the laborer is John Stuart Mill's open rejection of the paternalistic view of class structure. Mill views the situation as being described by two opposing theories: 'The one may be called the theory of dependence and protection, the other that of self-dependence' (Mill 1848b [1965]:759). In the former, the position is taken that it is the responsibility and duty of the upper classes to provide for the well-being of the lower classes and in return the lower classes shall respond with willing obedience to the dictates of the employers. This familiar view of social structure Mill discards in favor of the second: 'The poor have come out of leading-strings, and cannot any longer be governed or treated like children. To their own qualities must not be commended the care of their destiny' (Mill 1848b [1965]: 763). Thus Mill, to a greater extent than all of the classical liberal writers, advocated the elevation of the laboring population to an equal footing with middle-class English society, although the scope of his policy program was different and fell far short of Chadwick's.[6]

Chadwick's environmental theme (though not his and Mill's emphasis upon economic incentives) concerning labor's problems is reiterated in the writings of the Utopian Socialist Robert Owen, as well as in economic orthodoxy. Owen's view concerning the basic nature of man is plain and stark:

> Any general character, from the best to the worst, from the most ignorant to the most enlightened, may be given to any community, even to the world at large, by the application of proper means; which means are to a great extent at the command and under the control of those who have the influence in the affairs of men. (Owen 1821 [1927]: 14)

Owen is restating the theme that society can be shaped through manipulation of the institutions which direct and/or limit individual behavior. Owen's belief in this law of society was such that he was willing to risk his own fortune in experimenting with real world applications of the doctrine. Owen attempted to prove the thesis that the poor are wretched because they are poor, and not that they are poor because they are wretched. His experiments of restricting child labor, providing education, raising wages, shortening hours, and subsidizing housing must be reckoned a success in both social and economic terms. Owen's social thought represents one of many examples that may be put forth for the non-exclusiveness of thought between supposedly divergent schools of economic doctrine. This non-exclusive nature of economic thought is a major complicating factor in the taxonomy of economic doctrines. However, before proceeding to a discussion of how Chadwick was unique in recommendations for the improvement of the laborer, his conception of the English laborer's circumstances vis-à-vis that of the Continental workforce will be considered. The importance of this issue for the discussion is that the subjective evaluation of national workforce gives an indication of the progress that can be achieved with regards to the state of the laboring population.

Chadwick, unlike Owen in this regard, was not a socialist at least to the extent of advocating direct government involvement. Rather Chadwick rested his case for improvement of labor on education, machinery, and on sanitation and infrastructure reform (to be considered in Chapter 8), and on the role of technology. Government was to be involved, but not in the direct manner supported by traditional socialists and communists.

BRITISH LABOR AND THE INFLUENCE OF MACHINERY

The primary *macro*economic theory of the British classical writers was, as noted in Chapter 2, comprised, in addition to Say's Law, of four 'cornerstones' – the wages fund theory; a theory of investment in fixed (machinery) and circulating (wages) capital; the Malthusian population doctrine; and the principle of diminishing returns to agriculture. Many, most notably John Stuart Mill, envisioned the arrival through a kind of 'dynamic' process at some 'stationary state' wherein population was a maximized 'optimum,' land rents were at a maximum, and wages were at subsistence (see Ekelund and Hébert 2007: 161–2 for details). Naturally, some technological shock to the system would alter the process, but astonishingly, most classical writers, while understanding the impact of machinery on labor productivity and prosperity, did not fully appreciate the full impact of the technological revolution taking place before their very eyes. That was not the case with Chadwick.

In his analysis of the influence of technology, Chadwick found a potent source of optimism for the future improvement of the laborer's condition. At every stage of his thought, Chadwick was undeniably in favor of introducing capital to improve the state of those who had to use it; the laborers. Chadwick espouses the opinion that '. . . as machinery is improved, the economical conditions of the labourers is everywhere, and must, I apprehend, continue to be, improved with the character of the machinery . . .' (1856a: 804).[7] Chadwick continues from the preceding thought to explain why the laborer's state is necessarily improved by the introduction of labor-saving machinery.

The primary consequence of the introduction or improvement in machinery, as Chadwick viewed the process, was an increase in wages. (Naturally the increased largesse for some laborers did not mean that there was not a mass of working poor and destitute in British society, but overall Chadwick had a nationalistic pride in the abilities of the English worker.)[8] This increase in wages is evoked by two distinct market changes. The first being an increase in demand; the second a change in the supply of labor, through a change in the quality of labor which is requisite. With respect to the former, Chadwick writes: 'The whole manufacturing tendency in that county [Lancashire] during the last half-century, and before it . . . has been to displace handlabour, by the use of labour-saving machines; yet the more labour that has been displaced by machinery, the more labour has been wanted' (1856a: 804). The explanation proffered by Chadwick for this increased demand for labor is similar in concept, although not in terminology, to a productivity theory of wages. Chadwick notes: '. . . the efficiency of the laborer had borne its relation to the improved sources introduced' (1859a: 62), that is, the productivity of labor is directly related to the amount of capital employed. As additional units of capital are employed, productivity of labor would increase. Given some fixed amount of labor, the increased productivity would increase output and hence, lower per unit labor costs. Chadwick alleges that this decreased per unit labor cost resulted in decreased average costs of production, a fact drawn from empirical observation of the agricultural sector. He wrote: 'The farmer in Dorsetshire [using hand-labor] paid only 8s [in wages], and the farmer in Lancashire [where machinery was more pervasive] paid 16s a week, and the latter got his work done cheaper at higher wages than it could be done at the lower' (1859a: 62). Given constant product prices and lower average costs, the producer could then increase profits by increasing output through the employment of a greater quantity of workmen, hence the increased demand for labor.

The second cause of the increases was supply-related. The substitution of capital for labor resulted in a higher labor quality requisite to operate the machines and this increased quality requirement prohibited market participation by less qualified work. That is, the market experienced a decrease in supply, and in order to verify the validity of this market adjustment, Chadwick cites (1856a: 804) an anonymous industrialist:

> For working inferior and rude machines almost any man may be taken out of the streets and employed, at low wages without asking who he is . . . but not so with this improved machinery. It is a highly delicate and valuable property; it is a large amount of capital into one man's charge; a drunken or an ignorant man may in a minute do great damage; moral character and trustworthiness must not be sought for; inquiries as to these qualities must now be made before engagement; higher wages must now be paid for working the improved machine to workmen of higher character as well as of skill.

Chadwick is arguing that higher wages are due not only to the greater skills required for the operation of the machinery, but that there are other variables which enter the market equilibrium, namely, the moral character of the employee. With Chadwick's discussion of railway reform, the importance of the *moral stature* of workmen resurfaces. He notes that (1865a: 102):

> Intelligence, steadiness, and self-reliance, are important qualifications for the economical workings of such undertakings [railways], especially where costly and dangerous machinery is to be dealt with. Mr. Brunlus points out that the wages usually given by railway companies are too low, he says, 'inferior men are employed who are incapable of appreciating the importance and necessity of executing their duties with promptitude and exactitude.

Chadwick argues that, with the introduction of machinery, the employer must consider the full cost of purchasing labor, that is, the wage rate plus the expected value of damages resulting from the operation of the machinery by less qualified personnel. Chadwick recognized that the decrease in supply resulted from the elimination of unqualified participants, thus it could not be argued that the introduction of machinery was an unqualified benefit to labor as a whole. Obviously, the effects on the displaced laborers must be analyzed before such a sweeping statement could be made.

Did Labor-Saving Machinery Create Unemployment?

An incessant issue facing classical (and modern) writers concerned the impact of the introduction of machinery on employment. Chadwick admits that the introduction of labor-saving machinery will elicit a short-run increase in unemployment amongst those who do not have the necessary skills and moral character. However, technological unemployment was viewed by Chadwick as being readily eliminated by market forces and individual initiative. The most powerful force in eliminating technological unemployment is the increased demand for labor. Chadwick describes the process as follows: '. . . where labour is saved, or rendered more productive, thereby, capital is increased and the increased investment of capital increases the demand for labour, and thence, increased what I call the absorbent power of the labour market, to re-absorb the displaced labour' (1856a: 806). Chadwick has implicitly assumed that output increases are relatively greater than wage increases, causing average costs to fall and increasing profits. The increased profits present the entrepreneur with a larger investment fund, which, when applied, will increase employment.

Besides the action on the demand side, Chadwick observed the behavior of individuals who were technologically unemployed. While directly investigating the effect of the institution of labor-saving machinery on the pauper roles and Poor Law administration, Chadwick concluded that technological improvement was not a contributing factor to pauperism. As an example, to corroborate this conclusion, Chadwick presents evidence (1856a: 806):

> In one instance, where, by the introduction of Mr. Whitworth's street-sweeping machine into a large town district, the labour of the entire body of sweepers by hand had been displaced. I confidently expected that that class, at least, who were of the lowest labourers, and the least capable of changing the object of their labour, would be found, as a class, on the destitute relief list; but as a class, they were not there.

Chadwick continued his investigation of this situation and attempted to locate the displaced street-sweepers. The results were that 8 percent had since died (a percentage which Chadwick noted was not significantly different from his expected mortality rate), 6 percent were unaccounted for, and the rest had found employment elsewhere. This re-employment Chadwick attributed to the initiative of the individuals: 'Under the stimulus of an extraordinary necessity they had found for themselves miscellaneous services, for which, under that stimulus, they qualified themselves, – which services no one else could have anticipated or found out for them . . . and none had fallen below their former position, which indeed was scarcely possible' (1856a: 806).

Thus, the displaced workers, when left to their own faculties, will adjust to labor market changes. Chadwick also implies that the uncontrolled effect of market pressure results in the laborers actually improving their situation, and hence the efficiency of the market in providing alternatives when market conditions fail. Central to this adjustment problem is the matter of education and the laboring population (a topic to be considered later in this chapter).

Several other aspects of Chadwick's views on labor and machin-ery remain to be discussed. In addition to the pecuniary benefits of higher wages, the introduction of labor-saving capital contributed another advantage to the laborer, that is, increased job security. Chadwick believed that mechanical operatives were less likely to be subject to cyclical unemployment. Chadwick's arguments as to the reason for this stability are two-fold and are explained as follows (1856a: 804):

> When engaged they [the operatives] cannot be summarily dismissed with safety, for a substitute may not be found without great trouble, moreover, the wear and tear and interest on the machine is at least by per diem, and there is, therefore, a penalty to that amount on the owner of the machine for every day he omits to find work and keep the artisan employed at these high wages. Under these circumstances, the owner becomes, to a greater extent then may be supposed, the servant of the operative.

In the first instance, Chadwick is arguing that the employer is less likely to temporarily discharge workers, the higher the cost of rehiring. This analysis, upon consideration, is correct in marginal terms, although Chadwick did not consider the problem in a marginal cost sense. The latter reason for increased stability is not necessarily true, and exhibits the fact that Chadwick did not fully understand marginal analysis as applied to profit maximization. Chadwick has implied that, in every case, it would be optimal for the firm to continue production. He is considering the shutdown condition only in fixed-cost terms rather than the relationship between price and average variable cost. One should notice that there are disequilibrium conditions under which Chadwick's analysis is correct, that is, when the value of the marginal product is greater than the wage rate.

The effect of machinery on the laborer was an important facet of both Classical and Marxian economic doctrine. Principally, the effect on employment was the source of much controversy. The analysis of the employment effects of introducing labor-saving machinery has become known as the 'Compensation Controversy' (Beach 1971: 916–22; Hicks 1971: 922–5). As was noted previously, Chadwick took the position that the introduction of machinery would result only in temporary unemployment. On this question, Chadwick was in agreement with such writers as J.R. McCulloch, J.S. Mill, and T.R. Malthus. Malthus, considering the example of the cotton industry, where mechanization was progressing swiftly, 'argued that, for commodities in elastic demand, the end result of the introduction of machinery was likely to be an increase in employment' (O'Brien 1975: 227). McCulloch's analysis of the situation becomes difficult to follow because of his inconsistency in the definition of the demand for labor; at one point considering capital as demand for labor, while at another specifying consumption demand as demand for labor. However McCulloch's conclusion was that machinery resulted only in temporary frictional unemployment (O'Brien 1970: 302–6). J.S. Mill's analysis of the Compensation Controversy was not as unilaterally positive as was that of Chadwick, Malthus, and McCulloch, although his conclusion was the same. With a view of the introduction of machinery, Mill notes: 'that all increases of fixed capital, when taking place at the expense of circulating, must be, at least temporarily, prejudicial to the interests of the labourers' (Mill 1848a [1965]: 93). Mill then continues on to discuss the circumstances wherein laborers are injured by mechanization. Taking a practical view, Mill concluded, however, that the substitution of fixed for circulating capital does not ordinarily occur in an economy. Rather, 'improvements are always introduced very gradually, and are seldom or never made by withdrawing circulating capital from actual production, but are made by the employment of the annual increase' (Mill 1848a [1965]: 97). Mill is arguing that in a growing economy, mechanization occurs from the net increase in national output, leaving the wages-fund unchanged and hence, maintaining the demand for labor. The demand for labor being constant, Mill is in agreement with Chadwick, Malthus, and McCulloch and states: '. . . I do not believe that, as things are actually transacted, improvements in production are often, if ever, injurious even temporarily, to the labouring classes in the aggregate' (Mill 1848a [1965]: 97).[9]

The above mentioned authors (excepting Chadwick) had a common purpose in their expositions: they were directly responding to a controversy begun by Ricardo. The Compensation Controversy began when Ricardo included a chapter entitled 'On Machinery' in the third edition of *The Principles of Political Economy and Taxation* (1817 [1969]). In this chapter, Ricardo concluded that mechanization might be prejudicial to labor. He writes that 'I am convinced that the substitution of machinery for human labor is often very injurious to the interest of the class of labourers' (Ricardo 1817 [1969]: 264). Blaug summarizes Ricardo's analysis as follows: 'The basic argument is that if the introduction of machinery involves the diversion of labor previously required to produce wage goods, if instead of new machines being financed out of retained earnings they are financed by drawing down the wages funds, then output may fall for a time and produce unemployment' (Blaug 1978: 137–8). It should be noted that Ricardo based his analysis on an assumption – that is, that circulating capital (the wages-fund) is converted into fixed capital – which J.S. Mill was to reject at a later date. Ricardo's analysis of mechanization was taken further by a member of economic heterodoxy, Karl Marx, and became a central figure of Marx's 'Laws of Capitalistic Motion.'

The effect of the introduction of labor-saving machinery becomes the driving force behind Marx's 'Law of a Growing Industrial Reserve Army.' The permanent dislocation of labor by machinery creates a growing unemployed class as technological improvement advances. Marx (1906: 407) writes that:

> The self-expansion of capital by means of machinery is directly proportional to the number of workers whose means of livelihood have been destroyed by this machinery . . . that portion of the working class which machinery has thus rendered superfluous . . . either goes to the wall in the unequal struggle of the old handcraft and manufacturing industry, or else floods all the more easily accessible branches of industry.

Marx viewed mechanization as a necessary consequence of the capitalist system (the dynamic force of competition continuously forcing producers to discover less costly means of production; spurring the substitution of capital for labor), and one of the inherent contradictions of that system. Thus one side of the Compensation Controversy was used as an argument against the basis of classical economics, that is, capitalism.

The question of higher wages from the use of machinery embroiled Chadwick in a debate concerning the competitiveness of British industry. Writing in the *Journal of the Royal Society of Arts*, Chadwick refuted the notion that British manufacturers were consistently undersold, since labor was relatively cheaper on the European continent. Chadwick proffers the following opinion (1856b: 77):

> I know nothing of the manufactures of Spain; but from large manufacturers in France, Switzerland, Austria, Italy (several of them using the latest and the best of the English machinery) I know that, by whatsoever the English manufactures have been kept out it has not been by the cheaper labour of those countries.

Chadwick continues by arguing that higher wages do not necessarily entail higher per-unit costs of production. In making this observation, Chadwick

cites the importance of the productivity of the workers. Describing a group
of workmen from Lancashire known as 'navvies' (purportedly due to the
fact that they once were employed in excavating canals) Chadwick cites the
following fact (1856b: 78):

> A mile of road made by labourers of this superior class, earning 3s., 3s. 6d., or
> 5s. 6d. per diem has been executed in a much shorter time, and has been finished
> as cheaply as a mile of precisely the same sort of road done in Ireland by pauper
> labourers whose wages were only 1s. per diem.

As further evidence of the reduction of price associated with higher wages
and mechanization, Chadwick traces the fall in price of a particular type of
cotton thread from 1s. a pound, down to 3d. for the same quality of thread.
While at the same time, wages in the industry rose from 4s. to 6d. per week
(1865b: 5). This notion was widely accepted in classical economic thought,
as Coats noted that 'the classical economists fully appreciated that high
money wages did not necessarily mean high labour cost per unit of output'
(1971: 162).

CHADWICK ON RECESSION AND DEPRESSION

There was a close association between the beneficial effects of mechanization and the effect of recessions on the long-run condition of the working
class in Chadwick's works. Chadwick held the unique perspective that
manufacturing distress was, in the long run, beneficial to labor. His argument was that manufacturing distress resulted in technological improvements and the introduction of labor-saving capital and, as was noted
above, the introduction of capital results in an improvement of the laborers
situation. Chadwick was aware of the short-run effects of manufacturing
distress, but before discussing his proposals for the relief of the short-run
effects, it is interesting to investigate his analysis of the effect of recessions
on innovation.

When assessing the effects of the blockage of cotton shipments to the
British textile districts during the American Civil War, Chadwick notes:
'It was an axiom of the late Mr. John Kennedy, who was called the father
of the cotton manufacture, that no manufacturing improvements were
ever made except on "threadbare profits"' (1865b: 3). The argument is
that under conditions of low profits or even losses, entrepreneurs have
the greatest incentive to innovate. In periods of industrial expansion,
Chadwick attributes the following attitude to entrepreneurs: 'When the
trade is doing well, the axiom is, that they cannot be better than well, and
they remain as they are' (1865b: 3). On the other hand, during periods of

falling sales and profits, and rising inventories, Chadwick describes the entrepreneur's situation (1865b: 3):

> In such crises his nerves are strained, as much as any officer's in a military command, and his mind is tasked, even with the aid of new divisions of labor, of brokers to buy his raw material, and of agents to have an outlook and sell his produce. Being under heavy penalties for every day he fails to find work and wages for his corps, he is driven to his wits' end to exercise invention, and listens greedily to any which bids fair to cheapen production, lower prices and stimulate consumption.

Interestingly, Chadwick is implying that individuals are stimulated to exertion more by costs than by benefits. Obviously, any technology generated during recession could be produced during manufacturing expansions, but Chadwick alleges that during the latter, the profit motive is not effectual in simulative research and development.

Chadwick's view of invention is curiously diametrical to that advanced by Schumpeter (1942 [1962]: 106). Schumpeter's well-known view is that it is under monopoly, where profits are greatest, that the most effective research and development can take place. As one might expect, Schumpeter's thesis has been both advanced and attacked. Additionally, as one might also expect, the empirical evidence has yet to decide the issue as to which form of market structure is most conducive to effective market research.

Beyond the benefits of increased capital to work with, and the resulting higher wages, Chadwick foresaw yet another long-run benefit of manufacturing distress in the form of increased future economic stability. Chadwick (1856a: 805) delineates the economic consequence of recession-induced innovation:

> The reduced price rendered possibly the reduced cost of production, has brought the commodities within the reach of greater numbers, and has stimulated and extended the habitual demand. The restored and extended demand, as in the case of articles of what may deem primary necessity for civilized life, been from a higher to a lower class of consumers, who are least affected by fluctuations of fashion, or disposed to sudden changes of habit; and hence, the consumption is placed upon a wider and firmer basis, rendering employment at the improved wages less liable to extreme fluctuations.

Chadwick has argued that by lowering the price of goods, the goods then become accessible to lower income levels, and the increased quantity demanded provides more stable employment because of the greater relative stability in the consumption patterns of the lower classes. It is obvious, from the tone of the above, that Chadwick considered this constancy a virtue rather than a vice.

As previously mentioned, Chadwick was well aware of the temporary unemployment which resulted from manufacturing distress. However, since Chadwick predicted higher wages and increased stability of demand as being the final outcome of the distress, he was more concerned with alleviating the short-run costs rather than eliminating the cycle completely. Chadwick notes that 'Change must . . . be regarded as a normal condition of our manufactures to be provided for in the interests of ratepayers, as well as of the employed' (1865b: 10). For the alleviation of the short-run effects of recession, Chadwick had two suggestions for the laborer: (1) investment in human capital (which we consider later in the chapter); and (2) diversification.

On the issue of diversification, Chadwick was very straightforward. After having warned manufacturers against being dependent on only one source for a vital factor of production (in this instance, American cotton) Chadwick (1865b: 10–11) continues:

> there is a lesson on domestic prudence, on the like principle [diversification], the expediency of which, for families of the wage classes, ought to be strongly impressed upon them, namely to avoid, as much as they can, having all the working members of the same family engaged in the same manufacture.

Thus, by spreading the family's sources of income across several industries, a household would be less susceptible to the vagaries of manufacturing distress. This manner of protection is now a widely accepted strategy for minimizing risk (although Chadwick obviously did not develop the method fully), especially in the area of portfolio management.[10]

Irish Immigration, English Labor, and Unemployment

A critical issue relating to English laborers, unemployment, and poverty – an issue on which there was much disagreement – concerned Irish immigration. Was such immigration deleterious to the condition of the laborers and the poor? The general public opinion as to the effect of the Irish immigrants was that they depressed labor markets by increasing the supply of labor, and since they were willing to work for lower wages, they created unemployment amongst English laborers. Citing evidence contrary to this notion, Chadwick, as early as 1836, quotes from data collected in preparing for the reform of the Poor Laws (1836: 496):

> In our parrish (Christ Church, Spitalfields) it is a rare thing to find any labouring men working for less than twelve shillings a week: indeed, the average rate of wages throughout the year is not less than from fifteen to twenty shillings a

week . . . Are there many Irish in the parrish? Yes; there is a great proportion of them, and especially about Spitalfields Market. Do they usually receive the average wages you mention? Yes; they do. Why are English labourers not employed – or why are Irish labourers preferred? Because English labourers are not to be had for love or money to perform the labour.

Although, the economic foundations of the above-described situation can be analyzed suitable to either side of the Irish Question, Chadwick reported that 'the number of Scotch and Irish who had settled were found to be too few to have produced any effect on the rate of wages' (Chadwick 1836: 497).

Closely linked (at least in the minds of Chadwick and other policymakers) was the effect on public mores from the immigration of the Irish. Conforming with the general public opinion that the Irish were morally inferior to the English laborer, Chadwick was confident that the effect of the changed environment would improve the ethics of the immigrants. He writes (1836: 497–8):

> There are doubtless, moral and political evils connected with the permanent settlements of so undisciplined a people amongst our labourers. These results were cited as illustrative of the effects of the allowance system, and the law of settlement in England. If they had their due weight, they would, of course, dissipate so much of the [distaste] for legislation with regard to Ireland, that are founded upon the supposed mischievous effects of the immigration of Irish labourers into England.

Chadwick maintains the notion that the immigrants might have an effect on the local population, but doubts the strength of their influence.

The classical economists as a group were widely divided on the Irish question. Senior (1836 [1965]: 134) was adamant in his support of the Irish, although in a back-handed manner:

> We have heard it made a subject of complaint, that the uneducated Irish have dispossessed the English of the lowest employments in London and its neighborhood. We rather rejoice that the English are sufficiently educated to be fit for better things. If they are remained as ignorant as their rivals, many who are now earning 40s a week as mechanics, might have been breaking stones and carrying hods at 2s a day.

Even though Senior does exhibit a certain contempt for the Irish, he defends their right to immigrate on the grounds that they improve the condition of the English laborer, by forcing the more adaptable English laborer into other, higher paid occupations. However, there were dissenters to this belief including Malthus, McCulloch, Torrens, and James Mill.[11]

EDUCATION, HUMAN CAPITAL, AND INFORMATION

The attainment of a general system of education was one subject in which Chadwick became deeply involved. Although the particular mechanism for the provision of education is beyond the scope of this chapter, the *motives* for general education and to low-cost information and literacy for the entire populace were closely associated with the improvement of the wage classes. Chadwick ascribes both public and private benefits to education. Public benefits, or some of them, may be thought of as in the nature of an externality. The public benefits can best be described as the creation of public capital. The private benefits are those commonly associated with human capital.

Chadwick's public capital argument arises from the supposition that a higher general level of intelligence will result in greater social stability, a *societal externality*. The sources of this stability are threefold: the first is that intelligence reduces the propensity to violence; the second, that more informed voters will produce superior electoral decisions; the third, that greater worker intelligence will generate greater economic stability. On the first point, the causes of the increased stability are two-sided. One crucial aspect is distributing knowledge of the legal structure and the penalties entailed therein. To this end, Chadwick lobbied against what he labeled 'Taxes on Knowledge,' (that is, excise taxes on newsprint) and for extension of the skill of literacy. Speaking on agricultural riots during the winter of 1831, Chadwick writes (1831b: 245):

> At the commencement of the disturbances, addresses and proclamations were distributed, and exhortations were published in the newspapers, stating what were the penalties which the law attached to the commission of acts of the nature most prevalent. But the newspapers were entirely beyond the reach even of those of the laboring population, who happened to be able to read . . . Week after week whole parishes of labourers went on daily committing capital offences, but at the same time never suspecting that they rendered themselves liable to heavier penalties than fine and imprisonment.

Chadwick goes on to argue that there are no means other than the news media to produce the public capital of an extensive knowledge of the legal structure.

Another facet of the effect of increased intelligence on social stability is the alleged fact that informed individuals are less easily swayed to commit irrational acts, Chadwick notes (1831b: 246):

> A habit of reading the public journals, cannot fail to gradually loosen the authority of a certain class of ignorant popular leaders, whose governing

motives are less sympathy for the sufferings of the people and a desire to advance social happiness than insatiable vanity and love of power, and whose only claims to authority are reckless confidence and incessant action, which never waits, or allows others to wait, for evidence or deliberations. To such men as to the priests who sway an ignorant people, divided attention is divided power.

Expanding along these same lines, Chadwick blames the government for the political unrest that exists: 'In fact, the measures of government, whether by design or not, keep the immense mass of people in the state of ignorance which predisposes them to extravagant action, while it fosters and gives power to the fanaticism which takes the lead among them' (1831a: 115). To counteract this situation, Chadwick offers the following program:

The most pressing measure immediately called for is, however, the entire removal of the obvious taxes on knowledge. The reduction of the stamp duty, proposed by ministers, will benefit only the press and the middle classes; as regards the labouring classes it is paltry; and will keep the larger channels of public information as far out of their reach as before. Every penny of duty retained is a bounty on ignorance. (1831a: 116)

Going further, Chadwick (1831a: 116) concluded: 'There can be no safety from the most fearful outrages against life and property but in the intelligence and moral feelings of the labouring classes.'

At a much later point in life, Chadwick turned to the importance of education for the effective use of the electoral franchise. He writes (1887a: 348–9):

I submit that the public educational functions, instead of being set aside as a detail of no material account, and being relegated by party politicians to inferior hands, ought to be pressed for consideration as of the highest order of importance in its bearing on the early future of the people and of the realm. The result of the elementary education, such as it is, gives three and four times more of illiterates on the electoral lists of large districts in Ireland than in England. In the United States the illiterates are found to be elements of disorder and corruption, so that in those states the chief special agitation operates for their disfranchisement. The conclusion there is that sound education is requisite for the safe exercise of the local and general franchise.

Thus, information, public education, and literacy had widespread effects on individuals, markets, and societies. Most explicitly, literacy encouraged those acquiring it to detect charlatans within the ranks of politicians, especially local politicians. It brought down the costs of poor public decisions and helped prevent the ignorant and poor from being dominated and led without evidence or logic.

A third source of public stability gained from the instruction of the laboring classes would arise in the economic sector. Involved in a discussion of bank confidence at the annual conference of the National Association for the Promotion of Social Science, Chadwick noted that (1878: 591): 'one great factor against the revival of confidence was want of confidence, occasioned by . . . the conduct of the wage classes, who could not be depended upon for the performance of contracts.' Presumably, labor injected instability by attempting to renegotiate contracts during business slowdowns. To counteract this, Chadwick proposed to enlighten the wage classes (1878: 592):

> by instruction in the elements of political economy, which would show them how much they were misled by their leaders, through disaster after disaster, which intelligence foresaw, and by their attempting to sustain prices against fallen market and reduce consumption, which was only to be stimulated, as all experience showed, by reduced prices.

In this, Chadwick argues that labor destabilizes the economy by attempting to maintain wages in the face of decreasing demand for the output. In modern terms, this behavior would tend to increase unemployment, but Chadwick gives no indication as to the exact nature of the problem that organized labor's strategy entailed.

On educational questions, Chadwick saw the greatest benefits of education arising in private terms. Explicitly counting educational expenses as a form of capital expenditure, Chadwick viewed education as a prerequisite to the improvement of labor's condition. Specifically, education was expected to increase incomes and decrease job insecurity. On these two points, Chadwick was quite clear. He was adamant concerning the necessity of education. Within a discussion on the introduction of steam power to agriculture, Chadwick (1859a: 63) cites the lack of education as an inhibitor of economic advance, noting that, 'unfortunately, in the present state of education in the agricultural districts, if higher wages were offered, the men were not to be found to do the work with the greatest amount of economy, and in order to attain this end, their education must be improved.'

In other words, the education of the workmen was required in order to achieve maximum efficiency in conjunction with (then) modern machinery. Furthermore, the education of the laboring population was to provide for future improvement as well as the current improvement of the condition of labor in an industrialized economy. Chadwick argues that (1865b: 27):

> if the principles of economical and social science which I have indicated in their relation with the means of intellectual, moral, and physical improvement, be

duly regarded and applied, the conditions of the manufacturing population, instead of being deplorable, will, with the increased and increasing stages derivable by the people from the extraordinary improvements in the mechanical arts for which they are required as ministers and the servants, be brought up to a high state of moral and social advancement.

But education is only a portion of the necessary conditions for the advancement of labor; the other part being the continued augmentation of the capital stock. In addition to increased employment opportunities resulting from education, the increased choice set serves to lessen the effect of the business cycle. On this point, Chadwick concludes (1865b: 12) that advantaged labor are:

> the better educated, who can write and inquire for themselves, and find out for themselves new outlets and sources of productive employment which no one else can find out for them, and who can read for themselves, and act upon written or printed instructions. The really well-trained, educated, and intelligent, are the best to bear distress.

The comparative advantage at bearing distress comes about not only because of the relative efficiency at job search but also for the reason that the worker is better suited to learning new manufacturing skills. In the case of employment changes resulting from technological unemployment, Chadwick believes that 'to these changes sound education is advantageous, as increasing the aptitudes of labourers to learn new employments' (1856a: 806).

Chadwick's position on the importance of education for the wage classes closely paralleled that of classical writers as a whole. This similarity is found in terms of both the social and the private benefits. O'Brien summarizes the classical stance on education as predominantly an investment process. O'Brien notes that the classical economists 'saw it both as an individual investment giving rise to differences in earnings and as a social investment which would increase economic growth through investment in human capital' (1975: 283). Adam Smith (1776 [1937]: 740) pioneered the view of education providing social capital concluding that:

> The state, however, derives no inconsiderable advantage from their [the laborer's] instruction. The more they are instructed, the less liable they are to the delusions of enthusiasm and superstition, which among ignorant nations, frequently occasion the most dreadful disorders. An instructed and intelligent people besides, are . . . less apt to be misled into any wanton or unnecessary opposition to the measures of government.

As one can see, this closely resembles Chadwick's stance. This view was not unique to Smith and Chadwick. Coats contends that, on the whole, the classical economists 'believed that as time passed the workers' violence would diminish as their intelligence grew' (Coats 1971: 155). The difference between Chadwick and Smith is in their accent. Chadwick stressed the human capital aspects of education, whereas Blaug (1978: 226) notes that Smith 'favored education more for purposes of moral improvement than for the development of productive skills.'

The education of the laboring population is one topic on which Chadwick and J.S. Mill were particularly in agreement. Both writers stressed the need for the wider distribution of newspapers and news magazines, that is, information. Mill (1848b [1965]: 763) took the attitude that the media was an excellent aid to education, writing that 'There is a spontaneous education going on in the minds of the multitude, which may be greatly accelerated and improved by artificial aids. The instruction obtained from newspapers and political tracts may not be the most solid kind of instructions, but it is an immense improvement upon none at all.' Mill, in speaking of the workers' behavior during a manufacturing crisis, remarks on the salubrious effect of the removal of the taxes on newspapers: 'It is not certain that their conduct would have been as rational and exemplary, if the distress had preceded the salutary measure of fiscal emancipation which gave existence to the penny press' (Mill 1848b [1965]: 763). Additionally, Mill and Chadwick professed parallel views on the need for education in the exercise of the sovereign franchise, but in a back-handed manner. Mill states that 'the too early attainment of political franchises by the least educated class might retard, instead of promoting, their improvement' (1848b [1965]: 764). Chadwick's philosophical foundation, utilitarianism, was clearly similar to some of the classical economists. Chadwick also followed the classical school's pattern of renouncing the mercantilist contempt for labor with occasional lapses into mercantilist philosophy. But Chadwick differed from most members of the classical school in the extreme importance which he attached to environmental factors as behavioral determinants. On the question of the Compensation Controversy, Chadwick took the opposing view to Ricardo and Marx, but was joined by Malthus, McCulloch, and J.S. Mill. Chadwick did take an unusual stance with respect to the long-run effects of manufacturing distress (believing that the net effect of the disturbance was positive). On the Irish Question, Chadwick sided with Senior in denying a negative effect on the British labor market. Finally, Chadwick and J.S. Mill were in agreement on the importance of education as a factor in the improvement of the laborer's condition.

The characterization of Chadwick as the oppressor of the lower classes (that R.A. Lewis first set out to dispel more than half a century ago) is less credible given Chadwick's overall stance on labor problems. The former characterization was obviously a holdover from the controversy generated by the Poor Law reform that Chadwick helped author, wherein he sponsored constraints on labor's behavior. Certainly, the person who pioneered the sanitary reform movement and the many policy and economic reforms designed to promote the interests of the laboring population is deserving of even greater recognition than that proposed by Lewis. In particular, it is quite clear that Chadwick well understood that there were both societal externalities to education and, more importantly, that both the return to and ultimate condition of labor depended on education as a vehicle to human capital. Here the gains are both internalized by the individual whose enhanced productivity is also a gain to society. This was not the only path to the betterment of the poor and laboring classes, as we will see in Chapter 8, but it was a critical element in helping potential welfare recipients, the destitute, and the working poor to become productive, income-earning members of society.

CONCLUSION

Edwin Chadwick was most certainly not the first or the only writer of the nineteenth century to develop a role for education in the economy. (Most of the classical writers remained Mandevillian in spirit if not explicitly in print.) He was, however, one of the first to argue that education had a central place in the development of human capital and hence in the economic growth of the nation. Education, considered from a social perspective, was a capital expenditure in many roles, not only in formal state-supported schools, but in particular in keeping abreast of contemporary events and opportunities (the taxes on which Chadwick abhorred). In particular, lower information costs alerted British workers to new and more productive opportunities in the labor market. Uniquely, moreover, Chadwick envisioned immigration as a goad to educational and productive improvement of the British laborers, arguing that the Irish were willing to work for wages refused by the British. Finally, Chadwick was probably the most prescient thinker linking advancing literacy and education to economic growth. Rejecting the Malthusian trap, Chadwick, much more than any of his counterparts, recognized a 'Beckerian' mechanism through which prosperity brought restraint. Increased prosperity, achievable through investments in human capital, reduced population pressure and contributed to economic growth. The engine of growth was of a different sort than the 'top-down' mechanics espoused by the majority of classical writers and 'supply-siders' today, setting Chadwick distinctly apart from his more famous contemporaries.

NOTES

1. A review of the 1832 Poor Law Commissions Report will dispel the notion that Chadwick was acting out of humanitarian feelings only. Chadwick's concern was consistently for technical efficiency, that is, obtaining maximum output for available resources.

2. However, Chadwick's desires to concentrate liability for *all* accidents on employers and to require government inspection and regulation of employee living and working conditions were rejected by Parliament. The focus of the Lewis paper is historical in content and approach, tracing Chadwick's observations of the conditions of the railway laborers and following Chadwick's involvement in lobbying for a Parliamentary Committee to investigate the matter. The Committee was eventually organized and Chadwick played a major role in arranging the testimony that was to be presented to the committee, proposing major reforms. The final report was to include all of Chadwick's original proposals. However, when presented to Parliament for legislative action, the final legislation significantly reduced the extent of the reforms to be implemented. The incident represented a partial victory for Chadwick, in that his efforts did result in the adoption of some of his proposals. On the legislative level, an alteration of industrial accident liability was enacted. Previously, the law prohibited the collection of damages by survivors of victims of fatal work-related accidents. Lewis (1950) notes that Chadwick had proposed the principle of employers' liability thirteen years before the 1846 pamphlet and that this rule of jurisprudence was one of the earliest proposals for Workmen's Compensation. Chadwick was not entirely defeated on the latter issues. His recommendations for housing standards, the method of wage payments (with more frequency and hence, smaller amounts), and moral uplifting (through religion and education) were voluntarily adopted by some of the railway companies.

3. Even Chadwick was unable totally to rid himself of mercantile preconceptions. In 1885, later in life, argued that 'It may be maintained as a principle of political economy that a poor man must make a poor master, and that he had better serve a rich one, a capitalist, i.e., a work finder and a wage finder; that a poor man never works for so bad a master as when he works for himself' (Chadwick 1885: 26). Contempt for the laborer by Chadwick was also the product of his tendency to moralize. It is reflected in a discussion of the use of 'common labourers' as locomotive engineers in the construction of railways: 'High wages, with such a class of men, only increase the danger [of construction accidents]; for it generally leads to an increase in drinking' (Chadwick 1846: 25).

4. Again, Mandeville (1723 [1924]: 311) is the best source of this extreme attitude: 'Abundance of hard and duty labour is to be done, and coarse living is to be complied with: Where shall we find a better Nursery for these necessities than the Children of the Poor? None certainly are nearer to it or fitter for it.'

5. Smith reasons (in modern terminology) that in good agricultural years, real wages are rising due to falling food prices and increased demand for labor by farmers expecting higher profits from larger harvests. During these good years, there is excess demand for labor allowing suppliers of labor a larger choice set and greater economic freedom. However, in depressed markets, opposing forces result in an excess supply of labor, with the resulting labor market described as follows: 'Masters of all sort, therefore, frequently make better bargains with their servants in dear than in cheap years, and find them more humble and dependent in the former than in the latter. They naturally, therefore, commend the former as more favourable to industry' (Smith 1776 [1937]: 83). Hence, employers are reacting to conditions which promote their self-interest when they rationalize the adage that workers perform best when paid the least.

6. Mill's goal was intergenerational equality of opportunity. His view was that 'all must start fair,' as in a handicapped bowling game. Like Chadwick, moreover, Mill wanted to try to 'handicap' the working classes by providing incentives to save and progress but, most importantly, Mill advocated a high estate tax on grounds that each generation 'start fair.' He defended *intervivos* gifts and endowments but believed that ruin

generally accompanied the intergenerational transfer of great wealth (see Ekelund and Tollison 1976; Ekelund and Walker 1996; Chapter 9).

7. A certain optimism, characteristic of Chadwick, is revealed here. Chadwick never doubted the ability of technology to increase production, whether the technology affected the manufacturing or the agricultural sector. This outlook of continued economic growth is radically different from the stationary states as included in the economic models of Ricardo and J.S. Mill.

8. In the works of many British classical economists and certainly in Chadwick's, the reader will detect a strong feeling of nationalism. This is especially true in the case of Chadwick's attitudes respecting the relative stature of the English laborer and industry. Chadwick describes the state of the English textile industry as being able to import Indian cotton, produce a superior product, and export the finished cloth to India with the result that 'the labour of the poor Hindoo spinstress, and also that of the poor, rentless, and taxless Hindoo weaver, is undersold . . .' (1865b: 2). In Chadwick's opinion, the superiority of the English laborer was an undeniable fact and a major determinant of English manufacturing supremacy. He writes (1865b: 4):

> The great extent of production and consumption could not have been attained, and sustained under difficulties, and have prospered by the mechanical inventions and appliances, having got into the hands of a population whose power of patient steady work, especially the females, is by foreign workmasters admitted to be unsurpassed, if it be anywhere equaled.

As further proof of the superiority of the English worker, Chadwick notes that '. . . the lowest paid labour that has been tried, that of the Hindoo and the Fellah of Egypt, even with British machinery and British taskmasters, has everywhere hither to failed' (1865b: 5). Chadwick makes what he would deem a rational test of the hypothesis that British workers are superior by comparing performance holding other-factors (that is, capital and management) constant. However, in keeping with his views on the nature of mankind, Chadwick does warn against making generalizations based solely on race or national origin. He writes (1865b: 7):

> Nothing is easier, or more common, than to say of a particular class of men, that they are of a particular race – i.e., our own – and, therefore, infer that all is good about them; that another class are of another race, and, therefore, that they are essentially inferior, bad, and hopeless.

Having reduced the importance of genetic characteristics, this leaves one to suppose that the superiority of English labor is due to environmental factors. Chadwick does go on to express admiration for various clans of continental workmen, but he does maintain the overall superiority of British laborers.

9. Also see Blaug (1978: 196–7).

10. The literature suggests that the expected return to a diversified portfolio is increased by selecting investment opportunities that are negatively correlated.

11. Coats (1971: 158) notes that: 'Despite their belief in the influences of environment on character, the classical economists could not agree about the prospects of reforming the Irish. Some feared that Irish immigrants would contaminate the English labour force and favoured immigration restrictions.'

7. Criminal justice institutions, police, and the common pool

INTRODUCTION

Chadwick's quest to inculcate utilitarian principles into economic policy at all levels revolved, as we have seen, around palliatives for 'market failure.' And indeed, Chadwick envisioned market failure everywhere. The problems of decreasing costs and natural monopoly required, in his view, nationalization and franchising of the railways to private contractors (Chapter 4). Other types of market failure – high and asymmetric information costs and negative externalities – required urban franchising of local businesses including funeral supplies and the nationalization of graveyards (Chapter 5). Yet another possible form of market failure applied to the 'market' for the provision of crime prevention and judicial services. These services or parts of them were riddled with what it called the common pool problem – a problem whereby the property rights to some resources are non-existent or poorly defined, so that by default, anyone may use the resource, up to some limit of course. The result in many cases is the 'overuse' of the resource and its total or partial destruction.

Chadwick, who was concerned with crime and justice issues *throughout* his career, addressed a particularly modern problem in that failures with the contemporary criminal justice system are legion. Economists have sought to analyze criminal behavior (Becker 1968; Becker and Stigler 1974; Stigler 1970), economic efficiency in the law (Ehrlich 1973), and a host of matters relating to crime (drugs, gun control, and so on). A myriad of issues and problems are still in debate. While the mass of this literature has focused on crime deterrence and optimal enforcement (Polinsky and Shavell 2000), an interesting and interrelated line of analysis has sought insights into contemporary problems, issues, and characterizations in the study of the evolution of the received system.

Quasi-historical studies of the criminal justice system have centered on how institutional arrangements have affected incentives and outcomes within the system over the long span of English and US history. Some modern analytical work (Benson 1990; 1994; 1998), relying on the classic historical analyses of Pollock and Maitland (1895), Holdsworth (1903

[1966]), and others, evaluates the evolution of the system and the incentives that inure to ancient and modern systems. In doing so, and while recognizing free rider problems within the system, this perspective suggests how received institutions might be altered to produce crime prevention and greater efficiency within the overall criminal justice structure today.[1]

This chapter analyzes and evaluates Edwin Chadwick's early and powerful discussion of the institutions of Anglo-Saxon criminal justice and procedure within the context of common pool problems. His analysis is of high interest since the system he describes is largely unchanged to the present day.[2] Chadwick, premier utilitarian policymaker and analyst of nineteenth-century England, as we have seen in earlier chapters, was also a passionate and gifted legal scholar whose interests led him to analyze and contribute to policy debates over the received legal system.[3] With reams of interviews and evidence in hand, Chadwick unceasingly lobbied Parliament to completely alter the police and criminal justice systems (see, for example, his efforts in 1839b [1968]).

Particular aspects of Chadwick's lifelong quest have been discussed previously. Hébert (1977), in an excellent exposé, discussed Chadwick's psychological-economic foundations for criminal perpetrators' incentives to commit crimes, and discussed the probabilistic calculus of criminals, the preyed upon, and law enforcement. We discuss those matters in the present chapter, but Chadwick's contributions to interlocking problems of crime and criminal procedure within a common pool-open access system, which will be given special treatment here, have not been uncovered and analyzed. In particular, we focus on Chadwick's prognosis concerning the public provision of the criminal justice system as it evolved in England in his time. (That system was imported into the United States.) We will see how Chadwick offered theoretical support for the criminal justice system-as-publicly-supplied good view rather than return to a private system as had existed in early (Anglo-Saxon) England. Further, we develop Chadwick's goal of crime *prevention* by interrelated incentive alterations to the received system of common pool access, public policing, and lawyer-court-government rent-seeking. In particular we emphasize Chadwick's policy recommendations for the reform of criminal procedure in a little known paper on the subject he wrote in 1841.

Chadwick's views on these matters are not only of historical interest but have clear implications for the analysis and reform of contemporary institutions. All systems of justice have costs and benefits. In order to assess systems, a maximand or goal must be identified. Chadwick's primary goal, as is the case in some modern studies, was to prevent crime. As he wrote in 1829, 'A good police would be one well-organized body of men acting upon a system of precautions, to prevent crimes and public calamities;

to preserve public peace and order' (1829: 252). Within the context of this goal we show that Chadwick: (1) identifies the evolved system as a common pool; (2) presents a rationale for a centralized public provision of the entire justice system to deal with common pool problems because; (3) he believed that the system he observed, so like modern systems, misplaced property rights and incentives for crime prevention, creating dissipations within the common pool access to policing and other criminal justice services. Although Chadwick eschewed private solutions including those entertained today, he argued that particular alterations in property rights institutions affecting the criminal justice and other legal and societal institutions could affect desirable changes. In particular, altering property rights could lower the cost of participating in the system to obtain necessary cooperation of involved individuals in the justice system and in crime prevention. This analysis, as we show, speaks to some of today's problems and informs them with possible solutions to increase the efficiency of both policing and the courts in the criminal justice system.

EARLY EVOLUTION OF RIGHTS AND LAW

The early Anglo-Saxon system of private law enforcement, derived from the Germanic *wergeld* (or 'man price') system, was a feature of many early societies and is described by a number of classic legal scholars (for example, Maine 1861 [1986]). Chadwick interpreted the system through the prism of incentives and property rights.[4] The Anglo-Saxon invasion (*circa* 600–750 AD) replaced the tribal system of English agriculture (based on 'commons') and with it, wrought important changes in societal organization.[5] Under the Anglo-Saxon territorial system, each shire had its own particular system, complicated somewhat by additional law enforcement by noblemen and through churches in their own courts. According to Benson (1994), the system initially contained critical characteristics leading to relative efficiency: (a) injured parties – in the early days civil and criminal offenses were treated equally – were entitled to restitution; and (b) the system was able to elicit cooperation of non-victim witnesses and fellow enforcers (the hundred) with the promise of reciprocation or through various punitive measures (for example, ostracizing or 'shunning'). Declarations of 'outlawry' and actual and potential 'blood-feuds' were inducements to settle claims. This was, of course, an implicit contract between individuals for the pursuit and prosecution of malfeasors and, according to most accounts, commitments were credible enough to make the system work up to about the eleventh century. Under this system (Benson 1994: 252, citing Sir James Stephen 1883 [1963]: 53), crimes against the state did not exist, but most of the offenses detailed in modern criminal codes were defined as illegal. Importantly, policing was a *private* rather than a publicly provided good in early medieval England.

Monarchical government, intensified by the Normal conquest, significantly altered the system around the eleventh century. Rent-seeking by monarchs gradually encroached upon the private system as monarchs perceived the profitability potential of intruding on the private criminal justice system. 'Outlawry' required forfeiture of goods to the king (Bentham 1776–82 [1962]: 512) and violations became a new source of royal revenues through fines on malfeasors, most particularly through violations of the 'King's peace.' Slowly a frankpledge system developed and the private system evolved into a publicly provided good. With this gradual transformation, private restitution was eliminated. There was a general diminution in incentives for voluntary cooperation among the populace, which led to the institution of a local frankpledge by the Normans.[6]

The new Norman system was coercive and relied on penalties, sometimes collectively levied on entire communities, to elicit enforcement and court participation of citizens. All free men were required to be in the tythe. As householders, they were required to provide joint suretyship (frankpledge) as part of the tything. They agreed that they would bring to justice any offender as well as pay for the expenses incurred by the offence. The development of Justices of the Peace slowly evolved from the Shire-reeve or sheriff. The tything-men, now parish constables, reported to the Justice of the Peace (Stead 1985). In general, these men, constables, and Justices of the Peace, were able-bodied citizens appointed yearly to an *unpaid* position, which was in addition to normal duties required to maintain a livelihood.

Law enforcement authorities consisted of the unpaid parish constables and magistrates or Justices of the Peace at the beginning of the eighteenth century, with larger towns incorporating nightwatchmen and the beadle (the constable's assistant). With the tremendous growth and mobility in population, this form of authority was threatened. It became difficult to monitor the rapid changes and the increased size of the population. Constables were appointed yearly and duties were rotated through the community. According to Tobias (1972a), people bought out the duty and by the nineteenth century, metropolitan parishes began a system of pay to encourage people to work as watchmen.

The Frankpledge System Evolves

Two primary duties were assigned to the Justices of the Peace before the nineteenth century. They were to carry out judicial duties in the form of settling cases, conduct preliminary investigations, and grant warrants; and they were responsible for public affairs such as restoring order in a riot. But the frankpledge system as it existed at the beginning of the nineteenth century was doomed for a number of reasons. First, the Justices of the Peace and other magistrates and enforcers were unpaid and lacked the incentive to engage in crime enforcement or, more importantly, crime prevention. Opportunistic behavior, malfeasance, and shirking riddled the system, and were encouraged by the structure of police at the local level.[7]

Second, incentives for private participation – witnessing, accusations by those injured, and crime prevention – were drained from the system by government takeover and the generalized tax financing of criminal justice. Third, emphasis shifted from crime *prevention* under a pre-rent-seeking, pre-frankpledge private system, to law *enforcement* within a common pool, as Benson (1994) has observed. Government rent-seeking and effective takeover of justice within the late medieval and early mercantile English system did create incentives for victims and all potential victims to underinvest in the common pool and to invest in the private benefits from the system. Market failure was, in effect, created by the rent-seeking monarchy when the private Anglo-Saxon system was abandoned. But, as Chadwick emphasized, problems of the frankpledge system as it had evolved over the early Industrial Revolution were exacerbated by other forces.

Transactions Costs, Criminal Justice, and Institutional Change

The blatant failure of the frankpledge system – now a common pool problem – became obvious as the Industrial Revolution proceeded. As Edwin Chadwick argued in his second published essay, 'Preventive Police' (1829: 253, added emphasis),[8] the early applications of the frankpledge system were relatively efficient:

> It must be acknowledged that the early state of the general police of this country possessed a degree of efficiency highly characteristic of a military people [presumably referring to the Germanic tribes and early Anglo-Saxon practices]. The organization of the force, which may be termed the police, in counties and hundreds: the system of frankpledge, by which each man was rendered responsible for the conduct of his neighbour at a time when that neighbour was always known, and when his course of life might always in some degree be controlled by the pledge: the appointment of honorary officers at a period when *the duties to be performed were few and simple, and the value of time amongst the labouring and trading classes of the community was inconsiderable*: the enactment obliging the constable or the chief officer of a subdivision to raise the hue and cry, and the inhabitants to join with horse and arms and their best means in the pursuit of a felon – a duty which from the excitement it afforded would mostly be

fulfilled with alacrity; must be admitted to have formed a system well adapted to the wants of our ancestors and to the rude state of society in which they lived.

But Chadwick believed that the evolution of English society and increased population, presumably with or without private restitution, rendered the fundamental institutional structure of police inadequate. The central supply-side reasons for failure were the problems related to time, and transactions and information costs:

> the changed condition of society requires a new combination of means to attain the ends of a good police. Labour has become extensively subdivided. The time and the attention of those who are usually called upon to perform the honorary duties of the constabulary force, have become more valuable, and those duties complicated and burdensome. In thinly peopled neighborhoods and small towns every individual is known, and his acts are subjected to the observation of his neighbors. As population advances, the opportunities for observation diminish. (Chadwick 1829: 252)

Whatever the extent of these costs, however, Chadwick seriously under-estimated the growing virulence of rent-seeking tactics by Norman crown interests. As Klerman (2001) and Benson (1998) have argued, the forms of Crown rent-seeking vis-à-vis restitution and other factors were prob-ably sufficient to doom the efficient operation of the frankpledge system. Klerman, using regression results from 12 English counties, finds dramatic fluctuations in the level of private restitution throughout the first full century of Norman control (thirteenth century), and the main reason was the changing judicial treatment of private settlements. A primary reason for activating private settlements was that further threat of prosecu-tion was eliminated. As the thirteenth century wore on, Norman judges changed this rule, demanding further prosecution so that the Crown could get a 'take.' When they did, private prosecutions fell dramatically. Criminals were, in consequence, far less likely to be pursued, although 'informal' settlements might have been made with formal prosecution used as a threat.

Incentive change, moreover, did not rest solely on the elimination of restitution. Benson (1998, Chapter 9) clearly notes that the rent-seeking apparatus of the Norman monarchs included a penalty 'tax' for 'false prosecutions,' so that the rents were collected whether or not prosecution was successful. Furthermore, while restitution was the aim of victims, they had to bear other costs as well, such as court fees, costs of witnesses, and so on.

Chadwick did not recognize these deficiencies of the early frankpledge system, but rather laid emphasis on the costs wrought by institutional change and concomitant increased transaction costs within evolving English society. And institutional changes put onerous pressures on the system as it existed at the beginning of the nineteenth century. The English population had grown dramatically over the two previous centuries,[9] and urbanization over the period was dramatic (Tobias 1972b; Walvin 1988: 8). Settlement laws, whereby welfare receivers had to remain in the parish of their birth, reinforced the lack of labor mobility and increased poor rates, as recognized by Adam Smith (1776 [1937]: 135, 437). No wonder there was clamor, no more loudly than among prominent classical economists, for reform of the system (which ultimately came about in 1834).

Within this milieu Chadwick recognized that the institutional incentives created by publicly provided law enforcement were a criminal's dream. He in fact argues that any foreigner coming to England as an observer could view the English institution of criminal justice and bring forward 'plausible reasons for believing that it was craftily framed by a body of professional depredators, upon a calculation of the best means of obtaining from society, with security to themselves, the greatest quantity of plunder' (1829: 254). Chadwick recognized that the failures of the frankpledge system were not the result of the ancient system itself, but from a bastardized approach that was not truly private. The creation of a common pool through Crown rent-seeking had created perverse incentives that all but eliminated efficiency in all aspects of criminal justice.[10] As Chadwick put it, the English system (as then constituted) '. . . does not use the adequate means either to obtain full information from the public [concerning crimes], or to conciliate their aid' (1829: 307).

THE ENGLISH CRIMINAL JUSTICE SYSTEM, *CIRCA* 1830–41

The breakdown of the modified frankpledge system was becoming fairly obvious long before Chadwick's time, and certain policies were introduced to help close the 'incentives gap' as it existed in the late eighteenth century. In 1748 Henry Fielding, the magistrate of Bow Street from 1748 to 1754, set up six constables with outstanding records as 'thief-takers.'[11] These 'Bow Street Runners,' initially paid out of Fielding's salary, were the first full-time professional detective agency, establishing headquarters at Scotland Yard at Charing Cross.[12] Later, a horse patrol of eight men was activated in London and covered an area of 20 miles in and around Charing Cross. In 1782, a 68-man foot patrol was established, amid incessant calls for a professional public police force for urban crime control among some observers (Hanway 1775). Seven police justices were added in 1792 under the *Middlesex Justices Act*, a reform instituting paid magistrates and constables with support of government funds.[13] Police in London were strengthened in quantity over the early nineteenth century, but mobility of depredators and lack of crime prevention continued to be a central problem. In 1822 Robert Peel was elected Home Secretary and he worked steadily to reform the system. After a grisly series of murders (the Ratcliffe highway murders),[14] Select Committees of Parliament met in 1812, 1816, 1818, 1822, and 1828, resulting in calls for reform (Tobias 1972a).

Chadwick's direct involvement with Peel's Select Committee of 1828 is the subject of some controversy,[15] but the fact that he devised 'principles of action' to close up the gaps in private incentives to crime prevention and societal protection by 1829 is beyond doubt. Chadwick focused on *economic* crime – robberies – calling other kinds 'indoor crimes.'[16] His foundation and aim was to underline the institutional changes that would alter marginal incentives of perpetrators (thieves), and may be summarized as Marginal Cost of Criminal Acts equals the Marginal Benefits of Criminal Acts or where the Marginal Benefits of Robbery equals the sum of the probabilities of Apprehension, Conviction, and Punishment (including its severity). The kind of marginal calculation described by Chadwick is the modern one underlying the 'economics of crime' as outlined by Issac Ehrlich, George Stigler, and Gary Becker. This is reported by Hébert (1977) and it is the foundation for contemporary economic research in criminal enforcement. Chadwick established three overarching principles regarding police, enforcement, and crime prevention in 1829, elaborating on them over the rest of his career (Chadwick 1863 [1887]; 1876–77 [1887]; 1881 [1887]; 1887b). Chadwick explains his three axioms:

> First. That every arrangement which renders increased exertion necessary to obtain property illegally, is so much gained to the prevention of crime . . . Secondly, That every arrangement which increases the difficulty of converting to the use of the depredator, property dishonestly acquired, is so much gained in diminution of the motives to commit crime . . . Thirdly, That every arrangement which diminishes the chances of the personal escape of the depredator, is so much gained in the diminution of the motive to commit crime. (1829: 272–4)

Some of the particular institutional changes that Chadwick attached to these principles, both in his earliest essay and in others, have been discussed at some length elsewhere (Hébert 1977). Probabilities ruled here, because as Chadwick noted (1829: 274), 'the doctrine of changes is applicable to every operation of a police, and when we say, that the chances of escape have diminished, it is in general to be understood that crime has diminished.' (The 'doctrine of changes' is of course probability.) We simply list some of them below:

- Chadwick clearly understood the reciprocal aspect of economic crime. That is, he adjured individuals to protect themselves and others of the community, reducing the marginal benefit from criminal activity (1829: 272).[17] Thus, the marginal benefit to criminal behavior could be reduced by potential victims, given the probability of victimization;
- Chadwick supported the development of new inks and paper to prevent forgeries together with post-dated checks – another reduction in criminal benefit to the thief;
- Chadwick strongly urged increased information through establishment of publicly provided registers for the recovery of stolen property. According to Chadwick, 'a police should, as regards expense, be conducted, so far as possible, on the principle of an association of the public to insure each other from loss by depredation' (1829: 273). This included a publicly funded *Hue and Cry Gazette* with as wide a dissemination as possible;
- Chadwick recommended 'random' enforcement on highways (where an officer may appear anywhere), lamps, turnpikes, and the improvement of by-roads. These all made recognition of felons and capture after recognition easier, increasing the probability of apprehension;
- Chadwick supported technological improvements that would increase the probability of apprehension. Chadwick cites the ability to move police quickly to areas of criminal activity as reducing the probability of crime. He avers: 'A thief driven into a strange neighbourhood is like a buccaneer driven to adventure upon a strange coast' (1829: 275). Chadwick knew and noted that technological improvements such as the invention of photography would aid police in capturing criminals. Later in 1887, he urged the employment of tricycles to increase the probability of apprehension, a technology that anticipated the modern squad car (1887b);[18]
- Chadwick advocated administrative changes in police organization, such as combining police, fire, and other services to reduce time costs and to achieve other economies (1829: 290; 1876–77 [1887]).

While Chadwick wanted to reduce crime and increase crime prevention with every means possible, he was not in favor of increasing the level of punishment. Capital punishment was common in the eighteenth and early nineteenth centuries, and many (including Fielding) defended the practice for a number of offenses. Chadwick did not believe that the practice had had much effect on economic crimes such as petty theft,[19] but he was aware of the tradeoff between severity of punishment and certainty of punishment. He believed, after consultations with convicted felons and empirical research, that certainty of punishment was a stronger deterrent, a finding that corresponds to modern research. This is a major reason, we believe, for Chadwick's acute interest in reform of the entire criminal justice system, including court and legal procedure.

CHADWICK'S ANALYSIS OF CRIME AND THE COMMON POOL

Chadwick's hold on the problems of police and criminal justice was greater and larger than simply suggesting reforms to marginally change the probability of criminal behavior. He fully understood that the whole institution as it had evolved from the earliest private system through the frankpledge system created an open-access common pool of the entire criminal justice system. As Benson explained (1994), there are weak positive incentives to cooperate with *public sector* law enforcement because publicly produced aspects (for example, some deterrence) are treated as free-access common pools.[20] Any private individual will underinvest in the maintenance of these kinds of benefits and tend to overinvest in those aspects of the system that produce internalized private benefits.[21] Clearly the government extraction of rents and the takeover of the justice system, the elimination or curtailment of restitution, and the emergence of an industrial economy with rising populations and urbanization, created the necessity for public provision of criminal justice services in Chadwick's England. Chadwick recognized, however, that the then-constituted system was incapable of performing or even approaching the first most desirable characteristic of justice which, in his view, was crime prevention. The main defect of the English system was 'that it does not use adequate means either to obtain full information from the public, or to conciliate their aid' (Chadwick 1829: 307) – essentially the problem described by Benson (1990; 1994).

Victim and witness cooperation was difficult or impossible to get because of high costs imposed on victims and the paucity of benefits and possible net costs to witnessing in the common pool. For victims, the absence of compensation did not act to 'insure each other from loss by depredation,' as did the frankpledge system that initially included compensation and restitution. Rather:

> by allowing no compensation, and making parties pay the expense of all proceedings for the recovery of stolen property, they [the public] are taught to view the crime as a matter with which they may act as best suit their own interests, without reference to the public, which can claim of them no sacrifice, since, in this instance, at least, it has failed to perform its first duty of giving protection. (Chadwick 1829: 273)

Both victims and non-victims weigh costs and benefits, a point with obvious and profound implications for contemporary policy.

For their part, the police had no incentive to collect or supply information on theft. However, 'an interest is silently created in the officers to search after no other than rich prizes' (Chadwick 1829: 276), when private and public awards are available. Little enforcement, let alone prevention, could be expected in rural districts (with unpaid enforcers under the modified frankpledge) or in cities where 'the salaries of police officers are below those of ordinary mechanics' and where 'no reward can be hoped for, no exertion will take place, and . . . no profit can be derived by them from the prevention of the great mass of depredation' (Chadwick 1829: 277). Crime is encouraged, in other words, by the rational behavior of both victims and police in the common pool.

The Reforms of 1841

The deficiencies of the common pool criminal justice system are no more apparent than in the kind of criminal procedure followed in Chadwick's day and, to a large degree, in our own. They are, furthermore, then and now, riddled with rent-seeking behavior within the court system. In a virtually unknown essay appearing in the January–April 1841 issue of the *Westminster Review* entitled 'Licence of Counsel: Criminal Procedure,' Chadwick takes the entire English legal system to task for contributing to a lack of crime prevention within the common pool.[22]

Chadwick's overall maximand was crime *prevention*. As noted in the previous section, he examined policies to increase the probability of apprehension, but in his little-known analysis of criminal procedure he aimed at maximizing the probability of conviction under constraint. The constraint, as Chadwick clearly noted (1841: 19 *et passim*), was to simultaneously avoid Type I and Type II errors – to maximize the probability of convicting the guilty while simultaneously minimizing the probability of prosecuting and convicting the innocent – in plainer language a Type I error is the probability that a guilty person would escape punishment (go free) and a Type II error is the probability that a person innocent of a crime would be found guilty and punished. Chadwick's thinking was proceeding along these lines in his earlier essay when he noted that 'simplicity, expedition, certainty, and freedom from expense, are the most desirable qualities for penal as well as other procedure' (1829: 294).

The problem – one not uncommon or unrecognized in modern day British and United States systems – is that people will not participate in justice or crime prevention due (in part) to the costs imposed by the criminal justice system by the nature of the court procedures.[23] Many will underinvest in the open-access common pool benefits when returns are neutral (as contrasted to the system of restitution under the *wergeld* and early frankpledge systems). The system practically collapses when the necessary participants bear a net cost. As Chadwick explains:

> It is said we abound in mercy, but we give so much of it to the guilty, that we have none to spare for the innocent. Criminal justice has been made to vacilate in this country between two sets of blind presumptions, – the ancient one, which presumed guilt in all who were accused, and the modern one, which presumes that all who are accused are innocent, and which even after conviction, over-looks the party injured and the tendency of the crime, and bestows unbounded sympathy on the criminal. (1841: 17)

The reasons were clear to Chadwick: (a) a labyrinthine formal judicial system, riddled by (b) an evolved judicial procedural that did nothing but increase costs to people participating in the system, overseen (c) by rent-seeking court interests, particularly lawyers. Before turning to the proposed institutional changes for both police and the evolved judicial system, we consider his view on each of these factors.

The Institutional Judicial System

The vagaries of the evolved English criminal justice system were already much on Chadwick's mind in 1829. Particularly, he alleged criminals could easily escape conviction through the sieve of the criminal justice system. Chadwick's careful study of the system led him to argue that in the great majority of criminal cases, four investigations had to take place. The first was before a magistrate, the second before the clerk of the peace, the third before a grand jury, and the fourth before a petty jury and the judges. (This is of course similar to contemporary procedure.) Most meritorious, in view of simplicity and expedition, was the examination before magistrates. It was at this stage that Chadwick thought the best and most probable chances for efficient justice to occur, and for amending judicial institu-tions, existed.[24] But a hearing before a magistrate, prior to the institution of reforms, was not the end of criminal procedure, only a bad beginning as the institution then existed.

From the very first level, victims and witnesses were taxed in the criminal justice system. The magistrate, often of little skill, was not open twenty-four hours a day, and when he did see witnesses giving testimony, examined them piecemeal. The latter practice, according to Chadwick, was an open invitation to *ex parte* influences by the accused and his or her counsel. Likewise, the in-place system (*circa* 1829) required that evidence be restated before a clerk of court who framed the indictment, requiring witnesses to spend one or two more day's attendance at court, and again allowing the possibility of bribes by the accused or his or her counsel. This practice, where time lapsed between the apprehension and the actual framing of an indictment, permitted errors and bribery to enter the justice system, increasing the probability of a guilty party going free (that is, a Type I error).

Once more, the full costs of seeking justice or giving information came to the fore:

> [T]here are few persons who have been engaged in making any legal or other investigations in which the examination of witnesses is involved, who have not experienced the frequency with which persons of respectable character will evade the disclosure of facts known to be in their possession, when it is made apparent that they may be called upon to give their testimony upon them in a court of justice. When an outcry, or sounds indicative of violence, or distress, or suffering, is heard in the streets, it is generally only the young, or the labouring classes, who are seen to yield assistance; the educated or the sensitive ride past or hurry from the spot, for fear of being drawn in as witnesses and forced on that repulsive stage, a court of law. (Chadwick 1841: 2)

Public outcry over the mild sentences handed down by magistrates, sometimes for serious crimes, are also explained: 'summary conviction is the one earnestly preferred and sought by the party injured, and the punishment is inflicted by the magistrate in the consciousness that to send the criminal to trial before a jury is to inflict another and a severe injury on the prosecutor' (Chadwick 1841: 2).

If abuses of victims and witnesses were common at the entry levels of the English justice system, they were legion under both the grand and petit jury systems. Here, Chadwick takes on the fundamentals of the English judiciary (and the US judiciary as well). He had already attacked the grand jury system as a 'hotbed of perjury' in his earlier assessment of 1829. The grand jury's 'secrecy is useless, for the culprit is in custody: they save no imprisonment to the innocent man, for without this process he would be as speedily enlarged by trial' (Chadwick 1829: 298), but worse, witnesses were in effect free to perjure themselves and to alter testimony from that given to magistrates and clerks, since they were secured by the oath of secrecy taken by the jurors. Professionals (lawyers for the defendants) are clearly able to take advantage of 'a timid female, a nervous man, or an ignorant lout,' and skillful solicitors would take any occasion to go before the grand jury as a witness to slant the case with particular portions of evidence and secure release for their clients. And, according to Chadwick, 'the most unskilful of the police magistrates can scarcely fail, with the aid of their clerks, to exercise a better discretion, than a grand jury, as to the propriety of a commitment' (1829: 299).

Abusive Lawyers

Legal vituperation, false accusation of witnesses, and the influence of 'monopoly judges' riddled the whole justice system, and particularly within the jury system. The police are derided and were the common subjects of 'disgraceful and unmeasured attack by the prisoners' counsel in our penal courts' (Chadwick 1841: 9). Chadwick claimed that the police were routinely pilloried as 'inquisitorial ruffians,' 'miscreants,' and 'bloodhounds.' Lawyers within this system were in an ideal position and had incentives to hoodwink and mislead through casting aspersions on the police and witnesses and by 'assaults upon the fears of the jury.' Through no fault of their own, *unpaid* jurors were easy to confuse. Jurors were generally 'untutored minds which are commonly called upon to exercise the new and, to them, difficult functions of weighing evidence and deciding on the fate of a fellow-creature' (Chadwick 1841: 11).

These legal practices permitting and encouraging Type I errors (non-conviction of the guilty) were, in Chadwick's belief, the result of English legal traditions. Prisoners were protected from laws against self-incrimination, and that encouraged litigation and almost guaranteed the spread and defense of falsehood by counsel and perjury by defendants. The system permitted lawyers to suppress the truth even if they knew their clients were guilty but, according to Chadwick (1841: 14), they went much further:

> If the *suppressio veri* be permitted as the privilege of counsel, and the Magna Charta of delinquents in England, still we must venture to propose as an innovation that the freedom of defence should be restricted so far as it may be conceived to consist in the *suggestio falsi*. Inasmuch as the law restricts the freedom of an accused person from the use of such physical means of defending himself against capture as a knife, so we think the use of foul weapons of mental assault and injury, such as perjury and false imputations on parties, may be beneficially forbidden to the prisoner, and, by consequence, to his counsel.

Lawyers commonly engaged in highly aggressive and, to Chadwick, immoral behavior as a result of these incentives.

Rent-Seeking by Judges and Lawyers

The attempt to provide efficiency in the court and justice system was thwarted at every turn by rent-seeking judges and lawyers.[25] Despite attempts at reform through Parliament, self-interested judges and lawyers were adamant defenders of the status quo. When an extension of the 'summary punishment' (or in modern terms, 'summary judgment') system for juvenile delinquents was proposed legislatively, the Old Bailey bar was 'on the same side with their lucre,' defending the right of jury trials and emphasizing the dangers to the innocent.[26] The legislature demurred. Again, when an accused person – one who even might be shown innocent in statements to a magistrate and be freed – is advised by counsel, he or she was always advised by an attorney and counsel 'not to disclose his defence' and 'to reserve himself until his trial'(Chadwick 1841: 19). This high tax on the innocent, who must be committed and endure a trial, is supported by legal interest groups. Opines Chadwick:

> Any lawyer who would prefer justice '*instanter*' at the first stage of the procedure favours a course in which some five or ten guineas of costs are obtainable, instead of a prolonged course of several hazardous stages, from which twenty, thirty, fifty, or a hundred guineas of emolument are obtained, or more, according to the means of the accused; who, independently of any question of guilt or innocence, may always in this position be termed 'a victim of the law. (1841: 19)

The substitution of a 'pure procedure' for the extant system of English jurisprudence:

> which gives to the ninety per cent of clear and undoubted cases of guilt, defences on such false assumptions of persecuted innocence, and of malice and dishonesty of witnesses . . . would present to the imagination of the practitioner the apparent loss of ninety per cent of his business . . . Summary convictions before the professional magistrate would, it must be confessed, occasion a dire diminution of business and professional emoluments in the superior courts; and we might put it to the gentlemen who practise in them, whether they are competent to judge calmly of anything which may so powerfully affect them. (Chadwick 1841: 19)[27]

Litigation, as Neely (1980: 182–3) portrayed the matter, is the 'bread and butter' of litigants and is a 'bonanza' to the 'tens of thousands' of new lawyers who graduate each year. Lawyers, then and now, have every incentive to fight reforms that would reduce their incomes. There is, in short, incentive incompatibility between efficient application of justice and the self-interested motives within the legal system.

Judges in the system had to share the blame. Their 'business' in the superior courts was a function of the long and protracted procedure through which 'justice' was obtained. Payment by the case had earlier led to corruption of judges and the courts, as Adam Smith observed in 1763 (Smith 1896 [1964]: 48–9). Chadwick believed, further, that judges had few incentives to protect witnesses who were unjustly and unfairly pilloried by counsel with incentives to suggest falsehoods and attack character. They were clearly part of the interest group that rejected reform of the system. In this system there was no real protection of the innocent, and the threat to the guilty was minimal.

THE COMMON POOL AND CHADWICK'S REFORM PROPOSALS

The English system of justice, as Chadwick found it and as still exists to a large extent today in England and the United States, maximized the possibilities of both Type I and Type II errors. The overall system, as constituted, had this effect and, more importantly, guaranteed little or no emphasis on crime prevention and efficient justice. Further, as Chadwick emphasized early in the nineteenth century, victims, witnesses, and potential victims all have an incentive to underinvest resources in the justice system.[28]

The Police System (Prevention and Apprehension)

Some of the institutional changes designed to apprehend criminals, along with technological improvement (such as tricycles) and administrative changes, have been mentioned by other writers (Hébert 1977). However, Chadwick's crime statistics and recommendations for changing the police system have not received attention. First, he used casual empiricism and parliamentary statistics to show that, for all the lack of organization, police establishments (*circa* 1820–29) in both Paris and London were far more effective in making arrests than were parish officers. But, Chadwick argued (1829: 288), only 'naked pecuniary interests can alone be relied upon as motives of constant and sure operation.' Further, if these interests were carefully and skillfully adjusted, they would act with the 'certainty of gravitation.' Rewards, both public and private, were not discounted, but they did lead to selective incentives on the part of the police.

The central issue is, then as now, how to *measure* success at crime prevention so that incentives would be effective.[29] Chadwick thought it could be done. One method would be to supply all police districts with accurate information on crime committed in their districts (for example, through means such as the *Hue and Cry Gazette*), making officers responsible for any increase of crime within their districts not followed by an increase in detection. But another method (Chadwick 1829: 288–9) held more promise:

> The amount of these services in the prevention of crime, might be determined by comparing the amount of depredations committed in their district, with that of others in which property was similarly situated, e.g. by comparing the burglaries and minor depredations occurring in one district, or one street of a district with another district or street; as Fleet-street with the Strand, etc. Their services in the detection of crime might be determined by comparing the number of their detections with the returns of crime committed.

Chadwick here envisions an *ex post* component to the pay of police, creating incentives to *prevent* crime. Further, he notes that such a system is not unlike common practices in private businesses and that the same method would bear fruit in the prevention of crime.[30] Adequate pay and administrative changes such as the institution of office ranks and lifetime tenure and pensions (as in the military), plus particular assignments of costs and benefits for crime prevention, would create an interest in, and incentives for, crime deterrence. The amount and value of service would determine promotions, ostensibly as in the army. As Chadwick put it, 'Responsibility should at each step be concentrated on individuals; and, as the best security against improper appointments, the officers ought in general to be chosen in the first instance by the magistrates, who should be considered responsible for the security of person and property within their districts' (1829: 289). Thus, the centralization of information on crime, only recently being achieved in the US through the use of computers, and the establishment and assignment of property rights in crime prevention, could mitigate the adverse incentive structure of publicly provided police. Chadwick's scheme would, in effect, 'price' resources used for prevention of crime by property rights assignments of costs and benefits to individual action.[31]

This is the supply side of crime prevention. It required participation by victims and potential victims in reporting and following through on criminal activity. Demanders of crime prevention and criminal justice had little incentive to invest in the common pool aspects of the system, but Chadwick believed that efficiency and reduced common pool problems might be had through reform of the court system. His suggestions for reform affect both the supply of criminal justice and the participation of victims and potential victims to help alleviate the common pool problems. A complete revision of the court system was required.

The Court System (Conviction and Punishment)

Modern observers appear transfixed by the theory and metrics of 'optimal deterrence' through a combination of enforcement and punishment procedures. Chadwick believed that wholesale restructuring of the court system would be required in order to elicit greater public protection. It began with the magistrates who would first adjudicate all cases. While Chadwick believed that, in an efficient system, magistrates would have to become men of knowledge, character, and integrity, he noted that the system did not encourage that kind of behavior. One reason that many victims failed to prosecute theft was that they were forced, in the English system, to bring charges only in counties where the offence was committed. In such a county, the magistrate might be reputed by respectable society for incompetency or 'harshness of manners.' The system, as it existed, encouraged witness and victim abuse and real flagellation by lawyers and judges. Legal bullying and outright lies under the system of presumed innocence were not conducive to truth (Chadwick 1841: 10–11). Judges, both magistrates and superior court judges, were sympathetic to the system since they came from the same bar and would profit from it. Voluntary prosecution was lost to the public. But if crime could be prosecuted in other jurisdictions – including the district where the culprit resides or the district where he was seized – costs would be lowered to victims and a kind of competition would be set up between magistrates.

The Role of Magistrates

Magistrates would, in Chadwick's system, compete for the adjudication of cases. They would eventually become individuals of the *highest qualifications* with great burdens of administering the bulk of the criminal justice system, presiding over all police activities in their districts and adjudicating cases *instanter* when an accused was brought before them. Information was the key: '. . . the magistrates presiding over such a police should possess superior knowledge and qualifications, as well to enable them to direct, in the best manner, the preventive labours of the officers under their control, as to administer the law most efficiently in furtherance of the general objects' (Chadwick 1829: 302). But information about criminal behavior could not be obtained by cavorting with criminals, so the magistrates would be required to get information from police and particular adjudications. One method was the post-procedure or post-trial inquiry into the 'former conditions' of prisoners vis-à-vis employment, habits, connections, and 'places of resort.' This knowledge, gained from friends and relatives of the malfeaser and subsequent to police investigations, would give magistrates particularized knowledge of district conditions, adding to crime *prevention*.

Chadwick, in short, was suggesting that a system or form not unlike the French system be set up, a system which was, in its results, abhorrent to the English.[32] The employment of spies, a feature of the French system, was but the use of one set of criminals to apprehend another ('set a thief to catch a thief'). Chadwick did not see much potential for prevention in this system – only the generation of supreme distrust of the police. He did not believe that a good police could only be had at the expense of liberty. Rather, the goals could be achieved through giving complete and speedy information on all offences committed, 'creating in a better organized police an interest in the prevention of crime; and rendering penal procedure more simple, expeditious, cheap, and certain' (Chadwick 1829: 307).

Penal Procedure

Chadwick's most radical reform recommendation was to allow magistrates to examine accused persons with neither witnesses nor attorney present. Evidence would consist of a comparison between the accused statements and witness statements, with both being segregated from the other. This would, according to Chadwick, produce instant justice, greatly reduce time costs, and lead to the severe reduction of both Type I and Type II errors. This reform would require the revision of the laws against 'self-incrimination' and the abandonment of the accused being 'presumed guilty' or 'presumed innocent' – long traditions in the Anglo-Saxon law. Rather, Chadwick appealed to practices in Scotland which he thought much superior, with evidence to back up his opinion. As he stated (1841: 21–2):

> One result of the careful preliminary examination [in Scotch law] is that fewer doubtful cases are sent to trial, and fewer persons tried escape conviction. Suspected persons obtain ready discharge on accounting for themselves, and the pursuit of criminals is better directed . . . The procedure being shorter, and private individuals being relieved from the burthen of prosecution, parties come forward with greater readiness, and fewer persons who have once prosecuted will hesitate to go forward a second time in the aid of public justice.

In Scotland account was given for 'contrition,' and attempts were made to distinguish between first accusations, first offenses, and first convictions.[33] Allowances, in short, were made for first offenses, whereas in England, with no such distinctions or considerations were made, first offenders were 'sent to indiscriminate confinement with hardened criminals, whose associates they become for life!' (Chadwick 1841: 23).

Examining the aggregate statistics from Scotland and from England, Chadwick found that from 10 to 12 percent fewer persons were committed to trial (after the magistrate's examination described above) in Scotland than in England. If the same proportion were brought to trial in England as in Scotland, about two thousand more persons would be convicted annually, that is, 'either that number of innocent persons are improperly committed for trial, or that number of criminals are annually set at large, in consequence of the defects of the [English] procedure. There can be no doubt of this last alternative being the true one' (Chadwick 1841: n. 21).

CONCLUSION

Institutions clearly matter, and Chadwick had a firm understanding of that fact as regards crime prevention and the criminal justice system. The

English were highly suspicious of a centralized or even of a highly organized police due to a feared loss of liberty and a predicted institution of the French system of spies.[34] Citizens' own experience with a judiciary tightly linked with the monarchy-fed resistance also.[35] Fear that the police would be used to enforce workhouse incarceration in the new Poor Law was one of the primary reasons that the poor rejected centralization. Interest groups also played a large part in the maintenance of the incumbent system. Politicians and magistrates, composed of the gentry-landowners of property greater than £100, were in opposition because Chadwick's proposal redistributed the 'contractual powers' and the wealth of the gentry to a centrally managed national police force. Chadwick put his finger on the true opponents of reform of the then-existing system – entrenched financial (rent-seeking) interests of the local Justices of the Peace, their bureaucracies, and the legal profession. As cover for these interests, they claimed that a Scotch or French-style system would result in the incarceration of innocent people (a Type II error). Chadwick knew that the then-contemporary issues were empirical, but he neglected to carry the rent-seeking idea to its logical conclusion. The evolution of purely private institutions may have provided an efficient criminal justice system with strong incentives of prevention. It was rent-seeking under the Normans, just as it was in the system Chadwick addressed, that prevented efficiency.

Ultimately, a public police force was adopted in England, with 179 separate police forces in England and Wales by 1900, but there was little consolidation of police until the twentieth century. High crime, rising after the mid-nineteenth century, especially following the end of wars, and union (Chartist) agitation help explain the acceptance of a publicly provided police. But the retention of judicial procedures that made private participation in the justice system costly remained. Open-access common pool justice remains to the present day, despite technological improvements and the institution of regularly paid police. Chadwick's analysis and empiricism led him to believe that both Type I and Type II errors would be lower under a radically revised system of criminal procedure, with the added benefit of lowering costs to public participation in criminal justice.

The implications of Chadwick's system are profound since the institutions he described and attempted to change are those of the modern US system. While technology has reduced information costs, the incentive problems in policing, in prevention, and in the legal system itself are essentially the same. The same rent-seeking interest groups Chadwick describes continue to coalesce against legal and court reforms. Thus, all of the solutions and their modern equivalents proposed within a publicly provided system deserve consideration. We believe, however, that Chadwick prematurely set aside the actual and potential successes of privatizing portions of the system. This is somewhat incongruous given the acute emphasis he placed on how financial rewards directed the system. There is evidence that partial privatization to internalize dissipations in the common pool was effective in Chadwick's day, as it is in our own.[36] But his fundamental characterization of criminal justice as a common pool raises the critical question of how and in what manner public and private systems may be joined to reduce dissipations. As such Chadwick originated a popular modern notion in the economics of regulation and institutions – that no state of the world is nirvana, and that, before committing societal resources to use, all feasible alternatives must be examined. Chadwick takes his place among the most modern of economists dealing with the ever-present vicissitudes of social and public policy.

NOTES

1. The survey of Polinsky and Shavell does not mention the common pool aspects of policing and focuses entirely on optimum enforcement issues. They explicitly eschew the possibilities of private participation by victims and potential victims in the production of criminal justice and crime prevention (2000: 46, n. 5).
2. Material presented here partly replicates the material found in Ekelund and Dorton (2003).
3. Polinsky and Shavell's (2000) survey on law enforcement dates the scholarship on the subject from Bentham to Gary Becker's seminal contribution (1968). This statement is off the mark. While it is correct that Bentham wrote brilliantly on creating 'artificial' identities of interest in criminal justice matters in *Principles of Penal Law, circa* 1882 (see Bentham 1776–82) as well as in *Principles of Morals and Legislation* cited by Polinsky and Shavell (2000) (see Bentham 1789 [1948], Chapter 17) and devised an idealized prison system in his *Panopticon*, his analysis of crime was solely 'theoretical.' Certainly Bentham and Chadwick shared common aims on crime prevention although Chadwick carried utilitarian principles much further theoretically, empirically and into the realm of policy analysis. In addition, Chadwick's 1829 essay was entirely independent of Bentham and occasioned Bentham's interest in and employment of Chadwick. Chadwick wrote on law enforcement, policing, and criminal justice throughout the nineteenth century as our references reveal. These works were cited and even formed the basis for parliamentary studies and inquiries on crime and the police force.
4. Friedman (1979) describes a system of private law enforcement in medieval Iceland, existing for over 300 years.
5. In this system the populace was made accountable to an appointed representative. This representative, a tything-man, oversaw a group of 10 people called a tything. Each tything-man was accountable to a 'hundred-man.' The hundred-man, as the name implied, had 10 tything-men under him. He, in turn, was responsible to the Shire-reeve, or sheriff. This structure later evolved into the Magistrate-Constable system, the system in place when Chadwick addressed crime prevention in the nineteenth century.
6. As Benson (1994: 256) explains:

> With the Norman's undermining of the Anglo-Saxon restitution-based legal system, one of the most powerful positive incentives to cooperate in law enforcement disappeared. Common-access benefits, such as deterrence, remained, as did some private benefits, such as the potential for revenge. But the remaining private benefits

apparently were not sufficient to induce voluntary cooperation, particularly given other disincentives . . . Many of the hundreds ceased functioning altogether under William, for example, although other local associations took over some of the non-policing functions of the hundreds, such as road maintenance . . . Thus, Norman kings were forced to attempt to establish new incentives and institutions in order to collect their profits from justice. The Normans instituted a local arrangement called the frankpledge, with similar functions to an Anglo-Saxon tithing.

7. Similar behavior worked to defeat mercantilism during the late Tudor and Stuart periods. The opportunistic behavior of local authorities in dealing with the Tudor Statute of Artificers (passed in 1563) led to black and grey markets at local levels in the English economy (see Ekelund and Tollison 1981; 1997).
8. It was in fact this essay that attracted the attention of Jeremy Bentham. An introduction of the two was arranged by mutual friend J.S. Mill and the rest is history.
9. Royle (1978: 42) cites that the population growth of England increased from just over five million in 1699 to approximately 6 million in 1757. The population increased to above 9 million in 1804, 12 million in 1824, and finally to 13 million in 1830. These figures are much higher than Tobias' figures (1972b) for similar years, following the Census conducted in the first year of each decade (1801, 1811, and so on). Both data sets, however, do match up with the actual Census figures provided by Woods (1996). Naturally either estimate reveals a rapidly growing population and rising poor rates. According to Porter (1990: 94), by 1800, 28 percent of the population claimed poor relief (about 2 490 000 people given the 1801 census numbers).
10. Chadwick neglects the possible manner under which purely private institutions in criminal justice might have evolved. As some observers have noted, English citizens strenuously resisted the development of criminal law, the loss of restitution and the elimination of private prosecutions. Attempts by victims to 'settle out of court' with felons made the victim a criminal as we have noted. As Pollock and Maitland noted (1895, 2: 521–2), the earliest misdemeanors were crimes of this type and additional laws made it illegal to: (1) pursue civil remedies to a criminal offense until criminal prosecution was complete; (2) retrieve stolen goods before giving evidence in a criminal prosecution; or (3) print advertisements of a reward for the return of stolen property 'no questions asked.' Thus, incentives to develop private institutions over the seven centuries of frankpledge were weak on a number of counts, a fact ignored by Chadwick.
11. Pay of constables, however, was partly based on rewards – private and public rewards.
12. In addition, at his own expense, Fielding created the *Covent Garden Journal* (later changed to the *Police Gazette*), one of the first police reports publicizing crime with descriptions of criminals. Fielding was an advocate of strict enforcement of laws, with a large capital punishment component for infractions that, on the surface at least, appeared less severe in nature (for example, starting a riot in a house of prostitution): see Fielding (1749). For a contrasting view on capital punishment, see Bentham (1776–82 [1962]: 532 *et passim*).
13. There appears to have been blatant rent-seeking in the publicly provided police protection in Middlesex. As Benson reports (1994: 258), Middlesex was a neighborhood with government establishments and the homes of parliamentarians.
14. Shocking highway murders in 1811 in Wapping, a subdivision of London, brought calls for improved police. The slaying of two families, a shop boy, and a domestic, caused the House of Commons to call a Select Committee on the Police in 1812 to study the situation of the London Police. Between 1812 and 1828, ten Select Committees were called on topics of the police, punishment, and drunkenness.
15. Emsley (1983) states that Chadwick presented evidence before the Select Committee, but Finer (1952) disagrees believing that Chadwick was asked by Peel to present the evidence but that the manuscript was lost by an assistant and not found in time. Brundage (1988) felt that despite Chadwick's ambition, he was unable to influence the committee or present the evidence he had prepared. After looking through the Committee's

Report, there is no recorded evidence credited to Chadwick or mention of him as a witness (*British Parliamentary Papers* 1968a). His manuscript is in the University College London Library's collection of his papers.

16. Later in his career, Chadwick analyzed murder: see Chadwick (1863 [1887]). In this essay Chadwick linked property crimes to murder and argued that hoarding or the business practice of keeping large sums on the premises was an incentive to murder. He advocates (1863 [1887]: 402–3) methods of self-protection through the use of banks.

17. As Hébert (1977: 543) points out, Chadwick 'noted that robberies were much less frequent in Scotland than in England because receipts were deposited daily in the former country instead of weekly, or monthly, as in the latter. He advised citizens not to invite theft by keeping large sums of money at home or at places of business, and to keep bank deposits and withdrawals as secretive as possible.'

18. Chadwick, perhaps due to his technological familiarity with matters and devices relating to sanitation, was an avid promoter of technology in all aspects of markets. (His emphasis on how technology affects markets is in contrast to the lack of such emphasis by classical writers generally.) With respect to crime, he urged the institution of any policy or device which would increase the probability of apprehension and punishment rather than increasing the severity of punishment. As Hébert recounts (1977: 547), he advised the use of patrols of tricycles 'by two men abreast' because it was faster than a foot chase. In addition he urged that patrolmen be armed, a recommendation that was not followed for many years; bobbies were famous well into the twentieth century for being unarmed, with the harshest punishments reserved for those who conducted acts of violence on them (see Chadwick 1887b).

19. Henry Fielding was an unabashed defender of capital punishment. In 1749 Fielding supported the execution of one Bosavern Penlez, a British sailor, who had caused a riot in a house of prostitution. Despite pleas from the jury that convicted him and from the public at large, he received the ultimate punishment. Fielding (1749) wrote a spirited defense of the sentence. Capital punishment, especially for 'crimes' such as petty theft, had been eliminated by the time of Chadwick's evaluation of the criminal justice system.

20. Weak, but positive, incentives to cooperate with public sector law enforcement might include the return of stolen property, revenge, or reporting crime for insurance purposes. But Benson (1998) does argue that there are strong incentives to cooperate if the benefits can be internalized, as is the case with gated communities, private streets, and so on. This view is supported by Friedman (1995) who offers argument and evidence that private pre-public prosecution efforts such as local associations for the prosecution of felons and 'out of court' settlements created a smoothly functioning system.

21. A contemporary form of dissipation is the high proportion of false alarms with the new home 'alarm systems,' as noted by Benson (1994). Also see Thornton (1991) on the impact of drug enforcement on the relative price and on incentives to demand and supply drugs.

22. It is extraordinary that Chadwick's essay on criminal procedure has not received attention of any kind in the literature we have surveyed. While his primary biographer Finer (1952) lists the essay in a compiled bibliography, we can locate no commentary on the essay in Finer's account or in any other source, including Lewis (1952), who develops a substantial bibliography of Chadwick's writings, and Hébert (1977). A survey of the sociological literature on the criminal justice system and its evolution yields the same results. Finer's opinion that Chadwick's most complete account of police was 'Preventive Police' (Finer 1952: 164 *et passim*) might explain the neglect, but Chadwick's essay on criminal procedure (1841) much goes further into reform of the court system.

23. A modern classic on this problem is by Judge Richard Neely (1980). Neely contrasts a 'myth system' and an 'operational system' of justice and courts. The former operates on 'political theory, idealism, and a healthy fear of human lust, avarice, aggression, and self-seeking' whereas the latter's departure from the myth system 'comes from lack of money as well as from the nature of the raw material of which it is composed, namely men and women. Lust, avarice, aggression, and self-aggrandizement are inherently part

of the makeup of people, and these qualities are reflected throughout the operational system' (1980: 18–19).

24.   There would be a higher probability of overcoming high costs in the common pool problem at this level: 'The inclination of parties to give information and to prosecute, is greatly strengthened by the knowledge that they can have their cases investigated by a magistrate whom they regard as possessing superior qualifications' (Chadwick 1829: 292). Chadwick also suggests that competition between magistrates for 'business' will create better qualified magistrates (1829: 292–3).

25.   That interest groups, including police, lawyers, judges, and court interests such as prosecutors (Benson 1990: 137) circumvent efficient justice and crime prevention is the very foundation of modern work on justice as a common pool (Benson 1998).

26.   This is on par with the vehement opposition of lawyers to state or federally supported arbitration agreements – agreements which would lower demand for their services.

27.   The emergence of the 'lawyerization' of trials has received kinder interpretations. Langbein (1999), for example, considers the emergence (in the 1730s) of the legal use of defense counsel to interrogate witnesses for the prosecution (the defendant used to do that). He finds that the 'lawyerization' of the prosecution and the payment for number of cases prosecuted meant that the accused did not get a 'fair shake' and that judges, increasingly, wanted to even the score. This is undoubtedly correct, but there may be other reasons for the increasing domination of the courts by lawyers. Naturally lawyers for defendants have a financial interest in promoting this judicial policy and judges come from the same class. Most importantly, it was a rent-seeking crown that captured the judicial system in the first place. Prosecutors were being paid by the crown, perhaps for political favors. Venality riddled the post-frankpledge 'public system' which spread to the defense and created the modern (and costly) system of lawyer-dominated adversarial trials.

28.   Chadwick's analysis of the *source* of the common pool problems differs somewhat from modern observers. Chadwick did appreciate the efficiencies of the early frankpledge system with restitution and the lack of incentives created by the common pool, but he believed that time and information cost, population growth and centralization in cities, and improved transportation (better methods of escape) necessitated a publicly provided police. As noted above, modern observers emphasize the declension from the purely private system as the source of the common pool problem.

29.   Benson argues that prevention is essentially unmeasurable so that the reward structure encourages both shirking (as to crime prevention) and an emphasis on arrests and waiting to respond to crime (1994: 262).

30.   As Chadwick argued (1829: 289):

> The principle has . . . been already tried, and found successful in commerce. In some large retail houses, the zeal and eloquence of the shopmen is constantly stimulated by an arrangement, which renders it certain and palpable that each successful act will directly contribute to their own advantage, while it adds to their employer's prosperity. An account is kept of the goods sold by each man, and at the end of the half-year or year, promotion, larger salaries, gratuities, or advantages in various shapes, are given to those who are found to have been the most efficient. These shopmen are said to be distinguished for their unremitting assiduity, skill, and civility.

31.   Most classical writers, it would seem, followed the lead of Adam Smith on crime and the justice system. Smith was grossly suspicious of a centralized or an enlarged or enhanced police presence in society as existed in Paris. In his lectures of 1763 (*Lectures on Justice, Police, Revenue and Arms*, 1896 [1964]), Smith argued that market-driven higher incomes reduced crime rates and made large police forces unnecessary, a situation he thought to be the case in England. An invidious contrast is drawn with France where feudal and monarchical institutions held on (see Smith 1896 [1964]: 154–6). Later, in the *Wealth of Nations* (1776 [1937]: 677–81 *et passim*), the provision of justice

is seen to be a role of government (with separated powers to be sure). Like Chadwick and Bentham, Smith believed that incentives mattered and considered how payment systems (for example, of judges) could corrupt the system. Unlike Chadwick, however, Smith entertained no detailed analysis of incentives in policing and criminal justice or wholesale alterations of the police and court system to obtain efficiency and crime prevention. Ostensibly, Smith fundamentally believed that the market 'failed' in the provision of justice.

32. The English fear of a loss of liberty with the inception of anything like the French system ran deep. In 1763 Sir William Mildmay (1763) described the French, actually the Paris, system as highly bureaucratic, military in character and in practice a ruthless spy system that had successes in preserving the peace. The British fear of this system reached far into the nineteenth century (see Finer 1952: 177). Ultimately, and for a number of reasons, a fully public police structure was adopted without centralization (achieved partly in the twentieth century). Chadwick did not defend the liberty-threatening aspects of the French system and thought that the French police system generally never was a preventive or good system. England, he thought, could achieve the results of prevention without this kind of control. Showing a wonderful practical knowledge of how markets function, moreover, Chadwick describes the French attempt to institute censorship of books and pamphlets, both political and sexual, through the use of French police. This group of police was called *Colporteurs* 'whose real avocation was to smuggle and sell prohibited books and pamphlets. When vigorous pursuit was instituted by the police against any particular work, the price rose so high as to tempt the officers to become agents for the circulation of those which they seized' (Chadwick 1829: 306). A similar criticism might be applied in reference to some contemporary enforcement in the 'war on drugs.'

33. The Scotch justice system is reminiscent of modern Japanese practice. Contrition and remorse are large parts of the latter system but private restitution is also (see Benson 1998: 251–3). Unfortunately we are unaware of the nature of 'restitution' in the early nineteenth-century Scotch system.

34. At the time of the Radcliffe murders in 1811, John William Ward opined that:

> these things make the people cry out against the laxity of our police . . . it is next to impossible to prevent outrages of this sort . . . in those parts of the town that are inhabited exclusively by the lowest and most profligate wretches . . . except by entrusting the magistrates with powers vastly too expensive to be prudently vested in their hands . . . I had rather half a dozen people's throat should be cut in Ratcliffe Highway every 3 to 4 years than be subject to domiciliary visits, spies, and the rest of Fouche's contrivances. (Philips 1980: 174)

35. Monarchical hegemony over the judiciary and use of the Star Chamber (abolished in 1641) lingered in the minds of citizens. The gentry understood the potential for centralization and abuse of the judicial power and (initially at least) opposed it, preventing a police force of any consequence until well into the eighteenth century. According to Neely (1980: 15, n. 3) capital punishment was substituted as a deterrent for serious crimes (and, according to some observers, for minor crimes) and as a substitute for police. With the sharp reduction in capital punishment by Chadwick's time, other forms of deterrence had to be considered.

36. Chadwick eschewed private policing due, ostensibly, to the misdirected incentives of police and potential police. Justice under such patchwork systems, which clearly existed and was supported by businesses in Chadwick's time, would be disparate and non-uniform. Low or no pay would direct police incentives to work for private firms and a lack of coordination in pursuing and apprehending criminals would ensue. (This was Chadwick's objection to the decentralized post-frankpledge system as well.) There are, of course, free rider aspects to the use of private police, but short of instituting a system of national police, private police (in both time periods) do bridge some common pool problems. (See Finer 1952 who cites successes of private policing at the time.)

8. The economics of sanitation and the utilitarian agenda

INTRODUCTION

The whole process and engineering of sanitation reform is often (and justly) regarded as Chadwick's greatest achievement. Less recognized, perhaps, are the roles that sanitation reform and his prior investigations into English poverty played in shaping his analysis of the entire structure of the British economy. His firm aim of 'sanitizing' England had deep and broad implications and consequences for both economic and social well-being. His investigations into poverty and sanitation shaped his analysis of the entire structure of the British economy. Specifically:

- Chadwick's (and Mill's) acute interest in the urban sanitation issue was heightened by the cholera epidemics in the 1830s, 1840s, and 1850s, and created an interest in reform for both medical and social reasons;
- Chadwick's investigation into sanitation, prefaced by an analysis of the conditions and relative position of the poor in the 1830s, was an attempt to enhance the economic condition and productivity of labor and hence the overall economy;
- Chadwick's argument for centralized provision of sanitation and other social and economic projects was premised on an analysis of the inability of local governments to promote productive activities, and;
- Chadwick's theory of knowledge meant that voter apathy would prevail, he argued, at the local level.

In short, sanitation reform and centralized control were the keys to improvement of labor productivity, the elimination of poverty, and, ultimately, economic growth. We analyze some of these matters in the present chapter.

SIZE OF THE POVERTY PROBLEM

The exact dating of the Industrial Revolution in England may be a small matter of debate, but it is clear that the century between the mid-eighteenth and nineteenth centuries certainly qualifies. All of the characteristics of that revolution – including a massive movement from country to urban environments of people – have been clear to historians for many years. The penultimate question for our purposes is: 'how did that revolution impact the wealth and income levels of the entire population?' The quality of statistics on wealth and income distribution in nineteenth-century England, though relatively good, must necessarily be suspect. Without question the decades preceding Chadwick's evaluation of the conditions of labor and the poor was a period of massive growth in wealth and income. The flowering of the Industrial Revolution made the nineteenth century, 'England's century.' Statistics on wealth and income certainly confirm that fact as Table 8.1 shows.

There is no doubt of progress in the growth of wealth, even allowing for the quality of this early data from the United Kingdom. Progressive increases were translated into equally dramatic increases in per capita national income, according to most accounts. According to estimates reported in Baxter (1868: 66), national income (from all sources) expanded three-fold between 1801 and 1858. Per capita income increased from £14.7 to £20.15 between 1800 and 1858 according to Levi's estimate (1860: 7).[1] However, per capita income statistics say nothing about income distribution. The best statistics on income distribution tell a far different story – one that most clearly explains Chadwick's early concern for the working poor and the impoverished.[2]

Income Distribution

While all data sources for the period must contain important qualifications, official accounts of the distribution of income in Great Britain (England and Scotland) in 1801 and again in 1848 tell an important story. We have constructed Lorenz curves (see Figure 8.1) from data collected by William Farr (1852 [1968]) for the distribution of income in the years 1801 and 1848. Clearly income data is *self*-reported and huge discrepancies exist between estimates of the income earning population in various classes and the number of returns reported. This was a persistent complaint among observers and compilers of tax statistics well into the nineteenth century.[3] The dramatic inequality in income distribution is obvious from the Lorenz curves even allowing for the fact that only 1020 persons reported income above £5000 in 1801 and reportage was not much better in 1848. By 1848,

Table 8.1 Wealth and income estimates: United Kingdom (1700–1858)

Year	Population (millions)	Wealth estimate (millions)	Per capita wealth	Percentage increase in wealth	Income estimate (millions)
1700	8	£600	£75	–	–
1801	16	£1800	£112	300	£220
1811	18	£2100	£116	16	£250 (1822)
1841	27	£4000	£150	94	£450
1858	29	£6000	£206	50	£600

Source: wealth estimates: Gregory King estimate for 1700 (1698 [1936]); other wealth estimates Levi (1860: 6); income estimates: Baxter (1868: 66).

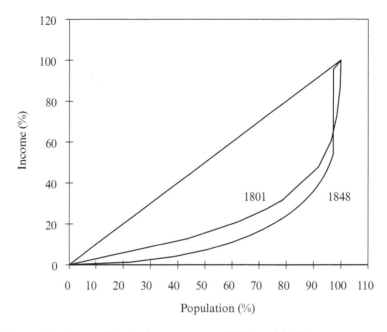

Figure 8.1   Great Britain Lorenz curves (1801 and 1848)

a year with finer estimates, about 60 percent of the population earned just over 10 percent of the income of Great Britain. The lowest 22.5 percent earned only 1.3 percent of income while the upper 3 percent earned 45.5 percent of reported income.

Two facets of these data should be noted at the outset. Wages – those earned by manual labor were exempt from taxation and thus a vast segment of the population was eliminated from the 1801 and 1848 data (and from tax liability). But a second point is that the inequality in income distribution most likely grossly underestimates the skewness in wealth distribution in England at the time. Underreporting and fraud by income earners and the exclusion (until later in the century) of income from landed estates are only two good reasons. There is also evidence of massive undervaluations of property over the period (Peto 1863: 45–6).

Robert Dudley Baxter, in a paper read before the Statistical Society of London in 1868, shed new light on the form of income distribution in the United Kingdom. Baxter estimated the population in each class along with estimates of income and wage earners (including 'dependent' classes). The 'dependent classes' included non-working wives, children and rela- tives at home, scholars, paupers, prisoners, vagrants, and manual laborers

Table 8.2   Population estimates by class: United Kingdom (1867)

Upper and Middle Classes		
With independent incomes	2 759 000	
Dependent	3 859 000	
		6 618 000
Manual Labor Class		
Earning wages	10 961 000	
Dependent	12 130 000	
		23 091 000
	Total estimated population	29 709 000

Source: Baxter (1868: 16).

above 65 years old (Baxter 1868: 81). His population estimates are shown in Table 8.2. Upper and middle classes comprised only 23 percent while the manual labor class is composed of 77 percent of the population. More than three-fourths of the entire population was working class. Wage earners in the United Kingdom outnumbered income earners by a ratio of four to one. Drawing upon the data on wages and earnings of the working classes collected in the previous year by Levi (1867), Baxter presented an estimate of income distribution for the year 1867.

The primary advantage of the Levi–Baxter calculations is that they include the wage income of the working classes as well as salaried incomes of those in middle- and upper-income groups. By modern standards, income distribution in United Kingdom in 1867 was comparable to that of an underdeveloped country today. Baxter's (1868: 64) income divisions, corresponding to Table 8.2 above, were Upper and Middle Classes: Class I (1) £5000 and upwards; Class I (2) £1000 to £5000; Class II £300 to £1000; Class III (1) £100 to £300; Class III (2) under £100; Manual Labour Class: Class IV (higher skilled labor and manufactures) £50 to £73; Class V (lower skilled labor and manufactures) £35 to £52; Class VI (agriculture and unskilled labor) £10 10s. to £36. By our calculations, taxes on large incomes of £5000 or more (Class I (1)) were assessed on 8500 individuals who received an average income of £14842. Those below the level of the income tax (£100 in 1867) were 12458000 individuals with an average annual income of less than £33!

Edwin Chadwick was well aware of this profile. Even given generous room for error, it appears as if the skew in English income distribution turned against the lower classes due to a lack of education and one prime factor that we will consider – the living and working conditions of labor. Notably, while there was not much of a 'middle class,' English workers with higher skills and some agricultural workers as well were moving toward that status.

Apocalyptic predictions of Marx and other heterodox writers of Chadwick's generation focused public attention on the state of the laboring population. These 'romantics' espoused a general belief that the situation of the working class had worsened due to the Industrial Revolution and appealed for reform of the economic system. This might have been correct given some of the above statistics relating to those in the lowest and 'dependent' classes. But in his investigation of the *laboring class* (unspecified as to rank) Chadwick concluded that degradation of the laboring class was not due to any fall in real incomes. He had wage data for many occupations showing increases in money wages, but did not accept this data as proof of increased real incomes. Instead, Chadwick offered the growth of thrift institutions as indicative of the improved circumstances of the laboring class. In an 1836 paper in the *Edinburgh Review*, Chadwick (1836: 492) had this to say:

> No body of men save money whilst they are in want of what they deem absolute necessaries. No common man will put by a shilling whilst he is in need of a loaf, or will save whilst he has a pressing want unsatisfied. The circumstance of there being nearly fourteen millions in the savings banks, and the fact that, according to the last returns, upwards of 29,000 of the depositors were agricultural labourers . . . justify the conclusion, that a condition worse than that of the independent agricultural labourer, may nevertheless by a condition above that in which the great body of English labourers have lived in times that have always been considered prosperous.

Independent agricultural workers were generally considered the lowest strata of the wage class, and if this group was capable of net saving, the real incomes of at least some of the working class must have increased. Chadwick thus eliminated 'falling incomes' as the source of deteriorating living conditions, concluding that a major cause of suffering was the faulty institutional structure of sanitary administration.

CHADWICK, POVERTY, AND SANITATION

Poverty, to Chadwick, had many dimensions. We have seen, in Chapter 6, that Chadwick understood the value of human capital – investments in education in particular– as one means to an improvement in the condition of labor and the poor. Worker (and English) productivity was enhanced through such investments in human capital. Additionally, improvements in medical science had actually improved life expectancy among middle-

and upper-class citizens from the eighteenth century. This conundrum – increased life expectancy *on average*, but wretched conditions and early death amongst the low income working poor and the destitute (the 'dependent class' a large part of these requiring welfare payments), was part of what led Chadwick to attack the problem in his famous *Sanitary Report* (1842a). The other influence was, of course, his work on the impact of Poor Law reforms of the 1830s.[4]

Chadwick's 1842 *Sanitary Report* investigated every corner of the United Kingdom and every facet of sanitary conditions and, from these statistics, Chadwick proposed two generalizations: (1) life expectancies had increased; and (2) substantial benefits would be realized through restructuring sanitary administration. As proof of the first proposition, Chadwick offered the insurance company life tables, compiled as early as 1828 (Chadwick 1828: 384–421). He gathered and compared, with what must have been an arduous data assembly, statistics from Northampton and Sweden. Life expectancy from Northampton was the table used by most insurance companies in calculating insurance premiums and had been in use for over thirty years. Statistics on expectancies (with the exception of those in Northampton) were based on more current data compiled by medical and governmental authorities, and a major insurance company (the Equitable table). Eyeballing the data, Chadwick recognized that in almost every category, life expectancy had increased.

Chadwick compiled his data in 1828 to show that insurance companies were overcharging purchasers of annuities, but the table had important ramifications for his sanitary investigations in that there were apparent differences in life expectancies for individuals in different circumstances. This early observation became the focus of his sanitary investigation, that is, Chadwick sought the circumstances which promoted sickness and death. To this end, Chadwick compiled the data summarized in Table 8.3. Here he separated the death statistics by county and by source (disease vs non-disease; Chadwick considered the former preventable). Then, using his general knowledge of the physical conditions of the counties, Chadwick concluded that a substantial portion of all illness was caused by environmental factors. Areas with the highest death rates from disease were characterized by impure physical conditions – inadequate supplies of fresh water, excess ground moisture, and inadequate waste removal. The number of deaths due to respiratory problems and epidemics of various kinds dwarfed the number from other sources. Most importantly, the number of deaths from these two sources alone produced the greatest number of orphans, most of which became charges of the state. This was a clear cost to government. Chadwick proposed changes in sanitary engineering and administration to reduce these costs and eliminate the disease promoting

Table 8.3   *The chief causes of death producing widowhood and orphanage*

Diseases, and conditions	Manchester Union No. of deaths	Whitechapel Union No. of deaths	Bethnal Green Parrish No. of deaths	Strand Union No. of deaths	Oakham and Uppingham Unions No. of deaths	Alston-with-Garrigill Parrish No. of deaths	Bath Union No. of deaths	Total No. of deaths	Total Average age of deceased	Total No. of orphans
Respiratory organs	500	212	147	95	69	47	40	1110	51	2218
Epidemic, endemic and contagious	146	65	73	28	34	9	4	359	46	862
Digestive organs	60	16	10	10	14	5	3	118	54	180
Nervous	74	41	38	17	25	3	5	203	55	296
Violent deaths	94	44	20	16	23	13	5	215	46	508
Old age	84	104	46	13	47	5	–	299	74	56
Other diseases	129	68	104	32	36	7	8	384	54	694
Undescribed	63	40	7	9	6	–	2	127	47	171
Total	1150	590	445	220	254	89	67	2815	53	4985

Source: Chadwick (1842a: 192).

factors. The solution was a comprehensive water and sewer system to which every house was connected, a system that he sought to show was privately profitable as well as socially efficient.

Potable water – with health and time costs high under the old system – could be altered (which we discuss later in this chapter). Renovated and modernized water delivery systems would work to eliminate disease and water-borne epidemics. All manner of water contamination was possible under the old system. Water-borne and air-borne contaminants from funeral and graveyard 'externalities,' as Chadwick exhaustively analyzes in his book-length appendage to the *Sanitary Report* (and as we discuss in Chapter 5), were to blame for much illness. Human excrement disposal, a negative externality under the old urban systems, was another source of disease and contamination. Here, however, Chadwick believed that human sewage, called 'night soil,' could be turned into a positive benefit. The English sewer system consisted of cesspools and bricked sewer lines which although designed to drain, acted like septic tanks requiring hand cleansing at considerable expense. 'Night soil' was being tested as fertilizer so Chadwick collected the data in Table 8.4 and noted its effectiveness as a fertilizer, and how its use would be substantially increased if its cost to users could be decreased. Chadwick determined that the major determinant of the cost were transportation costs, and his primary suggestion was an *arterial drainage system* that would greatly reduce transportation cost to the operator of the system, providing added revenues from fertilizer sales. Sewer systems were to benefit the public by decreasing disease and by increasing agricultural production. A prime benefit, however, was a healthier and cleaner population.

Such 'statistical reasoning' was typical of Chadwick's research. Clearly, when Chadwick argues 'from general knowledge' that a 'substantial' portion of illness was caused by 'environmental factors,' the modern investigator longs for a formal regression of factors leading to death caused by illness. Naturally, other possible factors may be at work in the counties that Chadwick identifies as 'death by illness'-prone, including genetic factors, diet, and so on. Further, low incomes could lead to poor diet, illness, and premature death, and vice versa. What was the channel of cause and effect? The answer is that the tools for discovering answers or tentative answers to questions such as these were half a century to more than a century away. Chadwick appeared unaware of such difficulties and made do with the kinds of descriptive statistics he had. This of course gave him a good deal of latitude in assessing the influence of 'other factors,' but modern recapitulations of his evidence appear to bear out the major parts of his analysis (Hanley 2002).

Table 8.4   Fertilizer productivity

Fertilizer	Application per acre	Produce of wheat per acre (bushels)
Soil sample	–	12½
Bushels of night soil	320	37½
Bushels of night soil	240	32½
Bushels of night soil	160	31¼
Cubic yards of farmyard compost	60	25
Cubic yards of farmyard compost	30	23¾
Cubic yards of farmyard compost and 1 cubic yard of chalk	30	25

Source: Chadwick (1857a: 498).

Changing *Economic* Constraints with Sanitation

We argued in the introduction to this chapter that sanitation reform was a
key to improving the economy. Indeed, the idea that one need only change
the constraints in order to alter the laborer's condition is strongly evident
in Chadwick's *Report on the Sanitary Condition of the Labouring Population
of Great Britain* (1842a). The many prescriptions in this report reflect what
can be done for the laborer rather than what the laborer can do for himself.
Clearly, as discussed in Chapter 7, investment in human capital was one of
the two pillars of progress. Changes described in the *Sanitary Report* go
further and can be grouped into two categories: (a) those to be provided
publicly or by contract management; and (b) those to be provided by
the employers of labor. It should be noted that all the changes proposed
involved providing a more aseptic environment.

Chadwick's statistics led him to summarize the condition of the
laboring classes, and to conclude 'That the various forms of epidemic,
endemic, and other disease caused or aggravated, or propagated chiefly
amongst the labouring classes by atmospheric produced by decomposing
animal and vegetable substances, by damp and filth, and close and over-
crowded dwellings prevail amongst the population in every part of the
kingdom' (1842b [1965]: 422). The problems to be corrected: the overcrowding, excessive dampness, and accumulation of the by-products of
human existence. To eliminate these problems, Chadwick proposed a

multi-dimensional program, all facets of which were designed to encourage the development of sanitary habits by lowering the cost of hygiene. The first problem was to remove waste from the individual habitations and then to remove it from the vicinity of the population. Next, there came the problem of instilling habits of personal hygiene amongst the population. Finally, the improvement of housing and working conditions was to be achieved. All but the latter were to be instigated on behalf of the public by the government.

The actions to be undertaken publicly consisted of the installation of a complete water and sewer system with extensions to every household. Chadwick was adamant on the inclusion of a water supply to all buildings not only for personal use but also for the immediate removal of the waste. He notes that 'it will be manifest that for an efficient system of house cleansing and sewerage, it is indispensible that proper supplies of pure water should be provided' (1842b [1965]: 135). Critically, it must be noted that Chadwick and virtually all other 'sanitation reformers' believed in the 'miasma' theory of cholera, a persistent plague throughout London and other large cities over the nineteenth century. In other words, they thought that breathing unhealthy air, whatever the source, could cause the disease. It was not until physician Dr John Snow's (1813–1858) suspicions of this theory and his subsequent research of the early 1850s that showed that cholera was water borne (the germ theory did not appear until 1861). In spite of these facts, Chadwick knew intuitively perhaps that clean water and separation from sewage disposal was a principal cause of disease in the metropolis. With the installation of the water and sewer system, 'the chief obstacles to the immediate removal of decomposing refuse of towns and habitations,' namely, 'the expense and annoyance of the hand labour and cartage requisite for the purpose' (1842b [1965]: 423), would be eliminated. Chadwick estimated that costs would be reduced to one-twentieth or one-thirtieth of the former costs and at the lower price, a greater quantity of public hygiene would be consumed. Along with the reduced cost of removing waste, Chadwick notes that the delivery of water to every household will promote personal hygiene. Under the old system of cisterns located in each neighborhood, 'the minor comforts of cleanliness are of course foregone, to avoid the immediate and greater discomforts of having to fetch the water' (1842b [1965]: 141). Chadwick (1842b [1965]: 141) does not limit this tendency resulting from a higher cost to hygiene to the laboring classes:

> Even with persons of a higher condition, the habits are greatly dependent on the conveniences, and it is observed, that when the supplies of water into the houses of the middle class are cut off by the pipes being frozen, and when it is

necessary to send for water to a distance, the house-cleansings and washings are
diminished by the inconvenience.

Chadwick, then, is arguing that the full-cost (including time costs) of cleanliness has an effect on the quantity of cleanliness consumed, a very modern
manner of viewing the problem.

Beyond the provision of water and sewer systems publicly, Chadwick
saw opportunities where employers of labor could greatly improve the
conditions of working people. The first action to be taken was the provision of housing to employees. Not only were the capitalists to provide
housing, but they are to undertake 'the erection of dwellings of a superior
order' (1842b [1965]: 298). Chadwick does not expect this to be done out
of benevolence by employers who have voluntarily attempted to improve
their employees' living conditions. He says that, 'though generally origi-
nating in benevolence, and without the expectation of a return, do in the
results, prove that in money and money's worth, the erection of good
tenements affords the inducement of a fair remuneration to the employers
of labour to provide improved accommodation for their own labourers'
(1842b [1965]: 298). The greatest gain to this arrangement is the workers
proximity to the place of work, and that the laborer 'avoids all the attacks
of disease, occasioned by exposure to wet and cold and the additional
fatigue in traversing long distances to and from his home to the place of
work' (1842b [1965]: 299). Although a healthier workforce is generally
accepted as being conducive to higher productivity (workers' vigor and
endurance having been increased), Chadwick goes further to amplify this
conclusion. He cites as evidence the experience of one entrepreneur, who,
strictly out of benevolence, invested in improved housing and provided
schools for the children of the employees. The results were that the capitalist 'was surprised by a pecuniary gain ground in the superior order and
efficiency of his establishment, in the regularity and trustworthiness of his
work people' (1842b [1965]: 301).

Besides the provision of housing, Chadwick maintained that the work
environment, per se, greatly affected the health of the working population, and that the factories could be designed to promote the well-being
of the workforce. To this end, Chadwick described a cotton mill which
had been engineered with the health of the workers in mind. The factory
was designed such that there was an abundance of fresh air and a means
of controlling the climate. Additionally, the machinery was installed
such that there was maximum protection against industrial accidents.
Chadwick was quick to admit that 'the first expense of such a building
is higher than a manufactory of the old construction, but it appeared
to possess countervailing economic advantages to the capitalist' (1842b

[1965]: 307). Again, Chadwick is not relying on benevolence, but is appealing to the profit motive. The above examples have been given to support the claim that Chadwick believed that the laborer's condition could be altered by altering the constraints faced by the working classes.

Sanitation and the Economy

Chadwick clearly envisioned public supply of sanitation (when possible through the franchise bidding process) creating improved systems of sewage disposal and clear water provisions. There is an economic link here between government 'savings' on various social expenditures (costs) and the benefits to be expected from implementing sanitation reform. Chadwick thought that part of the result of societal savings was a prolonged average lifespan. Although Chadwick investigated the difference in death rates between rural and urban districts (and within these categories as well) in the *Sanitary Report*, he based his arguments concerning mortality, correctly as it turns out, on class differences. Modern students of the adequacy of the statistical component of the *Sanitary Report* argue that Chadwick was correct in his conclusions, despite contemporary criticisms to the contrary. Hanley (2002: 40) concludes that:

> [C]lass-based death data were one of the central features of Chadwick's *Sanitary Report*. The significance of the data on average age at death in the report has long been recognized, but contemporary statisticians' disaffection with these statistics has led historians to conclude that this significance was mainly polemical or rhetorical. I would instead suggest that the class-based, average-age-at-death data Chadwick gathered over the course of the national sanitary inquiry provided new and compelling evidence in favour of his position, and we need to consider the role that these statistics played in his argument in order to appreciate fully the content and even the form of the *Sanitary Report*.

This means that early mortality was preventable by renovating and reorganizing sanitation – in particular by providing means of pure water delivery and cost-lowering waste disposal. Lower costs to the *individual* of personal hygiene saved lives by preventing the creation and spread of disease. Among the lower classes particularly, these improvements mean greater labor productivity and lower death rates. But these *private* benefits had spillover effects on the *public* economy. Lower death rates, as suggested in Table 8.3, reduce the number of widows and orphans that were highly probable to become wards of the state. Thus, the cost of sanitation reform – provided by government – had to be weighed against the benefits to government (cost saving) from reduced welfare and Poor Law relief to the lower and destitute segments of society. When private benefits – longer productive lives to workers, (possibly) higher productivity for businesses that provide enhanced working conditions to laborers (a net gain) – were added to the social savings, sanitation reform was, at least to Chadwick, a winning proposition. Preventable mortality would clearly support utilitarian goals. Critically, Chadwick, as had Bentham, appealed to private (net benefit producing) incentives as well as to public provisions to promote these ends.

CENTRALIZATION: THE LOCI OF SOCIAL CHANGE

Centralized control, in general, was the choice of Chadwick in so many matters, as we have seen. Railways were to be centralized, reorganized, and administered under a parliamentary-appointed contracting body (see Chapter 4). The conduct of funerals was to be 'let out' to private enterprise but with contractual clauses of given length and specifying performance standards (see Chapter 5). All of these administrative schemes, however, effectively removed some property rights from entrepreneurs. Whether based on economies of scale or high information costs, Chadwick's solution always involved the centralization of authority. This was certainly the case for sanitation, the results of which are interesting. Chadwick's urging of sanitation reforms came to pass in the Public Health Act of 1848, passed to implant sanitation reforms in the towns and parishes of England and Wales. Local bodies, administered by a centralized General Board of Health, could be formed in order to deal with sewerage, clean water, drainage, and throughout an evolutionary period, to deal also with burials, fire and fire prevention, and a myriad of other activities. If the death rates exceeded a particular limit, a local board could be set up. One could also be developed through petition from qualified ratepayers.

Chadwick's *Sanitary Report* had a huge impact on subsequent developments in sanitation. Rarely did Chadwick's proposals not feature a role for himself in administration, and he became a Commissioner of the Metropolitan Commission on Sewers (for London), as well as a Commissioner of the General Board of Health from 1848 to 1854. (His differences over the administration – and centralization – of the law caused him to be 'pensioned off' in 1854, but Chadwick researched and championed sanitation reform for the rest of his life.)

The point to be made here is that Chadwick advocated centralized control over local Boards and activities, not because he was a socialist or a Marxian or some other stripe (he was not), but because he did not believe that local governments could function well *for economic reasons*. Recall that he had a great distrust of the government operation of any service

– wherever possible, activities were to be leased with contracts to private enterprise. The same was true of sanitation. But that does not answer the question of Chadwick's particular distrust of local government. His interesting analysis again involves incentives respecting information costs and 'knowledge.'

Self-Interest, Centralization, and Voter 'Apathy:' Chadwick's Opposition to Local Government

Edwin Chadwick was an articulate proponent of centralization in both private and public activities. The concentration of responsibility for, and control of, economic activities was a common theme in all of his policy prescriptions, as with railways and sanitation.[5] One of the reasons for this view was that scalar economies existed in many economic activities, but another was a belief in the great inefficiency of local government and local authorities. The inefficiency resulted from the sheer extent to which public powers were subverted to private interests at this level of government. Chadwick's argument centered on time costs, or the lack of them. Chadwick believed that local governments 'generally fall into the hands of persons whose time is worthless, or into ignorant and wasteful hands, or into the hands of obscure persons who have some sinister interests to promote' (1885: 84).[6] The election of persons with undesirable characteristics to local government positions was far from accidental. It was due, in Chadwick's estimation, to a rational economic decision on the part of the electorate.

Chadwick objected to the traditional view of government at the local level as 'local self-government' arguing that 'The term "local self-government", signifying as it does the direct individual knowledge of the local affairs of the local unit of administration and the participation of the ratepayer in the expenditure of his money, is in the majority of cases a mischievous fallacy' (1885: 72). 'Self-government' was a misnomer because Chadwick alleged that local voters were not, as a whole, informed, nor did they participate in the political process. Such apathy was the result of *rational economic behavior* in that, Chadwick argued, the *costs of participating exceeded the expected benefits*:

> As the demands of attention to his own personal or private affairs increase, the citizen's power of attention to the public affairs of increasing magnitude diminishes, and he is obliged to let his local affairs go as they may to persons of whose fitness he has no knowledge, and with whom he has only an infinitesimal power of interfering; – that is to say, in a large London parish, he has, as a voter, some twenty-thousandth part of the self-government – if he neglected his private business to take a part. (1885: 72)

Thus, Chadwick recognized that it is costly for voters to become informed about issues and that the individual will optimize the amount of information that he purchases on the basis of the benefits that the information will provide. The citizen will typically (but not always) have a low pro-rata share in the benefits or costs of the outcome and high costs of obtaining knowledge about issues. Coupled with the fact that the individual has virtually no control over an election's outcome, optimal investment in information will approach zero. This means that the typical individual has only a minimal incentive to participate in the electoral process, an incentive that has been discussed in the modern literature on public choice, notably by Tullock (1998).[7] Whatever the empirical validity for Chadwick's positions, it is clear from his texts that modern theories of public choice would not have much surprised him.

Strategic Behavior and Collective Action

Besides analyzing the incentives faced by voters, Chadwick considered another case of the strategic (economic) behavior of individuals participating in the public sphere; that is, the behavior arising when unanimous consent is required to settle an issue. Rather than 'unanimity' or voting-rule theory as in twentieth-century formulations (Buchanan and Tullock 1962; Wagner 1973), Chadwick tackled a different problem involving collective action. The collective activity Chadwick dissected was the drainage of land for sanitary purposes. Land drainage physically depends on the cooperation of all landowners involved. Since the benefits of drainage depend on unanimous action, the possibility of strategic behavior and 'hold-up' arises. Chadwick refers to the factors preventing the advantageous drainage of both metropolitan and rural areas in the following way:

> But above all these [considerations] is to be added the circumstance of the power which the possession of a small part of a district gives to an individual, to thwart those operations of the majority which are for the common advantage and consequently the temptation which the possession of such power gives and almost ensures, of its use to exact unjust and exorbitant conditions. (1842b [1965]: 362)

Chadwick clearly describes the rent-seeking behavior which arises whenever an individual is placed in a monopolistic position. The holdout then can extract within an epsilon of the expected benefits of the project. The costs of obtaining the unanimous decision (bribing the recalcitrant) make the project uneconomical (costs would exceed benefits). To overcome such 'hold-up' situations, Chadwick proposed government provision of drainage since it has a cost advantage through the use of coercion. Whether or not government regulation or nationalization improves resource allocation and prevents socially wasteful dissipations over other possible institutional arrangements is a modern and important empirical issue, but Chadwick clearly identified the central problem of strategic behavior.[8] While he does not present an argument that would justify government intervention in all cases, his analysis presents a *possibility* that government ownership or regulation may be the low social cost alternative.

Naturally, Chadwick fully understood the 'interest group,' public-choice, aspects of change of any kind. Entrepreneurs or suppliers of existing facilities (such as the brick-based water and sewage systems) were often roadblocks on the road to progress. Their interests were concentrated in the outcomes of local (and other) 'boards' and, as such, they had influence on, and often the political power to thwart, progress. That story is, of course, a familiar one even in contemporary political processes.

A DIGRESSION ON 'KNOWLEDGE,' INTELLECTUAL PROPERTY RIGHTS, AND INFORMATION COSTS

The whole question of the assimilation of information, including information concerning education, social improvements, and sanitation reform, centered in part upon the ability of individuals to acquire knowledge of policies and events that affected them. Chadwick, employing something like a 'rationality assumption,' seemed at times to be arguing that rational individuals would vote 'correctly' if they could be properly informed. Matters relating to property rights and 'information costs' fascinated Chadwick from his earliest writings and in different contexts. In 1831 Chadwick wrote a newspaper article entitled 'The Taxes on Knowledge' for the *Westminster Review* (1831b), in which he analyzed the impact of taxes on the printed media to which we alluded in Chapter 6. A central theme in the paper was the decrease in output and related effects created by the imposition of a tax, but in a related context Chadwick considered the problem of patents and copyrights.[9]

The production of knowledge and technology presented problems not associated with the production of other goods and services. Chadwick (1831b: 259) cites the opinion of an anonymous manufacturer to illustrate the problem:

> in consequence of the impunity with which patterns of small works were copied immediately after they appeared, the only repayment which the manufacturer

can have for the labor of producing new patterns is a short and uncertain priority in the market; hence, it was not worth while to employ skillful artists to make designs; hence, the progress of an important branch of the arts was checked.

The producer has no assurance of recouping production costs in the absence of patents and copyrights, let alone earning a return on his investment. This is due to the fact that knowledge is a 'public good' with common pool properties. Given that there are resource costs to the production of these types of goods, individuals have no personal interest in pursuing an activity which is generally considered to be in the public interest. Patents as an artificial monopoly on technical processes had been granted in England since the Tudor era, although their origins were steeped in mercantile policies.[10] Chadwick, however, addressed a more general 'production of knowledge' in his paper and, more specifically, the protection of intellectual property rights.

Chadwick believed that an artificial identity of interest could be created, prescribing that 'protection should be given for a certain period to the copyright of the smallest paragraph, as for a whole book' (1831b: 260). Protection was to be enforced by granting summary judgment powers to local magistrates; the burden of proof being placed on the defendant. Chadwick equated copyright infringement with 'piracy,' advocating similar penalties, but tempered this attitude by suggesting a reduction in the fine to the production costs of the stolen article. If production cost was a 'floor' to the penalty, publishers would have no incentive to pirate an article and 'enterprise would have its proper reward, and would be more completely stimulated' (1831b: 261).

Chadwick's analysis of knowledge as a common pool resonates loudly in the minds of modern scholars. It is virtually identical to one of the aspects of knowledge that George Stigler delineated in 1968, namely that '. . . knowledge, once produced, is usually or at least often cheaply appropriable by any other enterprise which wishes to use it, in the absence of legal barriers to appropriation' (1968: 123).[11] The problem that Stigler addressed is the same one identified by Chadwick – the ease of appropriability leaves the producer of knowledge with great uncertainty with respect to capturing gains derivable from the knowledge. The issue is how to elicit the socially desirable allocation of resources to the production of knowledge. How long should the patent or copyright be? Stigler rejected a perpetual patent system, as would Chadwick, on grounds that 'the monopolistic sale of new knowledge would yield the same rate of return on resources as the competitive sale of other investment goods,' creating overinvestment in the production of knowledge (1968: 124). A time limit,

17 years in many applications, scales the rewards back to approximate the competitive exploitation of new knowledge. Chadwick's approach, similar to Stigler's in all essentials, was clearly modern.

Support for centralization, as we have seen, was in part placed at the door of the general (and rational) ignorance of local voters whose interest in most locally legislated activities was of small benefit to the average citizen. The general (and modern) argument for not voting is that the pro-rata share of benefits to an individual is overwhelmed by the cost of acquiring information. (This argument may of course be altered since individuals are generally more interested in services and provisions *closer* to them.) However, even in this area, Chadwick proffered a unique argument. He believed that there were physiological limits to 'mental labor.' There were, in other words, diminishing returns to the acquisition of information that were imposed by human physiology. This limit applied to voting, education, political speech, and conversation. Maturity extends this ability to concentrate and absorb, but there are limits. For example, consider Chadwick's view of education (1860 [1887]: 176):

> The business of education still requires for its successful prosecution scientific observation, and the study of the subject to be operated upon – the human mind. Even to empirical observation it should have suggested itself that the mind has conditions of growth which are required to be carefully noted, to adapt the amount of instruction intended to be given to the power of receiving it. It is a psychological law that the capacity of attention grows with the body.

The ability to concentrate varied with many factors – including temperature, the nature of the study (mathematics absorbed more concentration and could be studied only for shorter times), ventilation, lighting, overcrowding, and so on. But there were limits, even for savants (he cites Cuvier, Sir Walter Scott, and Sir Charles Lyell). More pointedly, Chadwick advocated physical training as well as educational instruction – up to the limits of capacity – as a means of pulling the poor and laboring classes into productive employments and lives:

> Where there have been good approximations to the proper physiological as well as the psychological conditions, as in the half-time industrial district schools, epidemic diseases have been banished, and the rate of mortality reduced to one-third of that which prevails amongst the general community in England and Wales alone, where upwards of a quarter of a million of children are annually swept away from preventable disease, which enervates those who survive. Four labourers, who have had the advantage of this improved physical and mental training are proved to be as efficient as five or more of those who have not. (Chadwick 1860 [1887]: 192)

CONCLUSION: TAXATION AS ONE KEY TO UTILITARIAN PLANNING

Clearly, sanitation reform – which is in all accuracy credited to Edwin Chadwick – was a cornerstone of the utilitarian agenda in nineteenth-century England. To this could be added education, health, prison, and many other 'reforms' of the system – much of it paid for out of taxation and local assessments. Chadwick had an insistent hand in all of these achievements. Chadwick's arguments, whether one accepted his recommendations for centralizing authority over these reforms (as well as over railways and other activities), were always empirically based – but also based, as we have seen in earlier chapters, on inventive and sometimes unique theoretical accouterments. Invention – or extension – of the concept of franchise bidding was only one example. Chadwick understood and applied asymmetric information, the common pool, time costs, and a myriad of other 'modern' microanalytic principles to economic issues and to the utilitarian agenda. In this regard, it is interesting to contrast Chadwick's approach to that of the other utilitarian master and Chadwick's very close friend, John Stuart Mill, to Bentham's program.

Clearly, Chadwick's approach was both theoretical and empirical, whereas Mill's was primarily a priori in nature. Both however, shared Bentham's belief in utilitarianism, incentive-based policies, creating artificial identities of interest, and in the principle – best enunciated by Mill – that 'all start fair.' The latter principle did not mean that individuals, due to differences in genetics, ambition, and energy (for example), should end up at the same place. Rather, the principle is that intergenerationally all should start out at the same place. Access to education, health, and other opportunities should be afforded to all but without guarantees that all end up in equality of income, status, and so on. This, of course, is a tall order for any society, but both Mill and Chadwick believed that the goal could be approached. Mill, for example, was an advocate of high or prohibitive death taxes. In order to gain some insight into Mill and Chadwick's notion of utilitarianism, it is instructive to look more closely at the tax structure of England at the time as a key to utilitarian goals.

The tax structure of England as Mill viewed it in the first edition of the *Principles* (1848a [1965]), and in testimony before Parliament in 1852 and 1861, was complex and filled with anomalies. Basically it was, as were many European systems of the day, a product of medieval (feudal) influences with particular elements from the more recent past. The form and amount of taxation in the United Kingdom was, of course, much conditioned by such 'exogenous' events as the Napoleonic and (later) the Crimean War (1852–56). Indirect taxes, including 'regalian' taxes in the form of customs duties and excises on particular commodities, were still a very large part of the tax structure in 1848. Out of total tax revenue of £51.4 million, fully 25 percent of the total was taken in the form of excises, and 38 percent in the form of customs revenues in 1848 (Shehab 1953: 90).

Direct taxes were (re)gaining favor in Chadwick and Mill's time. Wars with France at the end of the eighteenth century and the beginning of the nineteenth century had created extraordinary demands on the fisc. In 1798 Mr Pitt levied the first income tax (in Great Britain only) at a rate of 10*l.* per cent on incomes of 100*l.* and above and at various rates for incomes between 200*l.* and 60*l.* per year. That tax expired in 1815, but was reinstituted by Sir Robert Peel in 1842. After significant revisions of the entire tax structure under Gladstone in 1852–53, income taxes, despite continuous opposition, became a permanent part of the British tax structure.[12]

Death duties or a variety of other taxes (probate, legacy, and (later) succession duties, levied initially under the Stamp Act of 1815) had long been parts of the tax structure. In addition, other remnants of the medieval tax structure, especially the taxes on land and other forms of property, and a preponderance of indirect taxes, persisted into Mill's day. While it is not our purpose to provide details here, we find it significant that a radical restructuring of the British tax system (actually that of the United Kingdom) was in full swing during both Chadwick's and Mill's time.

Mill's views on a high and progressive inheritance tax – a view certainly shared by Chadwick – was designed as a focal point of an income redistribution program, but it was a centerpiece of their utilitarian program as well. While actual revenues from an inheritance tax were relatively small at the time, the tax became a major force in effecting a redistribution of wealth and income in the early decades of the twentieth century. Chadwick's and Mill's views of utilitarianism – in the form of taxation – are clear extensions of those propounded by Jeremy Bentham in *Escheat vice Taxation* (1795).[13] Bentham completely eschewed arguments defending absolute rights to property based on 'natural law' and other arguments. Bentham reveals his utter contempt for those who rely on an invoked 'natural law' to support one or another view of inheritance or of any other economic policy for that matter. Says Bentham (1795: 93–4, original emphasis):

> Quere, who is this same Queen '*Nature,*' who makes such stuff under the name of laws? Quere, in what year of her own, or anybody else's reign, did she make it, and in what shop is a copy of it to be bought, that it may be burnt by the hands of the common hangman . . . It being supposed, in point of *fact,* that the children have or have not a right, of the sort in question, given them by the *law,* the only rational question remaining is, whether, in point of *utility,* such a right *ought* to be given them or not? To talk of a *Law of Nature,* giving them, or not

giving them a *natural right*, is so much sheer nonsense, answering neither the one question nor the other.

As all know, Bentham based his argument on the 'utility' of the individuals receiving inheritance, and on the incentives or disincentives involved. Bentham's fundamental argument was as follows:

> Whatever power an individual is, according to the received notions of *propriety*, understood to possess in this behalf, with respect to the disposal of his fortune in the way of *bequest* – in other words, whatever degree of power he may exercise, without being thought to have dealt *hardly* by those on whom what he disposes of would otherwise have devolved – that same degree of power the law may, for the benefit of the public, exercise once for all, without being conceived to have dealt *hardly* by anybody, without being conceived to have *hurt* anybody, and, consequently, without scruple: and even thought the money so raised would *not* otherwise have been to raised in the way of taxes.

Bentham wanted to strengthen the law of escheat – the law dealing with the disposition of intestate property to the State and to limit the power of bequest. The law of intestate succession was to be eliminated except between close relatives with only half of the (then) current amount going to uncles and aunts, grandparents, and nephews and nieces. For those who died intestate, the State imposed a 100 percent tax on all inheritance. Bentham, unlike Mill, did not want to limit inheritance in direct lines, noting the possible disincentives of such limits on legators concerning 'the inducements to accumulate, and lay up property, instead of spending it' (Bentham 1795: 17). Death, in other words, meant that property rights are subject to limitations.[14] Bentham defended the (virtually) painless inheritance tax on collaterals (who had no cause to expect inheritance and whose utility was not appreciably diminished by not receiving one) as lightening the burden of taxes on the poor and working classes of society (Bentham 1795: 14). In other words, Bentham's arguments hinged on the utilitarian and incentive effects of various possible tax structures. Mill's views on income taxes were those of Bentham.[15]

Fundamentally, Mill and Chadwick (while in total agreement regarding aims) worked two sides of the utilitarian street. Two of the finest economic minds of nineteenth-century England provided utilitarian analyses of specific markets (Chadwick) and larger matters of taxation and income distribution as well as some basically a priori studies of markets (Mill). Alike though they were in their aims, moreover, there were very fundamental differences. While Mill was firmly in support of a high and progressive inheritance tax – defending intervivos gifts of course – and while he was keen to build incentives into government programs (Ekelund and

Tollison 1976; Schwartz 1972), he was not in favor of the kind of centralization espoused by his friend Chadwick. Mill's revealed preference was for income distribution leading to a strong middle class to take place within a market-oriented private property system. Social justice was from the beginning at root of his support of the Poor Laws but he worried that society's guarantee of an income to the destitute, if high enough to maintain them, would mean 'slavery' for society if the quid pro quo for welfare was not onerous enough. Chadwick had similar worries with respect to 'outdoor' relief for the poor, but he was led to the underlying problems – education and sanitation – which helped create the demand for poor relief.

Empirical investigations, the heart and soul of Chadwick's utilitarianism, were absolutely foreign to Mill moreover. Mill always deferred to Chadwick on matters of fact, as we have already mentioned. But he did not rely on a 'fact-based' analysis of economic questions and markets. He certainly reviewed Chadwick's voluminous writings and offered advice, but his reluctance to give an imprimatur to Chadwick's plan to nationalize industries (railways) or socialize property rights (for example, funeral and cabriolet markets) was met with stern resistance, despite Chadwick's evidence. Neither Chadwick nor Mill were socialists in any traditional sense, but Chadwick did countenance market interferences when he calculated a positive net utility outcome from his studies. Mill, often (unfairly, in our view) labeled a 'socialist' for his position on inheritance taxation, would abridge property rights, but only after a subject's death.

Strict rules regarding inheritance limitations (along with population control) formed the cornerstone in Mill's plan to redistribute and diffuse wealth, and to provide for *ex ante* equality in British society. It is correct that the rates of legacy and succession duties remained low throughout the nineteenth century, with the Stamp Act of 1815 supplying the basic rates until the Finance Act amendments of 1910.[16] These 'stamp duties,' which included a (regressive) probate tax on all inheritances and a legacy (and succession) duty depending on relationship to the legator, failed to get at real estate. Gladstone tried to levy new death duties on freehold and hereditary landed properties in 1853, but statistically the results were minimal (Peto 1863: 118–20). Assessment problems and evasion were unquestionably the reason for the failure of reforms.

Large increases and massive levies of death duties as a percent of property passed did not occur until the twentieth century. However, the 'take' of the death duties did rise during Mill's lifetime and afterward, to an extent with population, but also due to increased coverage, more accurate reporting, and a continued emphasis on direct versus indirect taxation. Death duty receipts (probate and legacy) grew from about £2 million in 1851 to £3.4 million in 1859 (Peto 1863: 135–6). Dramatic increases in the gross capital value of properties subject to estate duties took their amount to more than £31.7 million in 1918 (Soward and Willan 1919, Tables 10 and 14: 338–9 and 343). Death duties as a percentage of total government also rose over the last half of the nineteenth century, indicating that the kind of redistribution Mill envisioned was actually underway, at least until the massive growth of the state in England at the turn of the century.

Both Chadwick and Mill agreed on measures such as sanitation reform, and the urban cholera epidemics of the 1830s through the 1850s solidified that impetus to social, technological, and economic reform. Chadwick, who wholeheartedly supported Mill on these issues, went much further. He wanted to eliminate waste from many particular markets, believing that a transfer of property rights from open competition to a contract-letting body of 'experts' could maximize utility. The important point is that both Mill's and Chadwick's entire program – from sanitation and health reform, through reorganization of national and local markets, to a severe (proposed) revision of inheritance taxes – were inspired by Benthamite utilitarianism. Many of these proposals were the foundation for the change in income distribution and economic and social well-being in the latter part of the nineteenth century, and into the twentieth century as well. These altered programs were viewed by Chadwick, especially by Chadwick, as a cascade to progress and prosperity.

NOTES

1. Levi, using statistics collected in France, contrasted Britain's progress (20.15 per capita in 1858) with that of France (15 per capita) and Russia (5 per head).
2. J.S. Mill's view of the English tax structure, or so it is argued (Ekelund and Walker 1996) from which the discussion of this section derives, was motivated by the same condition of income distribution.
3. Chadwick's friend Mill argued that income taxes led to fraud and moral degeneration (1861 [1968–69]: 229). Many others complained of cheating. For example, the Draft Report to the Income Tax Committee of 1861 described the income from the trades and professions (Schedule D in the code) as depending 'on the conscience of the tax-payer, who often, it is feared, returns hundreds instead of thousands, and who is certain to decide any question that he can persuade himself to think doubtful, in his own favour' (quoted in Baxter 1868: 32). Also see Peto's (1863: 49) elaboration and documentation of enforcement problems.
4. Investigations surrounding the Poor Laws (as well as the insurance industry) were clear preludes to Chadwick's study of sanitation. He understood and was clearly impressed with incentive structures. Chadwick undertook the inquiry into the Poor Laws in his usual scientific manner determining: (1) the facts concerning the operation of the system; (2) the causes of the pernicious results and; (3) the reforms that would eliminate the ill-effects of the program. The first step resulted in city-by-city information concerning population, housing, employment, and welfare expenditures. The secular increase in relief expenditures attracted the greatest amount of Chadwick's attention. His investigations determined that the amount of relief and the method of payment

had caused the total expenditures on relief and the number of welfare recipients to increase. His proposals, as we mentioned in Chapter 1, attempted to alter incentives in the welfare system. His study led him to justify the further extension of the workhouse test. Districts (unions) cited were instances where his original plans had been followed to the letter. Where his plan was implemented relief expenditures fell drastically (£299 643 annually to £27 044 the first three months of operations) and the number of unemployed workers fell from 6160 to 124 (a 98 percent reduction). The data presented by Chadwick suggest that the old Poor Laws entailed a substantial disincentive for labor. Evidence supporting this conclusion has been the subject of much debate both in Chadwick's time and in our own. Testimony from local authorities that he presented to the Poor Law Commission attests to his thoroughness. As to accuracy, Tobias (1967), in a history of crime in English society corroborates Chadwick's evidence:

> Whatever use Chadwick made of it, the evidence was there. Enough of it survives to testify to the thoroughness of his investigations and to show that, on this issue as on many others, the view put forward in the report is a fair reflection of the opinions of the witnesses. (Tobias 1967: 151)

However, Tobias' conclusion may be biased by the fact that most of the data still in existence was actually compiled by Chadwick.
5. Centralization was vital in the kind of reforms Chadwick wanted to institute, as any of the numerous books on Poor Law reform reveal (see, for example, Brundage 1978).
6. One recent writer argues, with some empirical evidence, that Chadwick's distinction between artificial and natural identities of interest applies to politicians as well. Chadwick's distinction, in other words, could be used to support the public choice notion of term limits (Mixon 1996: 187–96).
7. Naturally there are many reasons why individuals vote – patriotism, close elections, and so on. But Chadwick's point concerning pro-rate share in outcomes would seem to apply with more force to 'federal' or 'national' elections where the voter's share (in the US) may be on the order of 1/150 million. Further, we take no position on the relative 'quality' of local versus higher level elections. Certainly one major consideration would be the site where tax and expenditure decisions, regulatory decisions, enforcement decisions, and so on were made. In a deToquevillian world of a large number of small local governments and a national government limited to provision of defense and justice, government competition and 'voting with one's feet' would appear to maximize citizen-voter utility (see Tiebout 1956).
8. The power of private arrangements to internalize rent dissipations in oil drilling and ocean and fishing resources vis-à-vis government solutions is developed in a number of contributions to the modern literature (see, for example, Bell 1986; Liebcap and Wiggins 1984). It goes without saying that Chadwick described only one form of strategic behavior in the case of 'drainage.' Different implicit assumptions about participant's conjectures would yield alternative outcomes. In other words, 'holdout' is only one possible outcome in the situation Chadwick describes.
9. Chadwick correctly concluded that a tax on news media would decrease circulation with the largest decrease in consumption being amongst the class with the greatest elasticity of demand– the laboring poor population. Chadwick thought a tax doubly bad for this class since he attributed their political 'unrest' to an uninformed state.
10. The Tudor monarchs used patents to attract 'foreign inventors' into England and subsequently as a rent-seeking device to further the private interests of both monopolists and the monarchs themselves (Ekelund and Tollison 1997). It was not until the Act on Monopolies in 1624, enacted under the Stuart monarchs, that such rent-seeking was restricted. Some of the issues linking the development of patents and the modern 'elasticity' in the granting of intellectual property rights are developed in a symposium on the subject in the *Journal of Cultural Economics* in 1995: see, in particular, Merges (1995).

11. Stigler's explorations (for example, see 1961), were stimulated by earlier important work on the impact of information in the functioning of markets developed by economist Frank Knight.
12. The tax imposed in 1842 was levied at 7*d.* in the pound on incomes of 150*l.* and above. In 1853 this rate was continued, plus a rate of 5*d.* on incomes from 100*l.* to 150*l.* and the tax was extended to Ireland. Rates rose and fell over the period of the Crimean War in the 1850s and in response to alterations in the excises and customs duties (see Levi 1860: 147–63 *et passim* for a useful summary of the entire British tax structure up to 1860).
13. The essay (written several years prior to 1795) was titled *Supply without Burden: or Escheat vice Taxation: being a Proposal for a Saving in Taxes by an Extension of the Law of Escheat: including Strictures on the Taxes on Collateral Succession comprized in the Budget of 7th Dec. 1795* (London: J. Debrett, 1795).
14. A similar argument was advanced in another connection – the rights to one's burial plot – in Chadwick's appendage to the 1842 *Sanitary Report* (1843). Chadwick, the utilitarian practitioner, appended a brief exposition of the English law with respect to perpetuities in public burial grounds (1843: 269–71). Rights, in a ruling judicial interpretation, consisted of a balancing act between those of the dead and those of the living and there were clear intertemporal aspects to the problem as in the case of intertemporal limits on property rights.
15. Mill went even further than Bentham in wanting to abolish collateral inheritance altogether with strict and progressive limits on direct heirs. His exact statements on these issues, admirably summarized by Hollander (1985: 876–9), include a defense of limitations on bequests, that is, limitations on private property. While suppressions of an unlimited right to bequest may have a marginal negative impact on accumulation during an individual's lifetime, such limits were more than acceptable in order to prevent the squandering of great fortunes by heirs who put no personal exertion into earning or developing them. The same went for intertemporal bequests with long chains of provisions far into the future. As Mill put it: '. . . property is only a means to an end, not itself the end. Like all other proprietary rights, and even in a greater degree than most, the power of bequest may be so exercised as to conflict with the permanent interests of the human race' (1848a [1965]: 226). Those in direct line such as children and parents were to be well protected in Mill's scheme so that they would not become a burden on society. But strict limits to inheritance for direct descendants were to be observed, not on grounds of diminishing marginal utility, but on Benthamite grounds of 'utility' maximization and on negative incentive effects to legatees (1852 [1968–69]: 309).
16. Rates (until the 1910 amendments) were with some variations, the following: husband or wife (0%); lineal ancestors or issue (1%); brothers or sisters or their descendants (3%); brothers or sisters of the father or mother or their descendants (5%); brothers or sisters of a grandfather or grandmother or their descendants (6%); other collaterals or strangers (10%). In 1910 rates rose, with a charge (1%) added to husband and wife (Soward and Willan 1919: 323–4).

9. If markets fail: Chadwick and contemporary society

INTRODUCTION

Edwin Chadwick was unquestionably a pioneer in addressing social and economic problems in a utilitarian manner. He has justly been lauded for his role in sanitation, labor, and educational reform. But in seeking 'the greatest good for the greatest number' Chadwick pushed the traditional (Smithian, classical) boundaries of both economic analysis and policy far beyond anything offered in the nineteenth century.

There are first the amazing inventions of particular microanalytic concepts that would not rise above water until far into the twentieth century. The issues of moral hazard, product and personal liability placement, and the role of possibly welfare-lowering incentives within markets were discoveries of the highest order. (Naturally it would be a serious error to claim that he possessed a comprehensive contemporary understanding of these concepts.) Additionally, the integral role that technology played in markets – and in economic progress generally – was emphasized by Chadwick and almost completely neglected by mainstream classical economists. The attempt to meld economic theory and policy with an anecdotal statistical complement is also unique for his time and place, and is elevated to high art by him. Multiple regression, time series, and sophisticated statistical techniques were more than a century away, but Chadwick marshaled and massed all the anecdotal evidence he could for sanitation reform and so many other projects.

Employing and integrating such tools into his research, Chadwick's primary contributions were to an analysis of markets that failed, and rules and regulations that created common pool problems. He is primarily known in economic circles for his notion of competition for the entire field of service rather than the standard competition within the field of service, but this was only one of his major and unique achievements. Markets, alleged Chadwick, in contrast to Smith's 'invisible hand,' could fail: (1) due to imperfect and/or asymmetric information about prices and exchange; and/or (2) due to common pool problems created by a failure to define property rights. A primary focus of this book has been an analysis

of how Chadwick dealt with such questions. But encased within his examples was both a theory and particular 'inventions' that only came to light
within microeconomic theory in the twentieth century. We must return
to the architecture of the Smithian tradition and its challenges in the
twentieth century in order to understand Chadwick's achievement.

TRADITIONAL MARKET THEORY AND ITS DISSENTERS: CHADWICK'S ACHIEVEMENT

Placing Chadwick's achievement within historical tradition requires revisit-
ing Adam Smith's view of markets and the critical amendments to his view.
Smith, as all know, held that, under particular and generally unspecified
conditions, self-interest promoted the general social interest. Naturally
this result could take place only under a wide array of assumptions.
Information concerning prices and preferences could be obtained cost-
lessly by buyers and sellers. All resource ownership was decentralized and
property was private. Production technology was such that there were no
economies of large scale production. These conditions in both Smithian
and later neoclassical (Marshallian) economics were assumed to produce
an efficient allocation of resources and, in most formulations, a maximum
of welfare.

We have seen in this book that Chadwick challenged these assumptions. In the case of railways he observed decreasing costs and 'natural
monopoly,' conditions whereby a single firm could most efficiently supply
the entire market and where consolidation would bring economies to
the English rail system. He looked to very real information costs to
market participants as an exception to Smith's (and the neoclassical)
argument that price and exchange information was costless. Further,
Chadwick identified a 'tragedy of the commons' in the forms of the
then-contemporary judicial and penal systems. The common property
character of the system encouraged overuse, indicating the absence of
another implicit assumption of the Smithian-neoclassical (private interest
= public interest) theory. These problems were not noticed – in any strict
theoretical sense – for generations.

In 1920 the British economist Arthur Cecil Pigou described a problem
where private costs were (allegedly) not equal to benefits. His famous
example (there were others) was of two public roads A and B from point
X to point Y. A was narrow but more direct and took less time to traverse,
but B was wider but more indirect. Congestion would occur on road A
because drivers would not take account of the congestion, imposing a cost
(or externality) on road A drivers. Road A would be 'over used.' Thus,

he concluded that markets could be inefficient and suggested a tax (or a subsidy for a positive externality) so that private and social costs would converge. Later (in 1924) economist Frank Knight brilliantly attacked this argument by noting that Pigou's result would occur only if the roads were public. If roads A and B were private, a congestion toll on A could be charged to bring private and social costs in line – that is, where entry was not costless and property rights were assigned (to a park, for example), overcrowding does not occur. It would not be in the interests of the road owner to let that happen unless the costs of monitoring the congestion were higher to him or her than the benefits of pricing the resource.

In 1960 Ronald Coase argued that so-called 'external effects' are two-sided in one of the most famous economic papers of the twentieth century. Consider an example of air pollution – a factory belching smoke over a nearby community. While harmful to the community, these externalities or 'spillover effects' do in fact create benefits to the firm. As the output of the firm rises, the firm's marginal benefits of pollution decline because the rate of return on additional production generally declines. On the cost side, the marginal cost of pollution is measured by the harm created by the smoke, which is an increasing function of production, since more production means more smoke. In Coase's conception, the marginal cost of pollution to the community must be balanced against its marginal benefits to the firm. The solution (as Chadwick recognized in the case of accidents) is to assign liability to one of the other parties and, in a world where bargaining costs nothing, the assignment of legal liability to a particular party does not matter. If the judiciary assigns liability to the low-cost mitigator (to homeowners in the area or to the factory owners, as the case may be), a private economy solution may be reached.

Modern Perspectives on the Externalities Problem

There is a catch to Coase's theorem, and its defense of purely private markets, at least in some situations. If the cost of defining and enforcing a system of ownership are significant, a role for government can be established. These might include taxing or subsidizing the externalities, selling 'rights' to pollute or engage in some behavior that creates the externality, or to regulate by monitoring behavior or, as Chadwick often argued, to take property rights from one or more parties to exchange and put them out for competitive bid. But there may be little or no reason to intervene at all, according to some contemporary theorists.

There are no perfect systems ('nirvana') in any world and the question of asymmetric information is an important case in point. Akerlof (1970) in a famous paper on 'lemons' argued that information asymmetries (we may call them transactions costs) prohibited some exchange or, in the limit, eliminated it entirely. Assume that A, who is purchasing a used car or appliance, has less information about the quality of the item than the seller, B. (One might think of Chadwick's buyers and sellers of urban funeral services described in Chapter 5.) If price is a signal of quality, a lowered price – that might bring buyers and sellers to equilibrium under other circumstances – might indicate a 'lemon,' causing demanders to reduce their demand for the car or appliance. In the limit, the market may actually disappear. But this is clearly not a solid case for government intervention. All manner of market devices develop to mitigate the information disparity – warranties by sellers, 'brand' names creating reputation and credence, money-back guarantees, independent certification, and so on. Competition and institutions arise to take care of such disparities in transactions cost.

Information, however, is not free, and that raises interesting questions. There are costs and benefits to acquiring information on all goods and services. Are private markets sufficient to develop solutions to transactions costs, or is some form of government intervention – licensing, regulation, certification, or other means – necessary? Economists are divided both theoretically and 'practically' over this choice. Some, notably Harold Demsetz (2011) and Thomas DiLorenzo (2011), have argued that the necessity for government resolution of such conflicts is extremely rare since only 'complex private negotiations' (that is, costly negotiations) between the two parties to the externality justify regulations. Demsetz further argues that private ownership generally resolves problems and that transactions costs must be an assumption in any economy but are generally the result of ignorance. Demsetz says: '. . . there exists an efficient amount of ignorance in an economic system if the cost of acquiring information is positive. The amount of ignorance that is efficient increases as does the cost of transacting (viewed as the cost of conveying information). Ignorance not only may be bliss, it also may be efficient' (2011: 9).

Therein lies the conundrum for modern practice if – a big 'if' – policy is to be based on rational economic principles rather than political forces and expediency. It is also a key to evaluating Chadwick's arguments from the nineteenth century. Is the fact that information regarding all goods or services is costly in terms of money and time a persuasive argument for no extra-market institutions – that is, the claim that, 'what is, must be optimal?' This position may be clear for the vast majority of goods but it has not been (at least in practice) for drug and food safety, physicians services, transport safety, and a myriad of other goods and services. Obviously the regulatory system in all of its manifestations is the product of both attempts to lower costs of information and blatant rent-seeking. Physicians and drug companies in the late nineteenth and early twentieth centuries in America pressed for licensing and regulation – which may have lowered information costs to consumers (over possible alternatives), but they also enhanced the income of suppliers in these markets.[1] The point is that there is a plethora of institutional alternatives that could amend so-called market failures. We do not deny that contemporary economists' arguments have merit, but the proposition that the status quo in real world markets is somehow 'optimal' is as unlikely as assuming that government can magically establish 'nirvana' (efficient equilibrium, always) in some low-cost fashion.

This is where Chadwick's nineteenth-century observations have relevance. He did not extend Smith's theory in the directions of Pigou, Knight, or Coase. Rather, he took Bentham's concept of the design of an 'artificial identity of interests' and a notion that 'incentives always matter given constraints' and presented actual case studies of what he deemed market failure, including information cost. Chadwick had a clear practical understanding of so-called market failure in its different forms – identified only in contemporary literature. Nirvana did not and does not exist in either government or market arrangements or restrictions in markets, but decisions must be made in some fashion when questions of possible market failure arise. (Too often they are based on politics, as Chadwick and modern analysts both understand.) We now consider the major forms identified by him and some of the difficulties associated with them.

The Franchise Solution

Chadwick applied the Bentham-inspired franchise solution to many of the types of market failure he identified: that included both failures due to decreasing cost (natural monopoly) and failures due to asymmetric information. One major economy-wide failure, in contrast to local economic problems with sanitation and health, was in the operation and management of the English railways. As we saw in Chapter 4, Chadwick advocated that English railways be purchased by the government and 'leased' via competitive bid to a private or to an interlocking set of private companies. He advocated the same system to cure inefficiencies that he observed in many areas – bread and beer sales being only two of them. There are of course problems with any such system, as we observed in Chapter 4.

A contracting body must be formed in order to design, modify, and administer the contract or contracts (in the case of multiple suppliers) to railway (or beer or bread) suppliers. Medieval practice (and that in some contemporary situations) would have been to ask 'what is the maximum price a business or individual would pay for the exclusive right to supply a good or service.' But this was not the Chadwick plan. The contracting body would accept bids (non-collusive bids would be required) for the lowest price that a concern would be willing to charge for pre-specified services, given that a normal profit was built into the bid. This would require that the contracting body be able to estimate demand and cost over the contract period. The longer the period, the more difficult it would be to estimate these magnitudes. Further, fundamental changes in demand or costs would produce either super-normal profits or losses.

The length of the contract would not only create estimation difficulties as outlined above, but it would affect the motives of private entrepreneurs to implant capital as well. The shorter the time horizon – contract length – the less likely that optimal (from society's perspective) emplacement of railway capital (rolling stock, and so on) would be installed by the entrepreneur. And, as has been pointed out in the modern literature, uncertainty would exist in anticipation of re-contracting by the initial bid winner. This would be the case for failures due to asymmetric information as well. Could the capital be sold at true opportunity cost at re-contract time if the initial winner loses the contract? Naturally, as Chadwick suggests, separate arrangements or an additional contracting process could be developed for capital deployment. Coordination problems would inure to this scheme however, and such matters may not easily be resolved.

One of the chief problems with traditional cost-plus regulation (with or without government ownership) is that the regulatory body tends to become captured by the regulated industry. Such regulation subverts the public interest to the interests of opportunistic actors, both regulators and regulated (Peltzman 1976). The formation of a contracting body controlled by either the industry or by political representatives could create the same effects. (Popular election of the contracting body might be a possible alternative, as Chadwick suggested.) Fundamentally, however, Chadwick assumed that those designing and letting contracts were possessed of high expertise in the subject of regulation – in this case, railway routes, rates, and operations. Such individuals must control all aspects of the industry and constantly monitor the contract terms and operators for cheating by inflating costs or creating x-inefficiency. In sum, should the alternatives of open competition or cost-plus regulation prove deleterious to societal welfare – as determined using the best statistical evidence – Chadwick's plan may be a viable alternative. Certainly the franchise/competitive bidding solution is a staple of the supply of military equipment (and some personnel) in the United States and many other countries.

Common Pools

Chadwick was the first economist and policymaker to demonstrate a thorough understanding of the common pool, especially in response to policing and the judiciary. He, unlike a number of modern observers, focused on crime prevention and the common property problems created by the evolution of the criminal justice system in England. The system, in Chadwick's time, was in hopeless disarray due to the lack of incentives on the part of police, victims, potential victims, and the public at large to participate in crime prevention as well as enforcement – a situation created by the Norman collectivization of the market. They had little or no incentive to do so! The criminal justice system as it existed (and still exists) did little to encourage the vital participation of the public in crime prevention. Indeed, the same kinds of problems apply in the present system. Chadwick's emphasis thus turned to instituting an efficient *public* system of police enforcement and crime prevention. He did not advocate a return to the old system of pre- and early-frankpledge, although theft victims could sue for property if recovered, but he believed that greater participation of the public could be obtained through a streamlined, *but publicly provided*, judicial system. These new benefits were of the nature of lower time costs to victims, the accused, and witnesses, with higher payoffs to private citizens through swifter and improved criminal procedure. Part of those innovations would be to make far less use of the jury system and lawyer-dominated trials. Incentives were the key – simply lower the full price of participation and system efficiency improves.

The incentives of police did not serve the ends of crime prevention or even of reasonable enforcement of laws. To mitigate these problems, Chadwick suggested numerous means, administrative and technological, to create more efficiency in the apprehension of criminals and enforcement of the law, and he continued to make these observations throughout the nineteenth century. He was not above hyperbole and exaggerated statistics in an attempt to scare the English into his system.[2] However, the important point to be made is that the non-existent incentives for crime *prevention* had to be changed. The argument that a system might be devised for rewarding officers on the basis of reduced crime rates in particular locales was truly unique. Accurate information and collection of statistics was vital to that end and, for Edwin Chadwick's entire life, that goal was paramount in so many areas of economic and social policy. Whether an *ex post* system of evaluating prevention and assigning property rights (benefits and costs) to particular officers would ever actually be possible or not, Chadwick, to the best of our knowledge, was the first ever to propose such a system. Further resources within the English system had to be 'priced' and incentives given to participate. Without that input, gross inefficiencies and lack of justice that characterized the system would continue. Further, part of these inefficiencies would be the build-up of private police forces, a trend that Chadwick vehemently opposed.

Thus, both a *public* and a *centralized* system were proposed to achieve the goals of efficient justice and crime prevention. The evolved system did not maximize social utilities and Chadwick wanted to eliminate the localized short-term agreements between local magistrates, the constabularies and the local communities they served. A nationalized system, Chadwick believed, created huge economies of scale. It would reduce negotiation costs of contractual agreements by standardization and internalization. Information costs would be reduced through interlinked organizations. Cost efficiencies would further be reduced by a centralized mobile force with reduced response time and forecasting the requirements of extra police due to riots, crime sprees, and so on. Through organization, standardization, and reduction of excess forces (mobile forces on standby), transaction costs could be reduced as compared with the localized and independent forces as then existed. Chadwick's was a comparative microanalytic and contractual approach to the study of economic organization, making the transaction the basic unit of analysis, and reviewing the details of governance and human action.

The Modernity of Edwin Chadwick

Economic theory is one thing – the world as it actually exists is another. This might be the mantra of Edwin Chadwick as it is for most policymakers in all countries today. Chadwick's modernity consists in a number of creative inventions, as we have seen. In addition to understanding how the action of incentives might not promote the general welfare and offering solutions, he understood how technology could be used to further societal goals, one of which was sanitation and health of all English persons. Not least, no writer of the nineteenth century had a more solid grasp on how technology and innovations could lower information and transactions costs in the economy: tricycles reduced time cost in the apprehension of criminals; literacy and knowledge created by the dissemination of newspapers enhanced social and market functioning; and time had an economic value equal to the wage rate. Such insights were unique among the savants of his time.

A final but critical issue remains to be considered in light of Chadwick's arguments. Is some economic rationale necessary for government interventions and, if so, what standard or standards of proof are (or should be) required for some particular form of intervention? Cynically but correctly, we might argue that rent-seeking forms of self-interest explain much regulation, as *endogenous* politicians balance the costs and benefits of supplying a regulatory apparatus to transfer rents in the fashion outlined in the famous research of Stigler (1971) and Peltzman (1976). In this public-interest-versus-private-interest or interest-group approach, coalitions gain control of the regulatory apparatus in order to redistribute rents in their interests. This familiar story has been given credence in much current research relating to government interventions in private markets.

The fall-back on public choice – however apt – nevertheless tends to mask the role of the economist as evaluator and analyst of basic costs and benefits in particular cases. Chadwick really believed that producing the best evidence possible would be a means of possibly overcoming entrenched political interests. While 'significant' economies of scale have always been an appealing rationale among economists for advocating regulation, the whole question of information costs and externalities was not brought into play until the modern era. So-called monopolistic elements found in markets may be sufficient reason to advocate regulation. The parent or parents of market failure – other than the so-called failure of long-term private contracts to provide adequate assurances of supplies to producers and consumers in the present – are not even identified in much of the literature providing rationales for regulation (Goldberg 1976). Allegations of market failure, whether based on tastes, asymmetric information, meddlesome preferences, transactions costs, or economies of scale, are of equal moment in comparative institutional approaches to property rights abrogation. Chadwick's approach to these matters was at least scientific, producing as he did the best evidence he could gather in order to promote change or to select a system of provision.

The nature of a nirvana versus a comparative institutional approach to efficiency norms is also relevant. Chadwick's funeral markets case, for example, even suggests a new approach to nirvana. Any conclusion as to the efficiency properties of an action must take place between alternative real and possible institutional arrangements. As Demsetz presciently observed, 'To say that private enterprise is inefficient because indivisibilities and imperfect knowledge are part of life . . . is to say little more than that the competitive equilibrium would be different if these were not the facts of life' (1969: 19). Chadwick's observation of transactions and information costs in the case of urban funeral supply led him to urge a *wholesale change* in institutional arrangements. Neither antitrust nor price regulation nor liability alterations were suggested. Rather, outright socialization of property rights was the essence of Chadwick solution. Unlucky funeral competitors would lose the right to freely supply their goods and services – it would be illegal to do so. They could only act as agents for government and then, only with a franchised permit.

The radical abrogation of property rights alters the basis for evaluating 'efficiency' in any real comparative-market-institutional framework, and introduces a new concept of 'socialized nirvana.'[3] A system of 'competitive' efficiency *cum* collective property rights is idealized. This solution is depicted as on equal footing with other systems (as is Arrow's nirvana) but without the caveat that others things are *not* equal. In particular, fundamentally different rules of agency and incentives inure to communal property rights, suggesting inefficiencies peculiar to that system. Any existing institutional arrangement, competitive or not, will fall short of some *idealized* Chadwick-style arrangement with completely socialized property rights.[4] To include a radically different system of property rights with costless information, omniscient and benevolent administrators, and transactions under franchising, would always tilt the balance in favor of some socialist 'nirvana' as an alternative.

Much of the enthusiasm for contemporary regulation, as well as in Chadwick's funeral market example, rests upon a misunderstanding of the competitive process within the context of comparative institutions. It is quite possible that Chadwick, for example, was sometimes describing a market in competitive *dis*equilibrium, but analyzing it within the framework of the results of the static 'equilibrium-always' model. In this sort of static world suggesting perpetual efficiency, costs are always at minimum and waste is eliminated. But in a world of 'tendencies' to equilibrium, some waste was a natural and *expected* product of the competitive process. Destruction of capital within the ebb and flow of unregulated competitive activity is cost effective when the costs of regulation and the reductions in value and efficiency from rent-seeking are considered. Allegations of monopoly may well be observationally equivalent to competitive disequilibrium which occurs, along with transaction costs, in all real markets. The attempt to provide an 'equilibrium-always' solution, as Chadwick did in his funeral markets example, has incomparable inefficiency properties of its own. Competitive 'nirvana' and socialist 'nirvana' are equally chimerical standards of efficiency. A central issue however, suggested by Chadwick, was the length of time monopoly or market imperfections would be tolerated. Here, time preference by demanders of goods or services comes into play, and with a universal positive time preference, business may be regulated or nationalized by government (Ekelund and Higgins 1982). The Chadwick plan of franchising might offer an alternative to government bureaucracies who manage industries or services in these circumstances. Clearly, the fact that such plans exist for products and services that do not undergo rapid technological change is proof that the scheme is viable. Hanke and Walters (2011) report that alternative schemes utilizing Chadwick's plan have been implemented and still exist in areas of France and in other areas of the world.[5] There is always a mix of public-private responsibilities, among the most important being capital emplacement. Who is responsible for providing capital, maintaining it, and for replacing it with more efficient technologies? All of these questions and many others must be addressed in a public-private partnership. A myriad of details attend such arrangements but suffice it to note that Chadwick's contract bidding plan is in operation in countries around the world. (That does not mean that some kind of nirvana is reached in any or all cases of course.)

Finally, it is interesting to comment on Chadwick as an economic theorist in both a narrow and in the broader sense of economic methodology. There is no question that no writer in the nineteenth century recognized the 'externality' problem (absent in traditional classical and neoclassical literature), the common pool issue, and the potential sources of market failure, more clearly than Chadwick. Bentham's 'artificial identity of interest' approach took on new meaning under his searing analyses of real world markets. How could accidents be prevented? Assign liability to the party most able to provide safety. How could public safety and sanitation be provided? Create market incentives that led to safety and sanitation. In other words, set up markets with liability rules that depend on incentives to achieve productive goals. These principles were not employed to deal with externalities until the second half of the twentieth century.

Then there is the broader context of Chadwick's achievements. Chadwick most likely did not think of himself as an economic *theorist*, even of the type that existed in his own day, and of whom he was acutely knowledgeable. Rather, he observed and gathered data on economic problems, finding *new* ways of approaching their solution. His method provides insight into a long-ranging 'environmental hypothesis' regarding the development of economic theory. His achievement was not a brick in the building up of economic theory from 'error to truth.' Rather, it was built on simple observations learned from Bentham and honed to fit economic problems as he found them. The environment – sanitation problems, information disparities among market participants in markets with no tendency to equilibrium, uncoordinated rail lines, and so on – helped Chadwick create new and alternative approaches to making practical advances in economic welfare. His analyses contain errors and important lacunae, but unlike any of his great contemporary thinkers in England, he did not simply ask 'what is it?' He went and made a visit by employing every empirical tool and every source of information at his disposal. Edwin Chadwick, to his everlasting credit, drew England's (and more recently, the world's) attention to the solidity of reason drawn from facts and the necessity of careful evaluation. This method of analyzing economic problems, and the tools used to do so, are his unique legacy. He was, in short, not only a great 'social reformer' – he was much more. He was an *economist* who in fact promulgated utilitarian analyses and possible solutions to social and economic problems that most of his contemporaries deemed impenetrable.

NOTES

1. Supply restrictions in the market for physicians – first at state and then at federal levels – may have been the foundation of the current 'health crisis' in the United States. First, physicians were licensed, after which hospitals were regulated, due to the fact that physicians could only be certified in 'approved' hospitals. The number of physicians and hospitals were thus conscribed by government regulations. Adding Medicare and other factors to the equation meant demand increases without supply increases as population and technology changed. The question is whether market forces – independent private evaluations of physicians and hospital services – would have been sufficient to create another path to health care in the United States.
2. In Chadwick's testimony for the first *Constabulary Report* of 1839 (see *British Parliamentary Papers* 1968b), for example, his statistics suggested that there were between 72000 and 120000 criminals at large (see Finer 1952: 168) and that the greatest danger was that many of them were migratory (requiring a centralized force).
3. Here we believe that Dnes is mistaken when arguing that 'externalities' created even by meddlesome preferences (as in Chadwick's recommended regulation of public houses) could conceivably be addressed by Chadwick's scheme (Dnes 1994: 531–3). Using some nirvana standard, virtually any industry at one time or another could potentially be improved upon – but at the cost of total economic freedom and private property.
4. The point is reminiscent of the idealized socialist solutions advocated as superior to the imperfect 'capitalist' market functioning in the former Soviet Union and the 'socialist calculation' debates thereby engendered. Chadwick's solution must actually be tried in order to assess the relative efficiency characteristics he alleged for the scheme. Without an actual test, for example, there is no way to assess statements such as 'From a comparative-institutionalist perspective, it may indeed be desirable to control an externality using Chadwick's idea of contract management. This may happen if other methods are infeasible or too costly and there is an increase in total net benefit from control' (Dnes 1994: 532). In 'nirvana' terms, the game is always won under perfectly functioning socialism. If systems are to be judged in other terms, what are those terms, what are their standards of proof, and where is the burden of proof to be placed in assessing alternative institutional arrangements?
5. Hanke and Walters (2011: 34) note in an excellent paper citing Chadwick that the water-supply industry appears 'well suited to the franchise bidding approach. The technology of water supply is well known and relatively static, and specifications about service standards ought to be readily formulable.' They go on to describe a series of alternative arrangements or combinations of public-private interactions, some of them operative in Brazil, Morocco, Peru, Indonesia, Kuwait, and several African countries. Our only reservation is that these schemes are not 'privatization' if that means direct private assignment of property rights. Only temporary property rights of some measure are acquired by winning bidders, a fact that attenuates incentives.

Bibliography

Akerlof, George A. (1970), 'The Market for Lemons: Quality Uncertainty and the Market Mechanism,' *Quarterly Journal of Economics*, **84** (3): 488–500.

Alchian, Armen A. and Harold Demsetz (1972), 'Production, Information Costs, and Economic Organization,' *American Economic Review*, **62** (5): 777–95.

Baumol, William J. and David F. Bradford (1970), 'Optimal Departures from Marginal Cost Pricing,' *American Economic Review*, **60** (3): 265–83.

Baumol, William J., John C. Panzar, and Robert D. Willig (1982), *Contestable Markets and the Theory of Industry Structure*, New York: Harcourt Brace Jovanovich.

Baxter, Robert Dudley (1868), *National Income: The United Kingdom*, London: Macmillan and Co.

Beach, E.F. (1971), 'Hicks on Ricardo on Machinery,' *Economic Journal*, **81** (324): 916–22.

Becker, Gary S. (1965), 'A Theory of the Allocation of Time,' *Economic Journal*, **75** (299): 493–517.

Becker, Gary S. (1968), 'Crime and Punishment: An Economic Approach,' *Journal of Political Economy*, **76** (2): 169–217.

Becker, Gary S. (1981), *A Treatise on the Family*, Cambridge: Harvard University Press.

Becker, Gary S. and G.J. Stigler (1974), 'Law Enforcement, Malfeasance, and Compensation of Enforcers,' *Journal of Legal Studies*, **3** (1): 1–18.

Beil, Richard O., Thomas Dazzio, R.B. Ekelund Jr, and John D. Jackson (1993), 'Competition and the Price of Municipal Television Services: An Empirical Study,' *Journal of Regulatory Economics*, **5** (4): 401–15.

Belidor, Bernard de (1729), *La science des ingenieurs dans la conduite des travaux de fortification et d'architecture civile*.

Bell, Frederick W. (1986), 'Mitigating the Tragedy of the Commons,' *Southern Economic Journal*, **52**: 653–64.

Benhan, Lee (1972), 'The Effect of Advertising on the Price of Eyeglasses,' *Journal of Law and Economics*, **15** (2): 337–52.

Benson, B. (1990), *The Enterprise of Law: Justice without the State*, San Francisco: Pacific Research Institute for Public Policy.

Benson, B. (1994), 'Are Public Goods Really Common Pools? Considerations of the Evolution of Policing and Highways in England,' *Economic Inquiry*, **32** (2): 249–71.

Benson, B. (1998), *To Serve and Protect: Privatization and Community in Criminal Justice*, New York: New York University Press.

Bentham, Jeremy (1776–82 [1962]), *The Works of Jeremy Bentham*, John Bowring (ed.), Vol. 1, New York: Russell and Russell.

Bentham, Jeremy (1789 [1948]), *An Introduction to the Principles of Morals and Legislation*, New York: Hafner Publishing Company.

Bentham, Jeremy (1791 [1995]), *The Panopticon Writings*, London: Verso.

Bentham, Jeremy (1795), *Supply without Burden: or Escheat vice Taxation*, London: J. Debrett.

Blaug, Mark (1963), 'The Myth of the Old Poor Law and the Making of the New,' *Journal of Economic History*, **23** (2): 151–84.

Blaug, Mark (1964), 'The Poor Law Report Reexamined,' *Journal of Economic History*, **24** (2): 229–45.

Blaug, Mark (1978), *Economic Theory in Retrospect*, 3rd edn, Cambridge: Cambridge University Press.

British Parliamentary Papers (1968a), *Crime and Punishment: Police*, Vol. 4, Irish University Press Series of *British Parliamentary Papers*, Shannon: Irish University Press.

British Parliamentary Papers (1968b), *Crime and Punishment: Police*, Vol. 6, Irish University Press Series of *British Parliamentary Papers*, Shannon: Irish University Press.

Brundage, A. (1978), *The Making of the New Poor Law*, New Brunswick, NJ: Rutgers University Press.

Brundage, A. (1988), *England's 'Prussian Minister': Edwin Chadwick and the Politics of Government Growth, 1832–1854*, University Park, PA: Pennsylvania State University.

Buchanan, James and Gordon Tullock (1962), *The Calculus of Consent*, Ann Arbor: University of Michigan Press.

Cantillon, Richard (1729 [1931]), *Essai sur la nature de la commerce en general*, H. Higgs (ed.), London: Macmillan.

Carnegie, Andrew (1900), *The Gospel of Wealth*, New York: Century.

Chadwick, Edwin (1828), 'On the Means of Insurance,' *Westminster Review*, **9**: 384–421.

Chadwick, Edwin (1829), 'Preventive Police,' *London Review*, **1**: 252–308.

Chadwick, Edwin (1831a), 'The Real Incendiaries and Promoters of Crime,' *The Examiner*, **1203**: 114–16.

Chadwick, Edwin (1831b), 'The Taxes on Knowledge,' *Westminster Review*, **20**: 238–67.

Chadwick, Edwin (1836), 'Testimony,' Second Annual Report of the Poor Law Commissioners, *British Parliamentary Papers* (Sessional Papers).

Chadwick, Edwin (with Charles Shaw Lefevre and Charles Rowan) (1839a), The Royal Commission on Constabulary Forces, *First Report of the Commissioners Appointed to Inquire as to the Best Means of Establishing an Efficient Constabulary Force in the Counties of England and Wales*, London: Her Majesty's Stationery Office.

Chadwick, Edwin (1839b [1968]), 'Testimony,' *British Parliamentary Papers, Crime and Punishments: Police*, Vol. 6, Irish University Press Series of *British Parliamentary Papers*, Shannon: Irish University Press.

Chadwick, Edwin (1841), 'License of Counsel: Criminal Procedure,' *Westminster Review*, **35** (January–April): 1–23.

Chadwick, Edwin (1842a), *Report to Her Majesty's Principal Secretary of State for the Home Department, from the Poor Law Commissioners, on an Inquiry into the Sanitary Condition of the Labouring Population of Great Britain*, London: W. Clowes and Sons.

Chadwick, Edwin (1842b [1965]), *On an Inquiry into the Sanitary Condition of the Labouring Population of Great Britain*, London: W. Clowes and Sons. Reprinted as *Report on the Sanitary Condition of the Labouring Population of Great Britain*, edited with an Introduction by M.W. Flinn. Edinburgh: Edinburgh University Press.

Chadwick, Edwin (1843), *Report on the Sanitary Conditions of the Labouring Population of Great Britain: A Supplementary Report on the Results of a Special Inquiry into the Practice of Interment in Towns*, London: W. Clowes and Sons.

Chadwick, Edwin (1846), *Papers Read Before the Statistical Society of Manchester on the Demoralization and Injuries Occasioned by the Want of Proper Regulations of Laborers Engaged in the Construction and Working of Railways*, Manchester: Simms and Sinham.

Chadwick, Edwin (1856a), 'Extracts from an Address on Improvements in Machinery and in Manufacturing Processes, as Affecting the Condition of the Labourers,' *Journal of the Royal Society of Arts*, **4**: 803–6.

Chadwick, Edwin (1856b), 'Improvements in Machinery – Races of Workmen – Nominally Low-Priced Labour,' *Journal of the Royal Society of Arts*, **5**: 77–8.

Chadwick, Edwin (1857a), 'The Application of Sewage Irrigation to Cereal Crops,' *Journal of the Royal Society of Arts*, **5**: 497–9.

Chadwick, Edwin (1857b), *A Lecture on the Economical, Social, Educational and Political Importance of Open Competitive Examinations*, London: Knight and Co.

Chadwick, Edwin (1859a), 'On the Forces Used in Agriculture,' *Journal of the Royal Society of Arts*, **8**: 62–3.

Chadwick, Edwin (1859b), 'On the Prevention of Accidents in Coal Mines,' *Journal of the Royal Society of Arts*, **8**: 43–4.

Chadwick, Edwin (1859c), 'Results of Different Principles of Legislation and Administration in Europe; of Competition for the Field, as Compared with Competition within the Field of Service,' *Journal of the Royal Statistical Society*, **22**: 381–420.

Chadwick, Edwin (1860 [1887]), 'The Physiological Limits of Mental Labour,' in B.W. Richardson (ed.), *The Health of Nations: A Review of the Works of Edwin Chadwick*, Vol. I, London: Longmans, Green and Co., pp. 176–92.

Chadwick, Edwin (1861), 'Some Accounts of American Implements and Economic Contrivances,' *Journal of the Royal Society of Arts*, **9**: 366–7.

Chadwick, Edwin (1863 [1887]), 'Prevention of Robberies and Murders for Money,' in B.W. Richardson (ed.), *The Health of Nations: A Review of the Works of Edwin Chadwick*, Vol. II, London: Longmans, Green and Co., pp. 398–405.

Chadwick, Edwin (1865a), 'Address on Railway Reform,' Transactions of the National Association for the Promotion of Social Science at its Annual Conference: 69–115.

Chadwick, Edwin (1865b), 'Opening Address of the President of the Department of Economy and Trade, at the Meeting of the National Association for the Promotion of Social Science, Held at York, in September 1864,' *Journal of the Statistical Society of London*, **28**: 1–33.

Chadwick, Edwin (1866a), 'On Modern Legislation in Regard to the Construction and Equipment of Steam Ships,' *Journal of the Royal Society of Arts*, **14**: 252.

Chadwick, Edwin (1866b), 'On the Proposal that the Railways Should be Purchased by the Government,' *Journal of the Royal Society of Arts*, **14**: 198–207.

Chadwick, Edwin (1867a), 'On the Economy of Telegraphy as a Part of a Public System of Postal Communications,' *Journal of the Royal Society of Arts*, **15**: 222–6.

Chadwick, Edwin (1867b), 'On Railway Reform in Connection with a Cheap Telegraphic Post and a Parcel Post Delivery,' *Journal of the Royal Society of Arts*, **15**: 720–726.

Chadwick, Edwin (1867c), 'Suggestions for a Mode of Supplying Cheap and Healthy Dwellings for the Working Classes, with Security and profit to the Investor,' *Journal of the Royal Society of Arts*, **15**: 313.

Chadwick, Edwin (1867d), 'What Action, If Any, Ought the Government

To Take With Regard to Railways?,' National Association for the Promotion of Social Science Transactions, 593–605.

Chadwick, Edwin (1875), 'The Proposed Alterations in the Railway System of the German Empire,' *Journal of the Royal Society of Arts*, **23**: 151, 210.

Chadwick, Edwin (1876–77 [1887]), 'The Police and the Extinction of Fires,' in B.W. Richardson (ed.), *The Health of Nations: A Review of the Works of Edwin Chadwick*, Vol. II, London: Longmans, Green and Co., pp. 418–30.

Chadwick, Edwin (1878), 'On Depression of Trade,' Transactions of the National Association for the Promotion of Social Science at its Annual Conference, 591–2.

Chadwick, Edwin (1881 [1887]), 'On the Best Forces for the Suppression of Riots,' in B.W. Richardson (ed.), *The Health of Nations: A Review of the Works of Edwin Chadwick*, Vol. II, London: Longmans, Green and Co., pp. 406–17.

Chadwick, Edwin (1885), *On the Evils of Disunity in Central and Local Administration Especially with Relation to the Metropolis and Also on the New Centralisation for the People Together with Improvements in Codification and in Legislative Procedure*, London: Longmans, Green and Co.

Chadwick, Edwin (1887a), 'Elementary Education Question,' *Journal of the Royal Society of Arts*, **35**: 348–50.

Chadwick, Edwin (1887b), 'Tricycles for Police,' in B.W. Richardson (ed.), *The Health of Nations: A Review of the Works of Edwin Chadwick*, Vol. II, London: Longmans, Green and Co., pp. 431–40.

Coase, Ronald H. (1959), 'The Federal Communications Commission,' *Journal of Law and Economics*, **2**: 1–40.

Coase, Ronald H. (1960), 'The Problem of Social Cost,' *Journal of Law and Economics*, **3**: 1–44.

Coats, A.W. (ed.) (1971), *The Classical Economists and Economic Policy*, London: Methuen.

Commanor, William and B. Mitchell (1971), 'Cable Television and the Impact of Regulation,' *Bell Journal of Economics and Management Science*, **2** (1): 154–212.

Committee on the Judiciary (1964), *Antitrust Aspects of the Funeral Industry*, US Government Printing Office: Hearings before the Subcommittee on Antitrust and Monopoly, US Senate, 88th Congress.

Consumer Reports (1980), *Funerals: Consumers' Last Rights*, New York: Pantheon Books.

Cournot, A.A. (1838 [1971]), *Researches into the Mathematical Principles of the Theory of Wealth*, Nathanial Bacon trans., New York: Augustus M. Kelley.

Cournot, Augustin (1843), *Exposition de la théorie des chances et des probabilitiés*, Paris: Hachette.

Crain, W.M. and R.B. Ekelund Jr (1976), 'Chadwick and Demsetz on Competition and Regulation,' *Journal of Law and Economics*, **19** (1): 149–62.

Cross, Melvin and R.B. Ekelund Jr (1980), 'A.T. Hadley on Monopoly Theory and Railway Regulation: An American Contribution to Economic Analysis and Policy,' *History of Political Economy*, **12** (2): 214–33.

Darmstadter, Ruth (1983), 'Blocking the Death Blow to Funeral Regulation,' *Business and Society Review*, Winter: 32–6.

Demsetz, Harold (1959), 'The Nature of Equilibrium in Monopolistic Competition,' *Journal of Political Economy*, **67**: 21–30.

Demsetz, Harold (1968), 'Why Regulate Utilities?,' *Journal of Law and Economics*, **11** (1): 55–65.

Demsetz, Harold (1969), 'Information and Efficiency: Another Viewpoint,' *Journal of Law and Economics*, **12** (1): 1–22.

Demsetz, Harold (2011), 'The Problem of Social Cost: What Problem? A Critique of the Reasoning of A.C. Pigou and R.H. Coase,' *Review of Law and Economics*, **7** (1): 1–13.

DeVany, Arthur S. (1970), 'Time in the Budget of the Consumer: The Theory of Consumer Demand and the Labor Supply Under a Time Constraint,' Professional Paper No. 36, Washington, DC: Center for Naval Analysis.

DiLorenzo, Thomas (2011), 'A Note on the Canard of "Asymmetric Information" as a Source of Market Failure,' *Quarterly Journal of Austrian Economics*, **14** (2): 249–55.

Dnes, Antony W. (1994), 'The Scope of Chadwick's Bidding Scheme,' *Journal of Institutional and Theoretical Economics*, **150** (3): 524–36.

Dupuit, Jules (1844 [1952]), 'De la mesure de l'utilité des travaux publics,' *Annales des Ponts et Chaussees: Memoires et Documents*, 2nd ser., **8** (2): 332–75. R.M. Barback trans., International Economic Papers, No. 2: 83–100.

Dupuit, Jules (1849 [1962]), 'Des péages,' *Annales des Ponts et Chaussees: Memoires et Documents*, 2nd ser., **17** (1), 207–48. Elizabeth Henderson trans., International Economic Papers, No. 11: 7–31.

Dupuit, Jules (1853a [1933]), 'De l'utilité et de sa mesure: De l'utilité publique,' *Journal des* économistes, **36**: 1–27. Reprinted in *De l'utilité et de sa mesure: Écrits choisis et republiés par Mario de Bernardi.* Torino: La Riforma Sociale, 163–91.

Dupuit, Jules (1853b), 'Voies de communication' ('Transportation'), in *Dictionnaire de l'economie politique*, Charles Coquelin (ed.), **2**: 846–54. In *Oeuvres Economiques Completes*, Yves Breton and Gerard Klotz (eds), Vol. I: 451–2. (Page references within text are to Breton and Klotz.)

Dupuit, Jules (2009), *Oeuvres Économiques Complètes*, Yves Breton and Gerard Klotz (eds), 2 vols, Paris: Economica.

Ehrlich, I. (1973), 'Participation in Illegitimate Activities: A Theoretical and Empirical Investigation,' *Journal of Political Economy*, **81** (3): 521–65.

Ekelund, R.B., Jr (1971), 'Economic Empiricism in the Writing of Early Railway Engineers,' *Explorations in Economic History*, **9** (1): 179–96.

Ekelund, R.B., Jr (1976), 'A Short-Run Model of Capital and Wages: Mill's Recantation of the Wages Fund,' *Oxford Economic Papers*, **28** (1): 66–85.

Ekelund, R.B., Jr and Cheryl Dorton (2003), 'Criminal Justice Institutions as a Common Pool: The Nineteenth Century Analysis of Edwin Chadwick,' *Journal of Economic Behavior and Organization*, **50** (3): 271–94.

Ekelund, R.B., Jr and G.S. Ford (1997), 'Nineteenth Century Urban Market Failure? Chadwick on Funeral Industry Regulation,' *Journal of Regulatory Economics*, **12** (1): 27–51.

Ekelund, R.B., Jr and R.F. Hébert (1981), 'The Proto-History of Franchise Bidding,' *Southern Economic Journal*, **48** (2): 464–74.

Ekelund, R.B., Jr and R.F. Hébert (1999), *Secret Origins of Modern Microeconomics: Dupuit and the Engineers*, Chicago: University of Chicago Press.

Ekelund, R.B., Jr and R.F. Hébert (2007), *A History of Economic Theory and Method*, Chicago: Waveland Press.

Ekelund, R.B., Jr and R.F. Hébert (2012), 'Dupuit and the Railroads,' *History of Political Economy*, 44: 97–111.

Ekelund, R.B., Jr and Richard Higgins (1982), 'Capital Fixity, Innovations, and Long-Term Contracting: An Intertemporal Economic Theory of Regulation,' *American Economic Review*, **72** (1): 32–46.

Ekelund, R.B., Jr and E.O. Price III (1979), 'Sir Edwin Chadwick on Competition and the Social Control of Industry: Railroads,' *History of Political Economy*, **2** (2): 213–39.

Ekelund, R.B., Jr and Mark Thornton (1991), 'Geometric Analogies and Market Demand Estimation: Dupuit and the French Contribution,' *History of Political Economy*, **23** (3): 397–418.

Ekelund, R.B., Jr and R.D. Tollison (1976), 'The New Political Economy of J.S. Mill: The Means of Social Justice,' *Canadian Journal of Economics*, **9** (2): 213–33.

Ekelund, R.B., Jr and R.D. Tollison (1981), *Mercantilism as a Rent-Seeking Society: Economic Regulation in Historical Perspective*, College Station: Texas A&M University Press.

Ekelund, R.B., Jr and R.D. Tollison (1997), *Politicized Economies: Monarchy, Monopoly, and Mercantilism*, College Station: Texas A&M Press.

Ekelund, R.B., Jr and Douglas M. Walker (1996), 'J.S. Mill on the Income Tax Exemption and Inheritance Taxes: The Evidence Reconsidered,' *History of Political Economy*, **28** (4): 559–81.

Emsley, C. (1983), *Policing and its Context, 1750–1870*, New York: Schocken Books.

Farr, William (1852 [1968]), 'Appendix No. 20, Tables 1, 2,' in *British Parliamentary Papers*, National Finance: Income Tax, Shannon: Irish University Press.

Federal Trade Commission (1978), *Funeral Industry Practices*, Staff Report, Bureau of Consumer Protection.

Fielding, Henry (1749), *A True State of the Case of Bosavern Penlez, who Suffered on Account of the Late Riot in the Strand. In which the Law Regarding these Offences, and the Statute of George the First, Commonly called the Riot Act, are Fully Considered*, London: A Millar.

Finer, S.E. (1952), *The Life and Times of Sir Edwin Chadwick*, London: Methuen.

French, Stanley (1975), 'Cemetery as Cultural Institution: The Establishment of Mount Auburn and the "Rural Cemetery" Movement,' in David E. Stannard (ed.), *Death in America*, Philadelphia: University of Pennsylvania Press.

Friedman, David (1979), 'Private Creation and Enforcement of Law: A Historical Case,' *Journal of Legal Studies*, **8** (2): 399–415. (Page references are to http://www.best.com/~ddfr/Academic/England_18thc./England_18thc.html.)

Friedman, David (1995), 'Making Sense of English Law Enforcement in the 18th Century,' *University of Chicago Law School Roundtable*, **2**: 475–505.

Friedman, Milton (1962), *Capitalism and Freedom*, Chicago: Chicago University Press.

Galt, William (1843), *Railway Reform, Its Expediency and Practicability Considered, with a copious Appendix Containing a Description of all the Railways in Great Britain and Ireland: Fluctuations in the Prices of Shares, Statistical and Parliamentary Returns, etc*, London.

Galt, William (1865), 'Address on Railway Reform,' from *Railway*

Reform, Its Expediency and Practicability Considered as Affecting the Nation, Shareholders and the Government, London: Longmans, Green and Co.

Goldberg, Victor P. (1976), 'Regulation and Administered Contracts,' *Bell Journal of Economics*, **7** (2): 426–49.

Grampp, William D. (2000), 'What Did Smith Mean by the Invisible Hand?,' *Journal of Political Economy*, **108** (3): 441–65.

Haas-Wilson, Deborah (1986), 'The Effect of Commercial Practice Restrictions: The Case of Optometry,' *Journal of Law and Economics*, **29** (1): 165–86.

Habenstein, Robert Wesley and William M. Lamers (1955), *The History of American Funeral Direction*, Milwaukee: Bulfin.

Hadley, A.T. (1885), *Railroad Transportation: Its History and Its Laws*, New York: G.P. Putnam.

Hadley, A.T. (1886), 'Private Monopolies and Public Rights,' *Quarterly Journal of Economics*, **1** (1): 28–44.

Hadley, A.T. (1888), 'The Workings of the Interstate Commerce Law,' *Quarterly Journal of Economics*, **2** (2): 162–87.

Hadley, A.T. (1890), 'The Prohibition of Railroad Pools,' *Quarterly Journal of Economics*, **4** (2): 158–711.

Hadley, A.T. (1896), Economics: An Account of the Relations between Private Property and Public Welfare,' New York: G.P. Putnam's Sons.

Hadley, A.T. (1899), 'Railroad Business Under the Interstate Commerce Act,' *Quarterly Journal of Economics*, **3** (2): 170–187.

Halévy, Élie (1928), *The Growth of Philosophical Radicalism*, New York: The MacMillan Company.

Hamlin, Christopher (1992), 'Edwin Chadwick and the Engineers, 1842–1854: Systems and Antisystems in the Pipe-and-Brick Sewers War,' *Technology and Culture*, **33** (4): 680–709.

Hamlin, Christopher (1998), *Public Health and Social Justice in the Age of Chadwick: Britain, 1800–1854*, New York: Cambridge University Press.

Hanke, Steve H. and Stephen J.K. Walters (2011), 'Privatizing Waterworks: Learning from the French Experience,' *Journal of Applied Corporate Finance*, **23**: 30–35. Reprinted from Steve H. Hanke (ed.) (1987), *Prospects for Privatization*, New York: The Academy of Political Science.

Hanley, James (2002), 'Edwin Chadwick and the Poverty of Statistics,' *Medical History*, **46** (1): 21–40.

Hanway, J. (1775), *The Defects of Police, the Cause of Immorality, and the Continual Robberies Committed, Particularly in and about the Metropolis*, London: J. Dodsley and Brotherton and Sewell.

Harris, Abram L. (1959), 'J.S. Mill on Monopoly and Socialism: A Note,' *Journal of Political Economy*, **67** (December): 604–11.

Hartley, D. (1966), *Observations on Man, His Frame, His Duty and His Expectations*, Gainesville, FL: Scholar's Facsimilies and Reprints.

Hawke, G.R. (1970), *Railways and Economic Growth in England and Wales*, Oxford: Clarendon Press.

Hazlett, Thomas W. (1991), 'The Demand to Regulate Franchise Monopoly: Evidence From CATV Rate Deregulation in California,' *Economic Inquiry*, **29** (2): 275–96.

Hébert, Robert F. (1977), 'Edwin Chadwick and the Economics of Crime,' *Economic Inquiry*, **15** (4): 539–50.

Hicks, J.R. (1971), 'A Reply to Professor Beach,' *Economic Journal*, **81** (324): 922–5.

Holdsworth, W.A. (1903 [1966]), *History of English Law*, London: Methuen.

Hollander, Samuel (1985), *The Economics of John Stuart Mill*, Vol. 2, Toronto: University of Toronto Press.

Hume, David (1936), *Enquiries Concerning the Human Understanding and Concerning the Principles of Morals*, Oxford: Clarendon Press.

Hume, David (1978), *Treatise on Human Nature*, Oxford: Clarendon Press.

Hume, L.J. (1981), *The Constitutional Code and Bentham's Theory of Government*, New York: Cambridge University Press.

Jenkin, Fleeming (1870 [1931]), 'The Graphic Representation of the Laws of Supply and Demand, and Their Application to Labour,' in *Recess Studies*, Edinburgh. Reprinted in *The Graphic Representation of the Laws of Supply and Demand and Other Essays on Political Economy 1868–1884*, London: London School Reprint.

Jevons, W.S. (1871; 1879 [1965]), *The Theory of Political Economy*, 2nd edn, London: Macmillan. 5th edn reprinted New York: Augustus M. Kelley (1st edn 1871).

Johnson, Steven (2007), *The Ghost Map. The Story of London's Most Terrifying Epidemic – and How It Changed Science, Cities, and the Modern World*, New York: Riverhead Books.

King, Gregory (1698 [1936]), *Two Tracts by Gregory King: Natural and Political Observations and Conclusions upon the State and Condition of England*, edited with an Introduction by George E. Barnett, Baltimore: John Hopkins Press.

Klerman, D. (2001), 'Settlement and the Decline of Private Prosecution in Thirteenth-Century England,' *Law and History Review*, **19** (1): 1–65.

Knight, Frank H. (1924), 'Some Fallacies in the Interpretation of Social Cost,' *Quarterly Journal of Economics*, **38** (4): 582–606.

Krieger, Nancy and A.E. Birn (1998), 'A Vision of Social Justice as the

Foundation of Public Health: Commemorating 150 Years of the Spirit of 1848,' *American Journal of Public Health*, **88** (11): 1603–6.

Lancaster, Kelvin J. (1966), 'A New Approach to Consumer Theory,' *Journal of Political Economy*, **74**: 132–257.

Langbein, J.H. (1999), 'The Prosecutorial Origins of Defense Counsel in the Eighteenth Century: The Appearance of Solicitors,' *Cambridge Law Journal*, **58** (2): 314–65.

Lardner, Dionysius (1850 [1968]), *Railway Economy*, London: Taylor, Walton and Maberly. Reprint, New York: Augustus M. Kelley.

Levi, Leone (1860), *On Taxation: How it is Raised and How it is Expended*, London: John W. Parker and Son.

Levi, Leone (1867), *Wages and Earnings of the Working Classes*, London: John Murray.

Lewis, R.A. (1950), 'Edwin Chadwick and the Railway Labourers,' *Economic History Review*, 2nd ser. **3** (1): 107–18.

Lewis, R.A. (1952), *Edwin Chadwick and the Public Health Movement, 1832–1854*, London: Longmans, Green and Co.

Liebcap, Gary D. and Stephen N. Wiggins (1984), 'Contractual Responses to the Common Pool: Prorationing of Crude Oil Production,' *American Economic Review*, **74** (1): 87–98.

Liebowitz, Stanley and Steven Margolis (1990), 'The Fable of the Keys,' *Journal of Law and Economics*, **30** (1): 1–26.

Loudon, John C. (1843), *On the Laying Out, Planting, and Managing of Cemeteries*, London: Longman, Brown, Green and Longmans.

Maine, Sir H.S. (1861 [1986]), *Ancient Law*, New York: Dorset Press Reprint.

Malthus, T.R. (1798–1826), 'An Essay on the Principle of Population', six edn (1st edn 1798; 2nd edn 1803; 3rd edn 1806; 4th edn 1807; 5th edn 1817; 6th edn 1826).

Malthus, T.R. (1820 [1951]), *Principles of Political Economy*, John Pullen (ed.), New York: Cambridge University Press.

Mandeville, Bernard de (1723 [1924]), *The Fable of the Bees*, B.F. Kaye (ed.), London: Oxford University Press.

Market Facts (1988), *Report on the Survey of Recent Funeral Arrangers* (prepared for Federal Trade Commission, 28 April).

Marshall, Alfred (1890), *Principles of Economics*, London: Macmillan.

Marston, Maurice (1925), *Edwin Chadwick*, Boston: Small, Maynard and Company.

Marvel, Howard (1977), 'Factory Regulation: A Reinterpretation of Early English Experience,' *Journal of Law and Economics*, **20** (2): 379–402.

Marx, Karl (1906), *Capital*, New York: Modern Library.

Mayo, John W. and Yasuji Otsuta (1991), 'Demand, Pricing, and Regulation: Evidence from the Cable TV Industry,' *Rand Journal of Economics*, **22** (3): 396–410.

McCulloch, J.R. (1824), *A Discourse on the Rise, Progress, Peculiar Objects, and Importance, of Political Economy*, Edinburgh: Archibald Constable and Co.

McCulloch, J.R. (1830), *The Principles of Political Economy with a Sketch of the Rise and Progress of the Science*, Edinburgh: William and Charles Tait; and London: Longmans and Co.

McKean, Roland N. (1972), 'Property Rights within Government and Devices to Increase Governmental Efficiency,' *Southern Economic Journal*, **39**: 177–86.

Merges, Robert P. (1995), 'The Economic Impact of Intellectual Property Rights: An Overview and Guide,' *Journal of Cultural Economics*, **19** (2): 103–17.

Mildmay, Sir W. (1763), *The Police of France; or, an Account of the Laws and Regulations Established in that Kingdom, for the Preservation of Peace, and the Preventing of Robberies*, London: E. Owen and T. Harrison.

Mill, John Stuart (1832), 'Thee Employment of Children in Manufactures,' *The Examiner* (29 January).

Mill, J.S. (1834), 'The Proposed Reform of the Poor Laws,' *Monthly Repository*, **8**: 361.

Mill, J.S. (1848a [1965]), *Principles of Political Economy*, W. Ashley (ed.), New York: Augustus M. Kelley.

Mill, J.S. (1848b [1965]), *Principles of Political Economy, Collected Works*, 3 Vols, Toronto: University of Toronto Press.

Mill, J.S. (1851 [1967]), *Essays on Economics and Society*, J.M. Robson (ed.), *Collected Works of John Stuart Mill*, Vol. 5, Toronto: University of Toronto Press.

Mill, J.S. (1852 [1968–69]), 'Testimony Before the Select Committee on Income and Property Tax,' House of Commons, Shannon: Irish University Press Series of *British Parliamentary Papers*.

Mill, J.S. (1861 [1968–69]), 'Testimony Before the Select Committee on Income and Property Tax (the Hubbard Committee),' House of Commons, Shannon: Irish University Press Series of *British Parliamentary Papers*.

Mill, J.S. (1963), *Earlier Letters of John Stuart Mill*, F.E. Mineka (ed.), 2 vols, Toronto: University of Toronto Press.

Mill, J.S. (1972), *Later Letters of John Stuart Mill, 1849–1873*, F.E. Mineka and Dwight Lindley (eds), Toronto: University of Toronto Press.

Mixon, Franklin G. (1996), 'Congressional Term Limitations: Chadwickian Policy as an Antecedent to Modern Ideas,' *American Journal of Economics and Sociology*, **55** (2): 186–96.

Neely, R. (1980), *Why Courts Don't Work*, New York: McGraw-Hill Book Company.

O'Brien, Denis (1970), *J.R. McCulloch: A Study in Classical Economics*, London: George Allen and Unwin.

O'Brien, Denis (1975), *The Classical Economists*, Oxford: Clarendon Press.

O'Donnell, Margaret G. (1979), 'Pigou: An Extension of Sidgwickian Thought,' *History of Political Economy*, **11** (4): 588–605.

Owen, Robert (1821 [1927]), 'An Address to the Inhabitants of New Lanark,' reprinted in G.D.H. Cole (ed.), *A New View of Society and Other Writings of Robert Owen*, London: Dent.

Patinkin, Don (1947), 'Multiple Plan Firms, Cartels, and Imperfect Competition,' *Quarterly Journal of Economics*, **61** (2): 173–205.

Peltzman, Sam (1976), 'Toward a More General Theory of Regulation,' *Journal of Law and Economics*, **19** (2): 211–40.

Peto, Morton (1863), *Taxation: Its Levy and Expenditure, Past and Future; Being an Enquiry into Our Financial Policy*, New York: D. Appleton.

Philips, D. (1980), 'A New Engine of Power and Authority: The Institutionalization of Law-Enforcement in England, 1780–1830,' in V.A.C. Gatrell, B. Lennman, and G. Parker (eds), *Crime and the Law: The Social History of Crime in Western Europe Since 1500*, London: Europa Publications, pp. 155–89.

Pigou, A.C. (1920), *The Economics of Welfare*, London: Macmillan.

Polinsky, A.M. and S. Shavell (2000), 'The Economic Theory of Public Enforcement of Law,' *Journal of Economic Literature*, **38** (1): 45–76.

Pollock, F. and F.W. Maitland (1895), *The History of English Law before the Time of Edward I*, Vols 1 and 2, Cambridge: Cambridge University Press.

Porter, R. (1990), *English Society in the Eighteenth Century*, revised edn, London: Penguin Books.

Posner, Richard (1972), 'The Appropriate Scope of Regulation in the Cable Television Industry,' *Bell Journal of Economics and Management Science*, **3** (1): 98–129.

Price, E.O., III (1984), 'The Political Economy of Sir Edwin Chadwick: An Appraisal,' *Social Science Quarterly*, **65**: 975–87.

Quetelet, Adolphe (1827), 'Recherches sur la population, les naissances, les décès, les prisons, les dépôts de mendicité, etc., dans le royaume des Pays-Bas,' *Nouveaux mémoires de l'Académie royale des sciences et belles-lettres de Bruxelles*, **4**: 117–92.

Quetelet, Adolphe (1835), *Sur l'homme et le développement de ses facultes, ou Essai de physique sociale*, Paris: Bachelier.

Ricardo, David (1817 [1969]), 'Principles of Political Economy and Taxation,' in Pierro Sraffa, *The Works and Correspondence of David Ricardo, Volume I*, for the Royal Economic Society, London: Cambridge University Press.

Royle, E. (1978), *Modern Britain: A Social History, 1750–1985*, New York: St Martin's Press.

Rubinovitz, Robert (1993), 'Market Power and Price Increases for Basic Cable Service Since Deregulation,' *Rand Journal of Economics*, **24** (1): 1–18.

Schmalensee, Richard (1979), *The Control of Natural Monopoly*, Lexington: D.C. Heath.

Schumpeter, J.A. (1942 [1962]), *Capitalism, Socialism and Democracy*, New York: Harper and Row.

Schumpeter, J.A. (1954), *History of Economic Analysis*, New York: Oxford University Press.

Schwartz, Pedro (1966), 'John Stuart Mill and Laissez Faire: London Water,' *Economica*, **33** (129): 71–83.

Schwartz, Pedro (1972), *The New Political Economy of J.S. Mill*, Durham: Duke University Press.

Senior, N.W. (1836 [1965]), *An Outline of the Science of Political Economy*, New York: A.M. Kelley Publishers.

Shehab, F. (1953), *Progressive Taxation; A Study in the Development of Progressive Principles in the British Income Tax*, Oxford: Clarendon Press.

Smith, A. (1759 [1976]), *The Theory of Moral Sentiments*, Indianapolis: Liberty Classics.

Smith, A. (1776 [1937]), *An Inquiry into the Nature and Causes of the Wealth of Nations*, New York: Modern Library.

Smith, A. (1896 [1964]), *Lectures on Justice, Police, Revenue and Arms* [delivered in 1763], Edwin Cannan (ed.), New York: Augustus M. Kelley.

Soward, Sir Alred W. and W.E. Willan (1919), *The Taxation of Capital*, London: Waterlow and Sons.

Spann, Rochard and E. Erickson (1970), 'The Economics of Railroading: The Beginning of Cartelization and Regulation,' *Bell Journal of Economics and Management Science*, **1** (2): 227–44.

Spengler, J.J. (1969), 'Evolution of Public-Utility Industry Regulation: Economists and Other Determinants,' *South African Journal of Economics*, **37** (1): 3–31.

Stead, P.J. (1985), *The Police of Britain*, London: Macmillan.

Stephen, Sir J. (1883 [1963]), *A History of the Criminal Law of England*, New York: Burt Franklin.

Stephen, Leslie (1950), *The English Utilitarians*, New York: Peter Smith.

Stigler, George J. (1961), 'The Economics of Information,' *Journal of Political Economy*, **69**: 213–425.

Stigler, George J. (1964), 'A Theory of Oligopoly,' *Journal of Political Economy*, **72** (1): 44–61.

Stigler, George J. (1968), *The Organization of Industry*, Homewood, IL: Richard D. Irwin, Inc.

Stigler, George J. (1970), 'The Optimum Enforcement of Laws,' *Journal of Political Economy*, **78** (3): 526–36.

Stigler, George J. (1971), 'The Theory of Economic Regulation,' *Bell Journal of Economics*, **2** (1): 3–21.

Stigler, Stephen M. (1986), *The History of Statistics: The Measurement of Uncertainty before 1900*, Cambridge, MA: Belknap Press of Harvard University Press.

Telser, Lester G. (1969), 'On the Regulation of Industry: A Note,' *Journal of Political Economy*, **77** (6): 937–52.

Thornton, M. (1991), *The Economics of Prohibition*, Salt Lake: University of Utah Press.

Tiebout, C.M. (1956), 'A Pure Theory of Local Expenditures,' *Journal of Political Economy*, **64** (5): 416–24.

Tobias, J.J. (1967), *Crime and Industrial Society in the Nineteenth Century*, New York: Schocken Books.

Tobias, J.J. (1972a), *Nineteenth Century Crime: Prevention and Punishment*, Newton Abbot, England: David and Charles.

Tobias, J.J. (1972b), *Urban Crime in Victorian England*, New York: Schocken Books.

Tullock, Gordon (1998), *On Voting: A Public Choice Approach*, Cheltenham, UK: Edward Elgar.

Viner, Jacob (1928), 'Adam Smith and Laissez Faire,' in *Adam Smith 1776–1926*, Chicago: Chicago University Press.

Wagner, Richard. (1973), *The Public Economy*, Chicago: Markham Publishing Co.

Walvin, J. (1988), *Victorian Values*, Athens, GA: University of Georgia Press.

Williamson, Oliver E. (1976), 'Franchise Bidding for Natural Monopolies – In General and with Respect to CATB,' *Bell Journal of Economics*, **7** (1): 73–104.

Williamson, Oliver E. (1979), 'Transaction-Cost Economics; The

Governance of Contractual Relations,' *Journal of Law and Economics*, **22** (2): 233–61.

Williamson, Oliver E. (1985), *The Economic Institutions of Capitalism: Firms, Markets, Relational Contracting*, New York: Free Press.

Woods, R.I. (1996), 'The Population of Britain in the Nineteenth Century,' in M. Anderson (ed.), *British Population History: From the Black Death to the Present Day*, Cambridge, MA: Harvard University Press, pp. 281–357.

Young, Gregory W. (1994), *The High Cost of Dying: A Guide to Funeral Planning*, New York: Prometheus Books.

Index

accident prevention 39–40
  and definition of liability 39–40
  see also railways
Akerlof, G. 9
  and paper on 'lemons' 211–12
Alchian, A.A. 101
Arnott, N. 10
Arrow's nirvana 218
  see also nirvana
artificial identities of interest 27–9,
  37–8, 45, 213, 219
artificial interests 22–9
  see also self-interest

bank confidence, discussion on 152
Baumol, W.J. 74
Baxter, R.D. 184, 186–7, 206
Beach, E.F. 144
Becker, G.S. 9, 22, 33, 35, 66, 158, 165,
  178
Beckerian
  mechanism 155
  restraint 30
Beil, R.O. 125
Bell, F.W. 74, 129, 207
Benham, L. 122
Benson, B. 158, 160–161, 162, 163, 167,
  178–9, 180, 181
Bentham, J. (and) xi, 6–7, 8, 11–12, 17,
  20, 21, 33, 34–5, 45, 55–7, 86, 93,
  99, 161, 178, 179, 196, 202, 203–4,
  208
  artificial identity thesis 27–9, 213,
  219
  Constitutional Code 12
  his critical legacy to Chadwick 22–9
  Escheat vice Taxation (1795) 203
  franchise solution 213
  the French Penal code 14
  *An Introduction to the Principles of
    Morals and Legislation* 28

  the *Panopticon* 28–9
  and theory of contracting 56–7
  philosophical pleasure-pain
    hypotheses of 35
  practical utilitarianism 103
  principles of individualism 32
  Principles of Penal Law 11
  Rationale of Evidence 11
  see also Halévy, É.; Smith, A.
Benthamite principles 32, 45
  applied to social phenomena
    34–42
Bigelow, Dr 123
Blaug, M. 5, 31, 44, 144–5, 154, 157
Bowring, J. 10, 11
Bradford, D.F. 74
Breton, Y. 90, 91
Brundage, A. 179, 207
Buchanan, J. 9, 198
burial market externalities 103–9,
  122–3
  disease transmission 106–7, 122
  and information costs 106–8
  moral and 'taste' 105, 118
  produced in the graveyard 103–4,
    191
burial clubs 107–9, 128
  and infanticide 109

Cairnes, J.E. 21
Cantillon, R. 6, 52, 53–5
cemeteries 72, 103–5, 110, 117–19, 126,
  129–30
  Abney Park 123
  Brompton 119
  Bunhill Fields 104
  emanations from 103–4
  nationalization of 102
  the Necropolis/Necropolis Company
    119, 129
  Nunhead 119